JOSEPH MADDREY

BEYOND FEAR

Reflections on Stephen King, Wes Craven, and George Romero's Living Dead

by Joseph Maddrey

BEYOND FEAR
Reflections on Stephen King, Wes Craven, and George Romero's Living Dead
By Joseph Maddrey

Published in the USA by:
BearManor Media
P O Box 71426
Albany, Georgia 31708
www.bearmanormedia.com

ISBN: 9781593935917
Printed in the United States of America
Book design by Robbie Adkins
Cover artist: Tom Mandrake. Colorist: Sian Mandrake.

Table of Contents

INTRODUCTION: PHILOSOPHIES OF FEAR

Why horror?

This is the question I have asked myself since I was eight years old, when I saw *Jaws* for the first time. In 2004, I published a book called *Nightmares in Red, White and Blue*, which explored one theory about the popularity of the longstanding genre: Horror films reflect the cultural fears of the time and place in which they are made. Universal's *Dracula* (1931) offered Americans relief from the Great Depression; *Invasion of the Body Snatchers* (1956) underscored the threat of communism after World War II; *Carrie* (1976) rebalanced the status quo for modern feminists. In 2008, while I was making a documentary film based on my book, I realized that this theory didn't explain why I *personally* was so attracted to horror. As I interviewed the modern-day masters of horror, it became clear to me that many of the genre's most successful storytellers—as well as its most avid fans—are often more deeply interested in timeless fears than in timely subtexts. We ask universal questions… and seek personal answers.

No serious-minded storyteller in any medium can produce a narrative that doesn't express his or her own beliefs and perspective on the world. In some cases, the primary concerns are sociopolitical. In my documentary, George Romero, John Carpenter, Larry Cohen, and Joe Dante all shared their criticisms of various aspects of modern American culture. In other instances, the storyteller's concerns are metaphysical. Dante spoke about the universal fear of death, and the great unknown that lies beyond. Carpenter spoke eloquently about the dual nature of evil—evil that lurks just outside the comfort zone of any tribal culture, and evil that lurks inside the human heart. What all these filmmakers share is a willingness to explore their personal fears through filmmaking. When we respond to their films, it is because we share those fears… and, sometimes, the worldviews behind them.

My own love of the horror genre is strongly related to the implied philosophies of three of its most prominent storytellers: Stephen King, Wes Craven, and George Romero. Some of my deepest beliefs—not just about horror, but about life—are reflected in, and perhaps partly derived from, the work of these three men. I'm thinking specifically of the romantic idealism of Romero, the intellectual spirituality of Craven, and the hard-won humanism of King.

The first filmmaker who tapped into my own feelings of metaphysical dread was George A. Romero. Romero's zombie films have been analyzed endlessly in relation to the filmmaker's sociopolitical views, but they appealed to me initially on a more primal level. *Night of the Living Dead* (1968), *Dawn of the Dead* (1978), *Day of the Dead* (1985), and *Land of the Dead* (2004) reflect more than the zeitgeist of modern America; they reflect on the essential nature of humanity. *Are we basically good or are we our own worst enemy? Do we pull together in times of crisis or do we fall apart? When the shit hits the fan, are we really any more "human" than cannibalistic corpses?*

Romero doesn't offer easy answers, which is one reason why his films have inspired so much discussion in recent years—along with countless imitations. In early twenty-first century America, zombies are everywhere; they are practically our national mascot. Because of that, it is easy to forget that zombies as we know them today were invented by one man. Romero realized a vision from our collective psyche by delving deep into his own psyche. Ironically, he wasn't half as interested in this new monster as he was in the way that humans would respond to them. Like all great horror films, Romero's Dead series holds up a mirror to the world we think we know. The zombies reveal us at our worst. Even more importantly, they reveal the possibility of a better world. It is this possibility—not the monster—that distinguishes the filmmaker's work.

Romero's contemporary, Wes Craven, takes an equally intimate approach to horror, excavating his personal demons onscreen. Craven's debut film *Last House on the Left* (1972) is not just a protest of violence in American culture, it is also the filmmaker's own therapeutic "primal scream." *A Nightmare on Elm Street* (1984) is not simply a reaction to the glut of unimaginative slasher movies in the early 1980s, it is also an exploration of the filmmaker's metaphysical beliefs. The *Scream* series (1996-2011) is not merely a tongue-in-cheek skewering of the horror genre, it is also a vigorous defense of dark art and its cathartic power.

I did not have an opportunity to interview Craven for my *Nightmares* documentary, because he was busy making his most recent film *My Soul to Take*. In 2010, however, the filmmaker kindly granted me an exclusive one-on-one interview, and I eagerly questioned him about those aspects of his work that appealed to me the most—namely, the spiritual aspects. Despite an endless stream of writings about Craven's most famous creation, no critic has ever traced the influence of Russian mystic George Gurdjieff on Freddy Krueger. But for Craven—one of the most erudite storytellers of his generation—the connection is absolutely vital. Drawing on links such as this, I'm inclined to argue that Craven's influence on the horror genre is actually subtler and more pervasive than even his most ardent fans realize. He has contributed much more than an imitable filmmaking style; he has imbued his films with an unorthodox religious philosophy, and that is why his work stands apart and endures.

For horror fans that came of age in the second half of the twentieth century, perhaps no storyteller is more influential than author Stephen King. The writer's sensibilities are inextricably intertwined with the genre as we know it today because King has created so many of our most popular modern myths. With more than fifty bestselling books to his name, along with countless film and television adaptations, he is a subject of constant speculation. Everyone seems to have a theory about what makes his stories resonate so strongly. My own theory is simple enough: King believes in the power of imagination as devoutly as any political pundit believes in an intellectual theory or any preacher believes in a religious creed. Most of all, he believes in *people*.

Some of King's stories have a sociopolitical bent (especially his recent novels *Under the Dome* and *11/22/63*), but all of his work hinges on questions of metaphysical belief. *Is there a God? If so, what does He want from us? If not, what do we want from ourselves?* For King, such questions are the best reason to write, as he explained in a 1988 speech:

> *The whole question of the exploration of belief is probably the only way in which pop fiction can be serious. I believe that*

> *that exposition of belief remains its greatest strength even more so than the social issues, which always seem to get the lion's share of the credit when it comes to critical analysis. Belief, and the exposition of belief, shows an amazing utility when it's merged with good story.*[1]

How does the world appear to those who confront (or even embrace) the supernatural, as opposed to those who blindly fear it? What is life like for those who adhere to a specific rationale, as opposed to those who remain forever open-minded to the unknown? Is it possible to lead a life full of optimism, even in the midst of constant horrors? Can conscious optimism—hope and faith—revolutionize the world we live in? Such questions are pivotal in King's stories, and central to the modern American horror genre.

Films like *Night of the Living Dead* and *A Nightmare on Elm Street*, and novels like *Carrie* and *The Shining*, remain relevant today because their storytellers dared to reach beyond the time and place in which they were writing, and to look for meaning beyond fear. If readers and viewers continue to believe in these stories, it will be because the storytellers believed in them first. Romero, Craven, and King have proven that they know how to get inside our heads and our hearts, so it's only natural for us to ask: *What's going on inside theirs?*

1 "Evening" 396

LIVING DEAD: ROMANTIC FEAR IN THE FILMS OF GEORGE A. ROMERO

"Romantic fear is anarchic, a libertarian free-for-all where the endlessly repeated concern is not of social collapse (the ultimate fear of aristocracy), but of psychic collapse."
– Clive Bloom

The first time I saw George A. Romero's *Night of the Living Dead* (1968) was in the early 1990s on home video. It was a cheap, public domain copy with abysmal sound and picture quality. Sometimes I wonder if my initial interest wasn't partly due to the grittiness of that copy. I watched it on a small black-and-white TV, the way Ben (the main character in the film) watches the world collapsing on a small black-and-white TV. I was twelve or thirteen years old, and it wasn't hard for me to suspend my disbelief and imagine that the casual everyday world no longer existed outside my window. In a way, that scenario was terrifying. In another way, it seemed full of hope.

I must have watched *Night of the Living Dead* a dozen times before I moved on to the sequels, *Dawn of the Dead* (1978) and *Day of the Dead* (1985). *Dawn* was epic by comparison, revealing a civilization at the height of its struggle for survival; *Day* showcased humanity in the throes of defeat. On the night I watched the third film, an ice storm swept through the small Virginia town where I grew up. It knocked out the power and buried our house. My parents and my younger brother gathered in the living room, in sleeping bags around the fireplace. After everyone else fell asleep, I sat listening to AM radio news on my Walkman until the batteries ran down. The storm kept us confined within the neighborhood for over a week, and all the while I kept wondering what it would be like if the snow never melted. My parents wouldn't go back to work. My brother and I wouldn't go back to school. Our neighbors would become like extended family. A much smaller community would take shape, and we'd have to talk to each other and trust each other as never before. We'd undoubtedly pay more attention to each other because in such a small world there would be fewer distractions. Questions about life and death, meaning and morality would be discussed more openly, because human life would be stripped down to its essence: not just survival but *survival for a purpose*. Part of me yearned for such a fate… though I thought it would be nice if that kind of world came without the zombies.

Through his films, George Romero suggests that zombies can change the world for the better by forcing us to focus on what's really important. Without an immediate threat, he suggests, we simply return to mundane habits. This truth is illustrated by the later films in Romero's series—*Dawn*, *Day* and *Land of the Dead* (2004)—and underscores the meaning of Romero's apocalypse: The force that really turns us into "zombies" is civilization. When we become too preoccupied with work, money, politics, news, weather, and sports, we forget about intimacy and human decency. It's no secret that Romero himself prefers the zombies to many of the human characters in his films. The zombies may be uncivilized, but at least they're not over-civilized.

When I had the chance to interview the director in 2008, I told him that his Dead films had exerted a profound influence on my life. He seemed genuinely surprised. How, he asked, could a cheap zombie movie made in 1968 have much of an impact on someone who came of age decades later? To Romero, *Night of the Living Dead* is inextricably linked with the zeitgeist of the late 1960s. "In my mind," he explained, "most of the power it has relates to the time that it was made . . . and the anger of that time . . . and the disappointment of that time." Since I wasn't alive in the 1960s, obviously I can't fully understand the film in that context. But something else Romero said made me realize that I have experienced *Night of the Living Dead* in an equally powerful context. While explaining that his Dead films are really about the human characters and about the ways they inevitably "screw up" their chance to create a new and better world, he said, "The zombies could be any natural disaster."

I suddenly remembered that, when I was in high school, I'd frequently had nightmares about natural disasters. In one particular dream, a hundred-foot-high tsunami descended on the hotel in Virginia Beach where my family was vacationing. That was the most powerful image of nature in revolt that my imagination could conjure. Had I grown up on the West Coast, I might have dreamed of a massive earthquake. If I lived in Middle America, it might have been a super tornado. Such dreams reveal the fear of death at its most basic: We cannot escape nature. Death is as *natural* as life, and physical survival is a game that we all lose eventually. The only way to survive, I figured, was to assess what was really important in life, and to live with a clear purpose.

As a precocious teenager, I didn't know how to talk about such things with friends and family. Barring the exception of a few late-night (often drug-induced) conversations, the ideas were too abstract for the everyday world I was living in . . . and yet I couldn't let them go. Neither could Romero. The filmmaker explains that this was his basis for *Night of the Living Dead*: "What would be a really earth-shattering thing that would be revolutionary and that people would refuse to ignore? The dead . . . stop . . . staying . . . dead."

Except it's even more dramatic than that. Romero adds with a grin, "Oh and there's one thing more . . . *They like to eat living people!*"

Much has been written about the cinematic precursors to Romero's slow-moving, cannibalistic zombies. The director says that he didn't conceive them as "zombies." Zombies, to him, were the voodoo slaves of Bela Lugosi in old Poverty Row flicks like *White Zombie* (1932) and *King of the Zombies* (1941). Romero acknowledges a comparatively larger debt to the films of Boris Karloff—*Frankenstein* (1931), *The Mummy* (1932), *The Ghoul* (1933) and *The Walking Dead* (1936)—by explaining that he initially imagined the living dead as "ghouls." In traditional folklore, a ghoul was a monster that dwelled in cemeteries and robbed graves in order to feast on rotting flesh. Over the course of his Dead series, Romero's zombies have gone from being shuffling, groaning ghouls (in *Night* and *Dawn*) to modern-day variations on The Mummy and Frankenstein's Monster (beginning with "Bub" in *Day of the Dead*).

Critics and fans have pointed toward many other potential sources of inspiration: Edward L. Cahn's *The Zombies of Mora Tau* (1957) and *Invisible Invaders* (1959), Hammer's *The Plague of the Zombies* (1967) and AIP's *The Last Man on Earth* (1964). The strongest case can be made for *The Last Man on Earth*, which was based on Richard Matheson's 1954 novel *I Am Legend*. In Matheson's novel, the monsters are vampires, hunted by the titular hero during daylight hours. The most thought-provoking aspect of Matheson's story is its ending, where the hero realizes that vampires are now the dominant species and, in their world, the last man on earth is the only monster—it's all a matter of perspective. Romero's series drives at the same type of revelation, because the filmmaker is not simply interested in making films about monsters in a fantasy world; he is telling stories about *us*, here and now.

Romero frequently names Orson Welles as his main filmmaking idol, and he's not alone. What aspiring filmmaker hasn't hoped for Welles's kind of success? After making a big name for himself in New York radio, Hollywood practically laid the world at this wunderkind's feet. RKO studio head David O. Selznick won the bidding war to put Welles under contract as a filmmaker, and the rest is history... with a touch of tragedy: Welles chose newspaper magnate William Randolph Hearst as the subject of his first film, *Citizen Kane*; Hearst tried to destroy the film and, failing that, he destroyed Welles's career as a filmmaker. Orson Welles never again had final cut on any of his films, but he had already secured a legacy that would influence an entire generation of filmmakers, including Romero.

Welles's earliest success—and probably his biggest influence on most horror filmmakers—was a radio adaptation of H.G. Wells's *The War of the Worlds*, broadcast on Halloween night 1938. Because of the way Welles presented the story—as a news broadcast rather than a dramatization—some listeners purportedly believed that Martians had actually landed in rural New Jersey, and they became hysterical. Welles promptly made a public apology, saying that he had not intended to create a panic. Secretly, however, he could not have been more pleased. Years later, he told biographer Peter Bogdanovich that the public reaction had exceeded his wildest hopes:

> *The size of it, of course, was flabbergasting. Six minutes after we'd gone on the air, the switchboards in radio stations*

> *right across the country were lighting up like Christmas trees. Houses were emptying, churches were filling up; from Nashville to Minneapolis there was wailing in the street and the rending of garments. Twenty minutes in, and we had a control room full of very bewildered cops. They didn't know who to arrest or for what, but they did lend a certain tone to the remainder of the broadcast. We began to realize, as we plowed on with the destruction of New Jersey, that the extent of our American lunatic fringe had been underestimated.*[2]

Once he had secured his reputation as a showman, Welles taught himself how to be filmmaker. He had loftier ambitions, however, than a repeat of his *War of the Worlds* experiment. While prepping *Citizen Kane*, he studied John Ford's breakthrough western *Stagecoach* (1939), a film that championed the common man and suggested that the "uncivilized" American represented the noblest strain of American life. Welles made a similar statement with *Citizen Kane*, by characterizing William Randolph Hearst as a megalomaniac who was wildly out of touch with his average reader. In this and other ways, *Citizen Kane* can be viewed as a kind of dark reflection of the values in *Stagecoach*. Whereas *Stagecoach* is bright, naturalistic, and open, *Kane* is shadowy, artificial, and claustrophobic. Ford's film sentimentally harkens back to a simpler time; Welles's film mourns its loss.

The cinematography of *Citizen Kane* was hugely influential on American filmmakers, particularly the visionaries behind film noir, but Welles later complained to Peter Bogdanovich that his film's themes "didn't seem to have much effect on anybody."[3] In response, Bogdanovich asked Welles about his "fondness for things of the past," and Welles said he longed "for that Eden people lose." He added, "It's a theme that interests me. A nostalgia for the garden—it's a recurring theme in all our civilization."[4] It is in this respect that George Romero is a cinematic heir to Orson Welles.

Most viewers probably do not think of the Summer of Love when they watch the original *Night of the Living Dead*, but Romero does. The ugliness of the film's ending, he says, reflects the way that the idealism of the Love Generation went sour. At the end

2 Bogdanovich 18
3 Bogdanovich 88
4 Bogdanovich 93

of the 1960s, the United States was fighting an unpopular war in Vietnam, and the carnage was being aired on the nightly news for mass consumption. On the night that Romero and his producer Russ Streiner drove the master print of their finished film to New York to seek a distributor, civil rights activist Martin Luther King Jr. was assassinated in Memphis. From a commercial standpoint, the duo realized that they had made the right decision to kill the black hero of the film—because the ending would now resonate with audiences in a way that no one could have anticipated. The bleakness of the film was amplified by a general sense in the following years that the American dream was dying. Things got worse at the 1968 Democratic National Convention in Chicago, which was followed by the Manson murders in Los Angeles, and the bloody fiasco at the Altamont Festival in northern California in 1969. The then-popular Joni Mitchell song "Woodstock," about a generation's yearning for a moment of possibility that had already passed, would have made an apt soundtrack for the final scenes of *Night of the Living Dead.* The singer laments, "We've got to get ourselves back to the garden."

Come to think of it, the contemporary Crosby, Stills, Nash & Young tune "Long Time Gone" would also work. It intones: "It's going to be a long, long, long time before the dawn."

Despite the film's timeliness, distributors initially failed to see the commercial potential of *Night of the Living Dead.* American International Pictures (AIP) offered to release the picture only if the filmmakers would shoot a more upbeat ending. The filmmakers declined the offer, realizing that this concession would rob the movie of its power. To their credit, the filmmakers understood that their greatest achievement was defying the conventions of traditional horror. Romero says that, if the film had produced made by AIP, "there probably would have been a scientist in the group, explaining what was going on."[5] In less capable hands, that single detail could have made *Night of the Living Dead* seem like a derivative variation on Roger Corman's *The Day the World Ended* (1954). (It is worth noting that Corman's latter-day ruminations on his first horror film sound very much like the philosophy expressed in Romero's Dead films. Corman says, "My belief, in general, is that civilization moves forward: Old civilizations end and new civilizations start."[6]) Instead,

5 Derry 119

6 Silver 33

Romero and company made a film closer in spirit to the source story for Alfred Hitchcock's *The Birds* (1963), which emphasizes the terrifying power of nature—both human and nonhuman.

Daphne du Maurier's short story "The Birds" is set in London during the early days of the Cold War, and it revolves around a family of four who take refuge in their house after local birds begin targeting people's eyes. The tale starts with a sense of foreboding—the lead character, Nat, interprets a bitter cold wind from the north as a harbinger of a hard winter ahead. He later rationalizes the frenzy of attacking birds as a reaction to extreme weather: "Like people who, apprehensive of death before their time, drive themselves to work or folly, the birds do likewise."[7] Other characters blame the Russians—the *real* cold from the north—for poisoning the birds. The "official" explanation from local authorities is just as ludicrous:

> *Reports from all over the country are coming in hourly about the vast quantity of birds flocking above towns, villages and outlying districts, causing obstruction and damage and even attacking individuals. It is thought that the Arctic air stream, at present covering the British Isles, is causing birds to migrate south in immense numbers, and that intense hunger may drive these birds to attack human beings.*[8]

Nat promptly boards up the windows, and gathers his family in the kitchen. After nightfall, they huddle together on mattresses beside the fire and listen to radio reports from the world outside. The London Home Office declares a national emergency, makes a few vague reassurances, and asks everyone to stay indoors, remain calm and conserve resources. After that the radio station promptly goes off the air for the duration of the night (and possibly the winter?). Realizing that he and his family are on their own, Nat mutters:

> *It's always the same . . . they always let us down. Muddle, muddle, from the start. No plan, no real organisation. And we don't matter, down here. That's what it is. The people up country have priority. They're using gas up there, no doubt, and all the aircraft. We've got to wait and take what comes.*[9]

7 Du Maurier 154
8 Du Maurier 164
9 Du Maurier 189

The characters in *Night of the Living Dead* express a similar attitude. Trapped in a rural farmhouse with a black-and-white television as their only connection to the outside world, they watch Congressmen bumbling and reporters fumbling with vague explanations about the cause of an outbreak that has brought the dead back to life. The misinformation leads to mass hysteria, not unlike in H.G. Wells's *The War of the Worlds*. Romero explains, "As far as the people on television not really answering questions and making it more confusing, that's been a conscious part of the zombie films. That's generally what it's about—'Ladies and gentlemen, there was just a plane crash that took out a small piece of Manhattan; more later.' It's never reassuring; it's always alarming, and that's been a kind of conscious through-line."[10]

Many critics have latched onto this aspect of Romero's mythology in order to advance personal theories. Gregory Waller, in his book *The Living and the Undead*, suggests that *Night of the Living Dead* is a criticism of modern man's faith in the "saving power" of rational knowledge: "*Night of the Living Dead* does not assume that knowledge is power, at least not for the people in the film whose fate we are most concerned with."[11] In his book *The Gospel of the Living Dead* (2004), Kim Paffenroth argues that the film dismisses all forms of secular authority and illustrates the Christian concept of original sin. In the end, Paffenroth suggests, the only thing that can save humanity is the grace of God.[12] In this interpretation, *Night of the Living Dead* leads the viewer back to a literal Garden of Eden. On the other hand, critic Robin Wood argues that the film presents a *godless* universe in which humans must make their own meaning. His point is the most fair, since the text of the film itself offers no religious solutions to the crisis. Wood states definitively, "Of one thing we may be sure: the films are not about 'punishment for sin.' Romero's universe is certainly not a Christian one (the occasional religious references are always negative)."[13]

This first film in the *Dead* series is obviously open to a wide variety of interpretations, but the filmmaker expounds his ideas more explicitly in the later films. An early scene in *Dawn of the Dead*

10 Gagne: *Zombies* 27
11 Waller 272, 275
12 Paffenroth 42-43
13 Wood: "Fresh Meat"

features a one-legged priest who issues a warning to the main characters: "We must stop the killing or lose the war." In this example, religion is clear-headed and well-meaning, but not very powerful. Science fares no better. Late in the film, a one-eyed scientist appears on television, ritualistically chanting, "We *must* remain logical." That repeated phrase is the whole of his contribution to a situation that has overwhelmed him completely. Romero's implication is that neither science nor religion alone is a sufficient coping mechanism for the crisis. The main characters turn instead to materialism, living out a consumer's dream inside an abandoned mall—a temporary fix that all but destroys them. At a loss for any kind of meaningful solution to the crisis of the living dead, the filmmaker says that he originally conceived *Dawn of the Dead* as a much darker story:

> *It centered around this couple—a guy and a pregnant woman—who were living up in this crawl space. He was like the hunter/gatherer, going down into the mall for supplies and food. They were really like cave people; they were naked all the time. I was really going out there, very heavy. It was too dark. It was really ugly.*[14]

In subsequent drafts, he moved away from this bleak vision toward something more carnivalesque. Instead of a stark, shocking newsreel, the film became a wildly garish comic book. Jaunty surrealism replaced heightened naturalism, and the black-and-white aesthetic of *Night* gave way to the brightly-lit locations and gaudy color scheme of *Dawn*. By removing the zombies from the shadows, and humanizing them, Romero made the point that the living dead are not simply a threat to the future of mankind. Rather, they *are* the future of mankind, if we keep living the way we've been living. The only hope lies in the recognition of our problems; once the survivors realize their own shortcomings, the filmmaker allows them to escape, and ends *Dawn* on a guardedly optimistic note.

Romero's story, however, was not finished. The filmmaker says that he always conceived his original Dead story as a trilogy:

> *During the first phase the cannibalism began, but the humans still outnumbered the zombies, and then there was a point later*

14 Gagne: *Zombies* 83

in time when things began to fall into equal balance, then, in the end, it seems as though the zombies were starting to run things. But in the very end you find out that, even though they're outnumbered, the humans still control the zombies. Nothing has changed after all those revolutions—if you want to look at it on an allegorical level.[15]

As it turned out, it took Romero four films to complete his would-be trilogy. Originally, Romero conceived *Day of the Dead* as an epic tale about a group of Latin American guerillas who stumbled onto a secret military installation on a remote island. There, they would incur the wrath of a megalomaniacal military dictator named Rhodes, who has turned the island population of zombies into an army of foot soldiers, using a combination of Pavlovian and *Clockwork Orange*-style conditioning. Budgetary problems forced Romero to scale down his vision for the film, leaving him with the seeds of an additional Dead movie.

In the filmed version of *Day of the Dead*, religion is mostly absent and science has gone mad. The film's central character, Sarah, is one of three scientists researching possible solutions to the zombie outbreak. While she searches for a way to reverse the plague, dotty old Dr. Logan tries to teach the zombies to "behave." The zombies begin to display some capacity for learning, but that specter of progress is short-lived because the other human survivors spend all their time squabbling over the remains of a dead society. Only one character, a West Indian helicopter pilot named John, offers genuine hope for the future. John suggests starting a new civilization with the emphasis on those age-old enemies of capitalism: peace, love, and understanding. Terry Alexander, the actor who plays the character, says he built the role around one particular monologue, which appears in the film as follows:

We don't believe in what you're doing here, Sarah. You know what all they got down here in this cave? Man, they've got the books and the records of the top 500 companies. They got the

15 Hickenlooper 346-347

> *defense department budget down here. And they got the negatives for all your favorite movies. They got microfilm with tax returns and newspaper stories. They got immigration records and census reports, and they got official accounts of all the wars and plane crashes and volcano eruptions and earthquakes and fires and floods and all the other disasters that interrupted the flow of things in the good old US of A. Now, what does it matter—all this filing and record keeping? Who ever gonna give a shit? Who even gonna get a chance to see it all? This is a great big 14-mile tombstone with an epitaph on it that nobody gonna bother to read. Now here you come, here you come with a whole new set of charts and graphs and records. What you gonna do? Bury them down here with all the other relics of what once was?*

In a 2008 interview, Romero told me bluntly, "That [character] is me. That is me entirely. That guy represents exactly what I would say in that situation." The message is simple. We are all going to die someday. Death is the great equalizer that puts us all on a level playing field with our fellow man. In the face of that undeniable reality, shouldn't we try to make the most of our time together instead of fighting for wealth or power (or the reestablishment of a dehumanizing status quo)?

At the end of the film, John and Sarah have escaped to a new Eden, a tropical island devoid of zombies . . . as well as other humans. As critic Robin Wood points out, this is not an entirely hopeful ending, because it proffers "hedonistic escapism" as the only means of maintaining a "qualified optimism."[16] Wood goes on to suggest that this cynical perspective may be responsible for the commercial failure of *Day of the Dead* in 1985. The critic notes that Romero's vision was ill-suited to the Reagan Era: "It was the last film a public duped into heaving a vast communal sigh of relief that radicalism was no longer necessary wanted to see."[17] Instead, audiences supported *The Return of the Living Dead* (1985), a comparatively lighthearted zombie farce.

For nearly two decades, *Day of the Dead* was George Romero's final word on Undead America. Other writers and filmmakers eagerly appropriated his universe, however, and kept it warm for potential

16 Wood: *Hollywood* 294
17 Wood: *Hollywood* 294

resurrection. In 1989, authors John Skipp and Craig Spector co-edited the first zombie fiction anthology, *Book of the Dead*, which included short stories by Stephen King, Robert R. McCammon, and Ramsey Campbell. The book boasted a foreword by Romero, who claimed that in the wake of *Day of the Dead*'s box office failure, he had been skeptical about the prospects of zombie fiction. "These are the eighties," he noted, "The self-centered, get-rich-and-look-good-at-all-costs eighties . . . I figured there were a few out there who knew the movements of the dead and that those few, fearing ridicule, would probably clam up when approached."[18] Despite his skepticism, *Book of the Dead* heralded a surprisingly healthy future for zombie fiction . . . eventually.

The following year Romero wrote the screenplay for a remake of his first film, transforming the heroine Barbara into a stronger character, and revising the ending to surprise audiences. The commercial and critical response to the film was tepid, prompting Romero to abandon hope for a conclusion to his series. He didn't return to the zombie subgenre until later in the decade, when he was briefly attached to a film adaptation of the Capcom video game *Resident Evil*—a popular game inspired by his own Dead trilogy. Romero wrote a prospective script for the film that closely followed the narrative of the video game, while emphasizing the game's inherent anti-corporate sentiments about ruthless capitalists who create and sell "soldiers who can't die." Had his script been shot, the film would have been an extension of the filmmaker's original ideas for *Day of the Dead*. Instead, the producers of *Resident Evil* opted to make a relatively mindless action movie.

In the wake of the films *Resident Evil* (2002) and *28 Days Later* (2002), the latter of which recycles many plot elements from *Day of the Dead*, zombie movies became popular again. Zack Snyder's remake of *Dawn of the Dead* (2004) and Edgar Wright's satirical *Shaun of the Dead* (2004) were major box office successes, prompting Universal Studios to give Romero the long-awaited opportunity to finish his series. Rumors of the filmmaker's return to the living dead circulated the working titles "Twilight of the Dead" and "Dead Reckoning," but the filmmaker eventually settled on *Land of the Dead*.

---

18 Skipp 2

Land of the Dead begins with a new world order already in place, and the human and zombie underclass in rebellion. In this new normal, reason and religion are valueless, because politics and power are the bases of "civilization." Romero, ever the revolutionary, employs his ghouls to bring the house of cards crashing down and make the point that America hasn't changed much since 1968. In a 2008 interview, he reflected:

> *We've been sort of relearning the same lesson over and over and over. Right now we are in the middle of a stupid war [in Iraq] and we're still learning the same lesson. It's very hard to get in there and change things. That was the frustration that a lot of us were living with when we made* Night of the Living Dead.[19]

To quote Pete Townshend: "Meet the new boss. Same as the old boss."

At the center of the narrative is a capitalist dictator named Kaufman, played by Dennis Hopper. Kaufman is not as maniacal as the Rhodes character in *Day of the Dead*, but he's just as contemptible. Like Rhodes, he craves personal power at the expense of everything else. The irony of casting of Hopper as a capitalist dictator wasn't lost on critic Robin Wood, who writes that Kaufman is "*Easy Rider* maturing into its most monstrous tycoon."[20] Like more than one hippie-turned-yuppie, the actor had morphed (onscreen and off) from a counterculture rebel into an ultra-conservative. Perhaps because Romero suggested that Hopper should base his performance on Defense Secretary Donald Rumsfeld, some critics read his performance as broad satire.[21] Hopper, a registered Republican, deflected this reading, saying, "Kaufman does things that are immediately illegal and very vicious. I don't really see that as representing the Republican Party."[22] In the same interview, however, he conceded that the film *does* have a strong political subtext, about "people out

19 Interview with author 4/26/08

20 Wood: "Fresh Meat"

21 Kane 90

22 Hopper

there who couldn't communicate before" learning to communicate and trying to overthrow the status quo.

At the end of the film, after the zombies invade Kaufman's empire, Romero's hero has a brief conversation with a street preacher about the future of human civilization. The preacher muses, "Now we can turn this place into what we always wanted it to be." Riley, who clearly speaks for the filmmaker, wonders, "Then what will *we* turn into?" The implication is that Romero still believes that it is necessary to escape civilization in order to save oneself. For that reason, Riley urges his friends not to kill any more zombies. Perhaps, in the wake of so much carnage, Riley is trying to adopt a "live and let live" approach to life. Or perhaps he sees the brightest glimmer of hope for the future in the behavior of the zombies. After all, at least they don't kill *each other*. They only eat the living.

By this point in Romero's Dead series, the zombies are longer operating on pure animal instinct. They have attained some measure of intelligence (at least, enough to use tools) and self-control. Most importantly, they have learned to work together. And if they can do it, Romero suggests, why can't we? As Riley and his friends head off in search of their utopia, they seem to accept the zombies as the new co-inhabitants of America. "They're just looking for a place to go," Riley rationalizes, "Like us." He's not talking about a physical place, so much as a mindset. Romero's message for humanity shines through the darkness: *We've got to get ourselves back to the garden.*

Bibliography

Bogdanovich, Peter. *Who the Devil Made It?* New York: Knopf, 1997.

Derry, Charles. *Dark Dreams.* Cranbury, NJ: A.S. Barnes, 1977.

Du Maurier, Daphne. "The Birds." *Daphne du Maurier's Classics of the Macabre.* Garden City, NY: Doubleday, 1987.

Gagne, Paul R. *The Zombies That Ate Pittsburgh.* New York: Dodd, 1987.

Hopper, Dennis. Interview. "George A. Romero's Land of the Dead Interview: Dennis Hopper." http://madeinatlantis.com/interviews/dennis_hopper.htm

Hickenlooper, George. *Reel Conversations: Candid Interviews with Film's Foremost Directors and Critics.* New York: Citadel, 1991.

Kane, Joe. *Night of the Living Dead: Behind the Scenes of the Most Terrifying Zombie Movie Ever.* New York: Citadel, 2010.

Paffenroth, Kim. *The Gospel of the Living Dead: George Romero's Visions of Hell on Earth.* Waco, TX: Baylor UP, 2006.

Silver, Alain & James Ursini. *Metaphysics on a Shoe String.* Los Angeles: Silman-James, 2006.

Skipp, John and Craig Spector, ed. *Book of the Dead.* New York: Bantam, 1989.

Waller, Gregory A. *The Living and the Undead: From Stoker's Dracula to Romero's Dawn of the Dead.* Chicago: U of Illinois P, 1986.

Wood, Robin. "Fresh Meat: Diary of the Dead may be the summation of George A. Romero's zombie cycle (at least until the next installment)." *Film Comment*—January/February 2008.

---. *Hollywood from Vietnam to Reagan... and Beyond.* New York: Columbia UP, 2003.

WES CRAVEN: TALES OF FAITH AND FANTASY TERROR

"To go against the order of society is always to risk plunging into anomy. To go against the order of society as religiously legitimated, however, is to make a compact with the primeval forces of darkness. To deny reality as it has been socially defined is to risk falling into irreality, because it is well-nigh impossible in the long run to keep up alone and without social support one's own counterdefinitions of the world. When the socially defined reality has come to be identified with the ultimate reality in the universe, then its denial takes on the quality of evil as well as madness. The denier then risks moving into what may be called a negative reality—if one wishes, the reality of the devil."

- Peter L. Berger, *The Sacred Canopy*

In the spring of 2008, I began pursuing interviews for my documentary *Nightmares in Red, White and Blue*, a history of American horror films. One of the first people I reached out to was Wes Craven. Unfortunately, he was not available for an interview; he had recently started preproduction on his new film *25/8* (eventually re-titled *My Soul to Take*) and he remained immersed in that project for the next two years. In the spring of 2010, he finally consented to an interview—but by then I had completed and delivered my documentary. I asked to meet with him anyway, knowing that the documentary would not be my final word on the subject of horror movies.

When I finally sat down to interview Craven in March 2010, I realized I could ask the questions I really wanted to ask. It was then that I decided to do what no interviewer should ever do. I started by talking about myself. I told Craven that my father was a Methodist minister, and that—in spite of my love and respect for him—I had struggled during my teenage years to believe in the benevolent God that he preached about on Sunday mornings. I explained that I had eventually turned away from the church and more toward philosophy, literature, and film. I told him about how I had become obsessed with horror movies while my mother was recovering from a near-fatal illness, and concluded that in some strange way I had always felt more comforted by films like *A Nightmare on Elm Street* and *Serpent and the Rainbow* than I did by organized religion. To my young mind, horror films seemed more honest—they acknowledged dark, secret forces at work in everyday life. Craven's stories suggested that by overcoming fear, it might be possible to overcome those dark forces. Over time, the filmmaker's truth became mine. Craven listened carefully, with a slight smile on his face that suggested he understood what I was saying. When I finished (and before I could start apologizing for my long ramble), he began telling me about his own childhood, which provided the foundation for his films.

Craven's work stands apart because of the filmmaker's lifelong philosophical commitment to broader literary and religious ideas. Not content to simply follow existing genre formulas, he has repeatedly deconstructed and rebuilt them to produce stories that are unique and personal. By creating his own myths from a heap of broken images, Craven offers his own philosophy of horror.

The Death of God, Timothy Leary and the Journey Out of Fear

In 1943, shortly before Wes Craven turned four years old, his father died of a heart attack. Even before that, the future filmmaker says he was living with a lot of anxiety: "I'm somebody who, in his initial impressions of the world, was very afraid. My father was kind of scary—I have few memories of him because he died when I was young—but, I knew he was a frightening, big man, and angry."[1] The world outside his front door was equally intimidating. Craven spent his early years in a rough neighborhood in Cleveland, Ohio. "There was violence in the street a lot of the time," he says, "and most of the schools I went to were quite violent and confrontational. I think I was sensitive to violence, because it was so much denied by the culture at large, and I was intrigued by the things that were denied by my religious background."[2]

Craven's mother was determined to shelter her youngest child from the ugliness of the world outside. Shortly before the death of her husband, Caroline Craven took refuge in a fundamentalist Baptist church. Her son stipulates that the church became, for him, "a second family," providing "stability and shelter."[3] He admits, however, that it effectively separated him from the mainstream of American culture—including Hollywood movies. He explained to me how the "secretive world" of his early youth put him at odds with other ways of thinking and living:

> *There was a song we were taught to sing as children: "This world is not our home / We're only passing through / The treasures are laid up somewhere beyond the blue." In sermons and everything else, [the message was] that everything that was not part of the church or the church's belief was "the world." And you were not part of the world, which is a great way to drive somebody totally insane. [The church said] "This is all we have." So I grew up not knowing how to dance. Sex was forbidden, so*

1 Russo 178
2 Russo 178
3 Craven: *Directors*

there was no early exploration of sex. You don't smoke. You don't go to the movies, unless they're Disney movies. You don't do any of those things, so you're not a part of the popular culture. I grew up feeling like I wasn't part of the world.

Ironically, he also felt like an outsider within the Church. Recalling vivid memories of childhood guilt, he explains that he eventually "grew away" from Christianity because he never had the type of religious experience he expected to have. Biographer John Wooley quotes him as follows:

I often felt that I was the one in the room who just had an irredeemable soul. They quite often would have the congregation all together for a revival, or they'd go overtime, and the pastor would say, "I know there's somebody here. I can feel there's somebody here. God is telling me there's someone here who still hasn't either truly, really given his or her soul to Christ or has backslidden and needs to rededicate his or her life to Christ.'" I can remember resisting that for years and years and years and finally going forward [to the altar], just feeling like my spirit was broken, like I had to do this. And still not feeling it.[4]

Speaking to me on the same day of Wooley's interview, Craven elaborated:

They would always talk about people who have gone through the motions of having given their heart to Jesus, but they haven't really. And [they said] if you do that, you're committing a sin against the Holy Spirit, and that's the one unforgivable sin. Of course, I immediately assumed I'd done the unforgivable. So now I'm really going to hell.

Although he yearned for a religious awakening, it did not come. Without that genuine experience, he could not bear witness to the faith. He ultimately realized that he had to reconcile himself to a new truth, or suffer endlessly.

4 Wooley 12

As a student at Wheaton College in the years 1957 to 1963, Craven became a voracious reader. "The whole thing about going to college," he explains, "was trying to fill in the blanks of all this stuff that was kept from me because it wasn't savory or it didn't fit the belief system or whatever."[5] Not surprisingly, he was drawn to popular studies of comparative mythology and religion: Sir James George Frazer's *The Golden Bough* and Joseph Campbell's *The Hero with a Thousand Faces*. He was also impressed with the American Gothic short stories of Edgar Allan Poe, Charles Dickens's picaresque coming-of-age novels, and the theodicy of Russian novelist Fyodor Dostoyevsky (particularly *Crime and Punishment*).

Although Wheaton was a fundamentalist college, Craven also managed to find a small ground of "radical" peers, "kids who were trying to juggle a belief that Christianity could still be relevant, but not include those archaic things about no dancing and no going to movies."[6] Students at Wheaton signed a pledge that they would not go to the movies—an infraction punishable by expulsion—but his fascination with film proved too strong to resist. In his senior year, Craven sneaked away to see *To Kill a Mockingbird* in the theater. It was just the beginning of his cinematic education.

"At the same time," he told me, "new ideas were starting to come into the culture. There was a book that was called *The Death of God*, which I read like you might read the *Communist Manifesto* if you were living with the general of a communist army." Gabriel Vahanian's *The Death of God: The Culture of Our Post-Christian Era*, published in 1961, theorizes that Christianity in modern America has become less a religion than a religiosity. "This religiosity," Vahanian writes, "is as shallow as it is intense, because it means that one believes merely for the sake of believing."[7] Vahanian goes on to say that it fosters empty faith by providing no room for doubt or contemplation. True belief in God, he concludes, requires "that one must rebel against Christianity."[8]

After graduation, Craven found some encouragement for this type of rebellion when he reached out to fellow Wheaton alumnus Elliott Coleman, a professor at John Hopkins University. "He and

5 Interview with author 3/12/10
6 Wooley 22
7 Vahanian 52
8 Vahanian 118

I talked about religion a lot," Craven explains, "and his feeling was that most of what people who say they're Christians say is bullshit."[9] Coleman, the son of an Episcopal minister, had studied to be a minister himself, but left the church to work in the publishing industry instead. In 1947, he founded one of the first creative writing MFA programs in the United States, through which he mentored some of the country's most prominent twentieth century writers, including Russell Baker and John Barth. Myra Sklarew, one of his former students, strives to sum up Coleman's influence on his students:

> *How to describe or even begin to characterize the form of deep freedom we felt in his presence in the Seminars. Not, however, freedom to abandon our purpose, but freedom to go into the depths as writers, as explorers, no matter the cost . . . As vitally different as his students were, as they embarked on routes not yet paved, their pages not yet inscribed, their tastes wildly divergent, he seemed to have knowledge for us all. He did not fear the new. I've long thought that it isn't possible to teach a person how to write, but it is possible to learn to read for the sake of one's writing. Elliott gave us that.*[10]

The initial encouragement that Coleman gave to Craven prompted the young writer to hitchhike to Johns Hopkins University for a face-to-face meeting. "[I] showed up," Craven remembers, "[with] no money, no plan, no nothing. And Elliott accepted me and gave me a scholarship. I became his assistant, and then I got a student loan to pay for the rest." He spent the following year studying James Joyce, T.S. Eliot and "all the great poets" of the Modernist age.[11] Those influences taught Craven to trust his own beliefs, as he later explained to journalist James Freedman:

> *Coming out of fundamentalism into the world as they call it—which is as good a term as any—can be wrenching, because you can't leave it without one part of your brain that's been inculcated with this stuff for fifteen, 20 years [saying], "You are backsliding, you're working with the devil," all these horrible things. Elliott was one of the first adults that said, "You know*

9 Interview with author 3/12/10

10 Sklarew

11 Russo 177

what, that particular version of Christianity is totally [messed] up, don't worry about it"... God bless anybody that's in that kind of religion, but if you're somebody who transitions out of it it's not an easy transition at all, and if somebody can help you feel OK about it that's really an important person. Elliott was like that.[12]

For his master's thesis, Craven produced an epistolary novel about "the reintegration of a mildly schizophrenic kid into a single person, through this journey to wisdom."[13] *Noah's Ark: The Diary of a Madman* now looks like an early version of *My Soul to Take*—and a trial run for Craven's cinematic journeys out of fear. If *Noah's Ark* contains an element of blasphemy, it is *genuine* blasphemy. And, as T.S. Eliot once wrote, genuine blasphemy is not the total rejection of belief: "Genuine blasphemy, genuine in spirit and not purely verbal, is the product of partial belief, and is as impossible to the complete atheist as to the perfect Christian. It is a way of affirming belief."[14] Craven was following Vahanian's prescription for "true belief," rejecting religiosity in favor of a search for something real.

Craven graduated from Johns Hopkins in 1964 and took a job teaching humanities at Westminster College in Pennsylvania, followed by an even longer stint at Clarkson College in upstate New York. During this period, he absorbed a host of new influences that contradicted the formative influences of his youth. Craven explains:

There was about a five year drift away from [Christianity]. I think [the war in] Vietnam had a lot to do with it . . . It just seemed like one lie after another was being revealed. At a certain point, I think the entire culture felt like everything had been a lie. Everything you'd been told about the government, about America trying to do good in the world, everything you've been told about sex, everything they told you about religion—it was all one big fabrication. Everything kind of fell apart. And sometimes in a rather joyous and raucous way . . . Rock and roll was very

12 Freedman
13 Wooley 29-30
14 Eliot: "Baudelaire" 373

anarchistic. It was just like, "Let's throw everything out and see what's real."[15]

As with many members of his generation, Craven's pursuit of the real led him to experiment with mind-altering drugs, and he names LSD guru Timothy Leary as a significant influence. A few years earlier, Leary had cowritten a book called *The Psychedelic Experience* (1964), in which he compared the stages of an acid trip with the stages of awakening outlined in the Tibetan Book of the Dead. "Of course," Leary stipulates, "the drug does not *produce* [italics mine] the transcendent experience. It merely acts as a chemical key—it opens the mind, frees the nervous system of its ordinary patterns and structures."[16] With this passage, Leary echoes the famous words of William Blake: "If the doors of perception were cleansed, everything would appear to man as it is, Infinite." Craven concurs:

> *If you trip, you suddenly realize that reality itself is a lie. It can be taken apart, and suddenly you are just looking at the molecules. Then you realize that there is this long history of drug-induced glimpses outside the whole structure of reality, into seeing something that's the bigger picture . . . That's when I started to think that God is much bigger than our concepts [of Him]. If God is infinite, then we're incapable of conceiving what any God could be. We make up these versions that are the most sophisticated versions we can think of, but the truth is still beyond us. At that point, I had a new awareness of [God as] just consciousness and the planet and nature. That's what's sacred. That's where the miracles are.*[17]

Craven concludes by saying that, as a result of such experiences, he simply "outgrew" the religion of his youth. He is quick to add, however, that he did not become an atheist and cannot imagine ever being an atheist, "because there's too much in the world that's wondrous."[18]

As Craven's beliefs changed, so did his life. He got married and had two children—another revelation, he says, remembering the

15 Interview with author 3/12/10
16 Leary 11
17 Interview with author 3/12/10
18 Interview with author 3/12/10

profound shock of becoming a father in 1965 and again in 1968: "You can't conceive of how that could ever come to be, that a kid in nine months would come out and have eyelashes in the right place and learn to talk and walk!"[19] Around the same time, he became obsessed with cinema. "In the town where I was teaching," he explains, "there was an arthouse theater. There wasn't a regular theater. It was the mid-Sixties, so they played all of the great European film directors: Buñuel, Truffaut, Fellini, Godard." He says his obsession began when he saw Michaelangelo Antonioni's *Blow-Up*: "I remember going back and watching it, like, six times in the theater—which, before that, I'd never done with any movie."[20] The films that followed forced him to recognize that film narratives could be as meaningful as literature and philosophy. Craven's newfound passion prompted him to serve as a faculty advisor to an extracurricular film club, and his fascination with filmmaking grew from there. He remembers:

> *[The students] had written a* Mission: Impossible *takeoff and I became sort of their advisor / cameraman. We made it and spliced it together on a projector—used a projector as an editing machine. Knew nothing about the technical side of film, really. We made the cost of our film, which I think was about $300, back ten times… And at the end of the year, my department chairman came to me and he said, "You know, it's time for you to get serious. You're not working on your PhD, you haven't published anything and you're running around with this stupid camera, acting like an idiot. It's time you became a serious Humanities professor. And I quit.*[21]

The following years were tense. Craven spent two summers in New York City, away from his family, trying to get into the film business—a decision that hastened his divorce in 1969. His first professional break came in 1970, when he met singer/songwriter Harry Chapin. Chapin was working as a documentary filmmaker at the time and he generously taught Craven how to edit on a flatbed machine. "I sat with him for about a week," Craven remembers, "just watching him cut. He explained to me why he was cutting, pacing, and a great deal of things which stuck with me to this day."

19 Interview with author 3/12/10

20 Interview with author 3/12/10

21 Craven: *Directors*

At the end of the week, Chapin fired his messenger and offered Craven the job.[22] Ten months later, Craven was assistant managing a postproduction house, and learning everything he could about filmmaking through hands-on experience with documentarians like Jim Lipscomb, Norman Mailer, Richard Leacock, and D.A. Pennebaker. Things were going well until he accidentally spliced a film in the wrong sequence—a mistake that cost him his job. For the next few months, the only job he could get was as a cab driver. At that point, he says, "I just thought, 'I've blown it,' like it was some sort of foolish fantasy."[23]

His fortunes changed when he met a twenty-seven-year-old producer named Sean Cunningham. Cunningham had recently scored a financial success with a Forty-Second Street documentary called *The Art of Marriage* (1970), a film that he describes as a "white coater," explaining:

> *At that time [. . .] they allowed you to get away with showing hardcore XXX-rated movies as long as they were under the guise of freedom of speech. You billed it as an "educational" or "medical" movie. At the beginning someone would come out in a white coat and say, "We're now going to show you marriage practices in Denmark and these are the ways you can improve your marital bliss." And then for the next 80 minutes you saw people fucking like crazy. At the end, the same guy with the white coat would come out again and say, "Now you have experienced these practices. Now you can go home with your mate and practice these things at home." We didn't have anybody actually fucking onscreen, just two people without clothes on lying on top of each other.*[24]

The Art of Marriage cost $3,500 and made over $100,000 in New York's grindhouse theaters, so Cunningham decided to make "a real version of it" that could play in suburban theaters.[25] He hired Craven to sync dailies for *Together* (1971), a film that Craven says "was essentially based on a lot of the sensitivity and human-awarenessbooks

22 Lofficier 232
23 Robb 17
24 Bracke 14
25 Bracke 15

that were coming out at the time."[26] Craven also worked closely with editor Roger Murphy, who he refers to as "my mentor," adding, "Between Harry Chapin and Roger Murphy, I learned in very quick time, from the point of view of two very bright men, how to cut material."When Murphy abruptly left the project, the eager trainee took over, and even managed to write and direct a couple of additional sequences.[27]

The resulting film was a financial success, so the film's distributor approached Cunningham about producing a follow-up. Craven remembers how he got involved:

> *[Sean Cunningham said,] "I have these guys who will give us $90,000 to make a movie, but they want it to be scary." My response was, "I don't know anything about scary movies." Sean, who was not an ex-fundamentalist, said, "You were raised as a fundamentalist. Just pull all of the skeletons out of your closet."*[28]

For Craven, it was the beginning of a long cinematic journey into fear.

26 Szulkin 31
27 Szulkin 28
28 Interview with author 3/12/10

Ingmar Bergman, *Last House on the Left* and Fairy Tales for the Apocalypse

Much has been written about the fact that Craven based his first film, *Last House on the Left* (1972), on Ingmar Bergman's *The Virgin Spring* (1960), which was itself based on a medieval Swedish ballad. Craven explains, "I had seen *The Virgin Spring* about a year before I wrote *Last House*, and I loved the turnaround of the story." Regardless, he points out, his film was hardly remake: "It wasn't as if I sat down and went scene for scene . . . the Bergman movie stuck in my mind, and that was about the extent of it."[29] Both films revolve around the rape and murder of an innocent young girl, and the revenge exacted by her parents. Each narrative, however, unfolds in its own way, revealing the differences between the storytellers.

For Bergman, *The Virgin Spring* was not a starting point, but a continued exploration of lifelong obsessions. The Swedish auteur had been making films since the mid-1940s, and his work had become increasingly personal, even confessional, since the making of *The Seventh Seal* (1957), an allegorical rumination on faith and death. That film, he writes in his 1994 autobiography, was one of the last manifestations of his dwindling childhood faith. When he made *The Virgin Spring* a few years later, his religious beliefs had morphed into something more complicated. He explained, "The God concept had long ago begun to crack, and it remained more as a decoration than anything else. What really interested me was the actual, horrible story of the girl and her rapists, and the subsequent revenge."[30] In other words, he was drawn to the story for the same reasons that Craven would be later.

The Virgin Spring is neatly divided into two parts. The first half tells the story of two young women. Karin is innocent and naïve and full of life. Ingiri, her adopted stepsister, is unlawfully pregnant and extremely jealous of Karin. And for good reason. Karin's parents, Töre and Märeta, dote on their biological daughter. They can't even

29 Szulkin 34
30 Bergman: *Images* 244

bring themselves to chastise Karin for sleeping late and shirking her sacred duty to bring candles to church for a festival honoring the Virgin Mary. Because of that, when Karin finally leaves for church, it is late in the day and she asks Ingiri to ride with her. Along the road, the two girls get into a fight and part ways. Karin rides on alone, and encounters three vagabond brothers—two adults and one child. The trio convinces the naïve girl to stop and eat lunch with them, and then the crudest of the bunch violently rapes her. Ingiri watches from the woods nearby, and does nothing to stop what's happening. Afterward, the rapist bludgeons Karin to death and steals her clothes.

The second half of the film begins when the three attackers unknowingly take refuge with Karin's family. That night, the youngest of the three attackers is literally sick with guilt, terrified of unknown forces that could steal his life as quickly and easily as his brother stole Karin's. The rapist, meanwhile, offers Karin's dress to Märeta as a gift, unaware that she is Karin's mother. When Märeta brings the dress to her husband, Ingiri confesses that she saw Karin murdered. Töre lashes himself in an apparent purification ritual, then goes after the brothers with a sword. In the end, he kills one with a knife and one with his bare hands. Märeta silently observes her husband's actions, and speaks up only to plead for the young boy's life. Töre disregards her plea and pitches the child's body against a wall, killing him. As the boy lies dead at his feet, the father looks down at his hands in sorrow and shame, and says, "God forgive me for what I have done."

The film concludes with a scene in which Ingiri leads Karin's parents to the place where their daughter was killed. When they discover her body, Töre falls to his knees and addresses God: "You let it happen. I don't understand you." The only response is silence, a moment suggesting that God is absent or uncaring. After a brief internal struggle, Töre breaks the silence, adding, "Yet still I ask for forgiveness. I know no other way to make peace with myself . . . I know no other way to live." Töre vows to build a church on the very spot where his daughter was killed, and God makes His presence known by opening an underground spring right in front of Töre's eyes. The silence that follows is God's silence.

This was not Bergman's final statement on the subject of God's silence, as the filmmaker explained in the 1963 documentary *Ingmar Bergman Makes a Movie*: "In *The Virgin Spring*, I let God answer in the form of a ballad, as the spring begins to flow. For me that was a timid way of closing in on the issue, and setting forth my own views on the reality of God." In his subsequent film *Through a Glass Darkly* (1961), the filmmaker proposes a much darker theory: that "every conception of a divine god created by human beings must be a monster."[31] In hindsight, he felt that this conclusion was tainted by his own preoccupations with his father, and with "that old idea of God, where God is the father . . . a God of security."[32]

He continued to wrestle with the idea of God in *Winter Light* (1963), a film in which the main character decides that, whether God exists or not, a man has a moral obligation to help his fellow man. What's most important is not the objective truth of Christianity, but its practical effects in the world. Bergman regarded this conclusion as a "moral victory and a departure":

> *With* Winter Light *I dismiss the religious debate and render an account of the result [. . .] The film is the tombstone over a traumatic conflict, which ran like an inflamed nerve throughout my conscious life. The images of God are shattered without my perception of Man as the bearer of a holy purpose being obliterated. The surgery has finally been completed.*[33]

Just as Bergman's films convey his changing worldview, so *Last House on the Left* reflects Craven's perspective at a particular place and time in his life. *The Virgin Spring* may have provided the story template, but a host of other influences profoundly affected the way the first-time filmmaker spun his variation on the tale. Just as Bergman's film embodies the austerity of the Scandinavian landscape, both physical and metaphysical, Craven's first film embodies the cultural anarchy in America after "the death of God."

31 Bergman: *Images* 238
32 Bergman: *Ingmar*
33 Bergman: *Images* 30

Craven is the first to admit that, when he started writing *Last House on the Left* in 1971, he knew almost nothing about the tradition of horror films. In later years he has referred to *Last House* as "the next logical step after *Psycho*,"[34] but he also admits that he did not actually see Hitchcock's 1960 film until "decades after it first played for audiences."[35] He did, however, take some inspiration from George Romero's *Night of the Living Dead* (1968), as he explained to biographer John Wooley:

> *My sole horror-film experience, when I set out to make* Last House, *was just coincidental. A friend had dragged me to see* Night of the Living Dead. *I knew nothing about it, but she said, "I just hear it's a lot of fun." So we went in, and this movie started, and I immediately found myself really scared. The audience was completely into it. It was almost a* Rocky Horror *kind of thing. They knew what was coming. They were laughing, they were screaming, and people were running up and down the aisles. There was tremendous energy in the theater [. . .] I went home after that and I thought, "My God, I'm not aware of this art form at all. It's raucous. It's bawdy. It's crazy. It electrified an audience. And it has something to say." It was amazing.*[36]

In his foreword to Joe Kane's study of *Night of the Living Dead*, Craven adds:

> *That movie, more than anything else I can think of, liberated me to make* Last House on the Left, *because I knew that after that there was a whole new kind of film blossoming in American cinema. It was something hybrid that mixed terror and laughter and social comment into one heady, totally unpredictable witches' brew of entertainment unlike anything I'd ever experienced before.*[37]

Just a few short years after he had discovered European arthouse cinema, Craven was discovering American exploitation cinema. And he didn't just study it: he got *immersed* in it. One of his earliest jobs was that of assistant editor on the counterculture comedy *You've Got*

34 Sharrett 219
35 Craven: "10 Movies"
36 Wooley 50
37 Craven: "A *Night* to Remember" xvi

to Walk It Like You Talk It or You'll Lose That Beat (1971), written and directed by a young filmmaker named Peter Locke. More significant at the time was his affiliation with producer Sean Cunningham, who was quickly making a name for himself in the burgeoning exploitation film business. Only a few months before *Deep Throat* (1971) brought hardcore porn into the mainstream of American culture, Cunningham saw the writing on the wall. "White coaters" were out. He needed something else to exploit.

According to an interview in the documentary *Celluloid Crime of the Century*, Cunningham and Craven found what they were looking for at a screening of one of the Sergio Leone / Clint Eastwood spaghetti westerns. Despite the graphic violence in the film, Cunningham says, "it didn't have anything to do with people dying and the real horror attached to people dying." The two young filmmakers decided that "if you could ever make a movie in which [the audience] *thought* somebody really died, it would be just dramatically different." They were not simply interested in making a gore movie. Herschell Gordon Lewis had been doing that for years. They wanted to make a *real* horror movie, something that would break all of the taboos about sex and violence.

Up to this point, Craven says, "I'd always written artistic, poetic things. Suddenly, I was working in an area I had never really confronted before."[38] In addition to drawing on the religious tension of his early life, he found himself incorporating his feelings about current events:

> *I think what was going on subconsciously was a pretty complex matrix of being raised as a fundamentalist [and] being alive in America at that time. The Vietnam War certainly was the first time where the country—that I could remember—had gone into this long, excruciating self-examination.*[39]

The outcome, for the nation and for the filmmaker himself, was a "tremendous coming of age that nobody would have wanted."[40] Craven's political awakening had a direct impact on his version of *The Virgin Spring*.

38 Wood 111

39 Craven: *Still*

40 Craven: *Still*

Last House on the Left begins by introducing the Collingwoods: mild-mannered middle-class parents John and Estelle and their free-spirited but naïve daughter Mari. Mari is preparing to celebrate her seventeenth birthday with her friend Phyllis Stone, a girl with a more sullied reputation. Unlike their counterparts in *The Virgin Spring*, however, they are not going to church. Together, they leave the bucolic setting of Mari's childhood home in rural Connecticut for the grime of New York City, intent on seeing a rock band called Bloodlust. The band name says everything that Craven needs to say about American culture in 1972.

1967's "Summer of Love" had been followed by violent rioting at the Democratic National Convention and the assassinations of Martin Luther King and Robert Kennedy in 1968, the Manson Family murders and the deadly Altamont Free Concert in 1969, the Kent State massacre in 1970, the untimely deaths of Jimi Hendrix, Janis Joplin, and Jim Morrison in 1970 and 1971, and the continued escalation of the war in Vietnam. By 1972, the idealistic dreams of the Love Generation had turned into vivid nightmares. Rock and roll had turned angry. (Bloodlust was undoubtedly a close cousin to shock-rock performers like Alice Cooper.) Drug use no longer connoted freedom: it connoted death. Free love had become marketable sleaze. In this milieu, Craven does not need to give Mari's mother a premonition of bad things to come (as Bergman did in *The Virgin Spring*). The writing is already on the wall—or, more accurately, in the landscape. *Last House* was filmed in October, amid the colorful beauty of slow death. "I guess winter's coming on," Mari observes, blissfully ignorant of the symbolic significance of her observation.

Before long, the film introduces a second family consisting of two escaped convicts, a homicidal maniac named Krug and his sexually deviant friend Weasel, plus Krug's heroin-addicted son Junior and "animal-like" girlfriend Sadie. This mini-Manson family abducts Mari and Phyllis and drives them out to the woods, vaguely contemplating the "sex crime of the century." In an uncomfortably protracted sequence, they torment and humiliate the girls, while laughing nervously and wondering (like the audience) how far they will go. Craven intercuts the extended sequence with a comic relief sequence, probably inspired by *In the Heat of the Night* (1967), which reveals the local sheriff and his deputy at their most bumbling and ineffectual. The message is clear: We can't rely on the "authorities" to restore order.

Whereas the attack in *The Virgin Spring* passes relatively quickly (Craven admits that his original script was "much more sexual," noting that the actors talked him out of shooting a hardcore rape.[41]) It is painfully drawn out in *Last House*. After Krug rapes Mari, the family members look at each other with disbelief and disgust, revealing for a moment their humanity. Craven says that the subsequent murder of Phyllis, heavily edited in all existing cuts of the film (though some of the raw footage was repurposed for a 1976 documentary *The Evolution of Snuff*), was intended to have the same effect:

> *The killing of Phyllis is very sexual in feeling, and ended with her being stabbed not only by the men but by the woman repeatedly. Then she fell to the ground and Sadie bent down and pulled out a loop of her intestines. They looked at it and that's where it all stopped. That's when they realized what they had done. It was as if they had been playing with a doll, or a prisoner they thought was a doll, and it had broken and come apart and they did not know how to put it back together again. Again, there were parallels with what I was seeing in our culture, where we were breaking things that we did not know how to put back together.*[42]

For Craven, it was important to show these murders in all of their ugliness and brutality, without flinching. He was implementing what he had realized while watching the Clint Eastwood spaghetti western. The violence had to be *real*, not stylized.

A few years earlier, Alfred Hitchcock had filmed a comparable murder scene for his film *Torn Curtain* (1966). It wasn't a particularly bloody scene, but it was emotionally exhausting, because Paul Newman spent nearly five full minutes of screen time in a knock-down-drag-out fight, with a man who was trying just as hard to kill him. Hitchcock, deviating from the then-popular James Bond-style screen violence, let the scene play without music and without the usual cutaways. He explained to Francois Truffaut that he did this for a very specific reason:

41 Craven: *Celluloid*

42 Wood 113

> *In every picture somebody gets killed and it goes very quickly. They are stabbed or shot, and the killer never even stops to look and see whether the victim is really dead or not. And I thought it was time to show that it was very difficult, very painful, and it takes a very long time to kill a man.*[43]

Craven was after the same effect. The MPAA censors, he told journalist Ian Grey, "want people to get shot and Bang! They're done. Like they're just disappearing." Craven argues, "The films are just so much better without those cuts. Much better. There's more humanity to them."[44]

Last House encourages us to empathize not only with the victim but with the victimizers. It demands a strong reaction to a cultural loss of innocence. When Craven talks about onscreen violence as a form of social protest, he is asking how Americans can, for example, watch nightly news footage of the atrocities in Vietnam, then casually return to our ordinary lives. How can we "take part" in a crime like this and, afterward, do nothing about it?

Many viewers were outraged by this unrestrained display of sadism and cruelty, and Craven was labeled instantly as the worst kind of deviant filmmaker: a pornographer of violence. Perhaps that response was inevitable, since the events in the second half of his film do nothing to morally redeem the events of the first half. As in *The Virgin Spring*, the killers in *Last House* unknowingly take refuge in the home of their victim's family. Once Mari's parents realize that they are harboring their daughter's murderers, they start planning their revenge. From this point on, *Last House* is geared toward exploitation audiences.

John Collingwood, not as accustomed to overt violence as Töre was in *The Virgin Spring*, sets up a series of elaborate booby-traps around the house. Estelle Collingwood is a bit more direct. She seizes an opportunity to seduce Weasel . . . and then seizes an especially vulnerable part of his anatomy. In the final sequence, John emerges from the basement with a chainsaw and savagely kills Krug. The bumbling sheriff and his deputy show up too late to stop the transformation of the once mild-mannered middle-class parents into brutal killers. Unlike Bergman, Craven does not allow

43 Truffaut 234

44 Grey 113-114

any time for reflection or remorse, and the film concludes without any sort of affirmation of the existence of a higher morality. In *Last House*, the violence goes unanswered.

At times, Wes Craven seems to be genuinely surprised and dismayed by the intensity of his first film. He has referred to *Last House* as a "primal scream," comparing himself as a filmmaker to the mad Captain Kurtz in Joseph Conrad's *Heart of Darkness*:

> *Certainly one of the things that the horror genre does at its best is express that rage that Kurtz expresses at the end of the river, a sort of primal scream, and its done by people who are in one way or another outside the usual mainstream of art who figure they have nothing to lose. When I did* Last House, *I was in this situation.*[45]

Craven is obliquely referring to a 1970 bestseller, *The Primal Scream: Primal Therapy, The Cure for Neurosis* by psychologist Arthur Janov. Janov encouraged his patients to release "the pressure of holding the real self back" through focused outbursts of concentrated emotion.[46] The goal, he explained, was to overcome lifelong neuroses by recognizing them as such:

> *Unfulfilled needs supersede any other activity in the human until they are met. When needs are met, the child can feel. He can experience his body and his environment. When needs are not met, the child experiences only tension, which is feeling disconnected from consciousness. Without that necessary connection, the neurotic does not feel. Neurosis is the pathology of feeling.*[47]

The primal scream, essentially, is an attempt to reconnect. Janov goes on to explain that neurosis causes a kind of psychic split, creating an "unreal self" that denies the real self's basic needs and feelings. Primal therapy aims at breaking down a person's socially-reinforced defense system "in order to release the real, defenseless self."[48] In the

45 Sharrett 219
46 Janov 84
47 Janov 24
48 Janov 209

simplest terms, Janov urged his patients to "let it all out." In his view, such a release is a dire necessity for some people:

> *The* Primal *view of rage is that it is a rage against someone trying to crush the life out of you. We have to remember that neurotic parents are unconsciously killing their children, in a sense; they are killing off the real selves of their offspring; psychophysical death is a real process where life is being squeezed out of them. The result is the anger: "I hate you for not letting me live." To be anything else but yourself is to be dead.*[49]

On some level, it seems as if *Last House on the Left* served this function for Wes Craven, allowing him to vent years of repressed rage. A recent interview with Jason Zinoman shows that he is conscious of having released some feelings that he'd repressed because his mother would not have approved of them. "For all of her genuine love toward me," Craven told Zinoman, "I never felt like she loved who I really was. Maybe *Last House* was just a flying in the face of my mother's judgment. You want to see violent? You want to see *sick*? Here it is!"[50] The filmmaker goes so far as to suggest that the alternative might have been venting that rage in a destructive manner, even climbing up in a tower and shooting people.[51] This is not, of course, how Craven's story ends. He unleashed his primal scream on celluloid, then had to face the world's reaction.

In 2010, Craven admitted that he was overwhelmed by the initial viewer response: "Everybody's reaction to us—especially me, since I had written and directed it—was: 'You are a perverse, horrible, twisted person.' That was scary. I thought, *Oh my God, I am everything my church warned me about.* (laughs)"[52] He can laugh about it now, because later audiences have embraced the film as the "primal scream" of an entire generation . . . and because he has never felt the need to repeat that primal scream. Janov predicted: "Make anger real, and it will disappear."[53] For Craven, that seems to have been the case. He says, "I felt it very strongly and I needed to get it out of my system [and] I've never felt the need to go and have quite the

49 Janov 323
50 Zinoman 82
51 Zinoman 70
52 Interview with author 3/12/10
53 Janov 323

same depictions in a film again."[54] According to biographer Brian J. Robb, Craven initially planned to write a sequel in which Krug and company return from hell and resume their killing spree, but he ultimately decided not to go there.[55]

That said, it was not easy for Wes Craven to escape the legacy of his first film. He told interviewer Randy Lofficier: "Because *Last House* was so upsetting to the Establishment, I think I had only one call in two years [after its release] . . . That was from the producers of *Let's Scare Jessica to Death*."[56] A film like *Let's Scare Jessica to Death* (1971), which emphasizes gothic atmosphere and psychological terror rather than overt violence, might have been a perfect sophomore film for Craven. Certainly it bears some similarities to the filmmaker's later efforts, which question the nature of accepted reality. For the time being, however, Craven was not quite ready to take on another horror film.

In the midst of the *Last House* backlash, Craven and producing partner Sean Cunningham tried to develop a biopic of Anthony Herbert, an ex-Army officer who spoke out against the atrocities in Vietnam in his best-selling book *Soldier* (1973). They also planned "a satire on American beauty contests."[57] When those projects failed to materialize, Craven went back to work for his friend Peter Locke, serving as assistant director and editor of the hardcore sex comedy *It Happened in Hollywood* (1973), a film with at least one scene that resonates in terms of Craven's mainstream filmography.

It Happened in Hollywood revolves around a horny girl-next-door type named Felicity Split, who is determined to make it big in tinseltown. She screws everyone, from the talent agent to the makeup girl, on her way to a breakthrough role as Delilah in a hardcore porn version of *Samson and Delilah*. The most inventive sequence in the film features Felicity Split masturbating while talking on the phone to a casting director, who is simultaneously getting a blowjob from another actress. After she spontaneously pops a hardboiled egg out

54 Robb 23
55 Robb 32
56 Lofficier 236
57 Robb 34

of her vagina (?!), the casting director literally ejaculates into the phone. His semen shoots out of the other end, onto Felicity. Freddy Krueger fans may recognize this absurdly surreal sequence as a hardcore variation of the Freddy tongue-phone scene in *A Nightmare on Elm Street*. (The casting director does what Freddy can only dream of in a mainstream movie.)

Hollywood was not Craven's last foray into the world of hardcore pornography. There are rumors that he also worked on Sean Cunningham's 1973 vampire porno *Case of the Full Moon Murders*, as well as a few films for *Flesh Gordon* director Howard Ziehm. According to Bill Landis and Michelle Clifford's *Sleazoid Express*, he also directed *The Fireworks Woman* (1975) under the pseudonym of Abe Snake.[58] The mysterious Snake is credited on the film as cowriter and editor, and it's true that there are some striking thematic similarities to Craven's later work.

The Fireworks Woman begins with a ritualistic dance sequence, primal and sinister. At the center of the dance is a man wearing a black top hat, a cape, and a sardonic smile. Sure enough, it's a young Wes Craven, playing the role of Nicholas Burns, "the fireworks man." Burns is a purely symbolic character who lends an ominous quality to the narrative. In some ways, he is a bit like the carnival leader "Mr. Dark" in Ray Bradbury's novel *Something Wicked This Way Comes*. (And now that I think about it, *Something Wicked This Way Comes* would have been a great title for this darkly philosophical porno.) Burns continues to reappear throughout the film, like a mischievous devil subtly orchestrating the chain of events.

The story revolves around a young woman named Angela, who recently emerged from an illicit affair with her brother Peter. In the wake of the affair, Peter has become a priest, leaving Angela alone to fantasize endlessly about their time together. There's a dreamy quality to her flashbacks, photographed in a gauzy white light and accompanied by percussion-free music (most notably Pachelbel's "Canon in D"), which suggests that the sex scenes are meant to be spiritual rather than simply lustful. As Angela's fantasies become increasingly desperate, "Canon in D" segues into David Hess's "Now You're All Alone," the song that was used to convey a sense of inconsolable loss following Mari's rape in *Last House on the Left*. These

58 Landis 127

flashbacks stand in sharp contrast with the kinky and frequently sadistic sex scenes that follow, as Angela descends into a world of impersonal, unthinking, primal lust with an assortment of strange characters. The juxtaposition reveals a filmmaker's attempt to distinguish between meaningful sex and exploitation, just as *Last House* attempted to make a distinction between real world violence and action-movie violence.

The secondary story, revolving around the character of Peter, is steeped in religious guilt. As Angela falls from grace, Peter begins to question whether his loyalty to the church should be greater than his loyalty to the woman he loves. At first, when she confesses that she still loves him, he flatly replies that their love is "forbidden," adding, "The soul can be tortured forever." Angela responds, "It's not my soul. It's my heart. Can't you see that?" Peter still rejects her, although he has to go home and self-flagellate in order to suppress his arousal. In Janov's terms, he is denying the needs and emotions of his "real self."

At this point, Craven's "fireworks man" reappears, offering Angela a Faustian deal to win Peter back. When she asks who he is, Burns simply smiles and responds, "No one special." He sticks to the facts: "There is something you want. And you can have it. There are no mysteries that can't be untied. No fight that can't be won. But it'll cost you something. Know what I mean?" For the moment she turns her back on him, but the devilish stranger keeps smiling. He can afford to be patient, because he knows that she is weakening. As it turns out, so is Peter. When he confesses his desires to a fellow priest, the priest echoes the sentiments of the fireworks man: "Leave it to God. There are no mysteries he cannot unravel. No fights he cannot win. No matter who the adversary might be. . . ." The filmmaker's implication is that God (at least, the Catholic God) and "the devil" are not so different from each other.

The story climaxes with a frenetic orgy at Angela's house on the Fourth of July. Ironically, it represents the moment when she has completely surrendered her independence. She says, "I realized I was the center of the cycle now and that everything was going to be sucked into it. I knew sooner or later Peter would be swept up into it . . . and I would have him!" As anticipated, Peter shows up and interrupts the orgy, claiming Angela for himself. It's a moment of triumph for her, and also seemingly a moment of triumph for Peter, who writes to his monsignor:

> *I've thought about what you said this morning, but I just can't leave it to God any longer. I've been doing that my whole life. Now it's time I took responsibility for things myself. Angela and I are going to go away together. I guess in a way it's just natural. We've never been apart really anyway. Not ever. I can't even be a decent priest anymore, not as long as this is in my life.*

Above all, it's a moment of triumph for "the fireworks man." Craven shows up onscreen one last time, revealing that he is also the monsignor who counseled Peter to "leave it to God." He laughs sardonically as the two young lovers sail away together, and the film ends on an ambiguous note. Have the young lovers overcome their fears and liberated their "real selves?" Or has the devil seduced them? Is Craven's laughter meant to be evil or merely cynical? It's difficult to tell and, in light of the fact that hardcore pornography has been so thoroughly dismissed or demonized by most audiences since the 1970s, it's difficult to view the film today with any kind of critical objectivity.

In light of Craven's other work, however, it is easy to view *The Fireworks Woman* as a reflection of the filmmaker's rejection of organized religion and religious dualism. If *Last House* is Craven's *Virgin Spring*, *The Fireworks Woman* is his *Winter Light*. If *Last House* represents his primal scream, *The Fireworks Woman* may reflect his "real self." That self is an enigma—at least to us.

Eventually Craven turned his attention back to the horror genre, mainly for financial reasons. He figured he had two options: he could continue to avoid the type of film that had made him notorious or he could accept the idea that maybe a bad reputation was better than no reputation at all. In a 2010 interview, he reflected on his decision:

> *Once you do a really violent film, people don't say, "Okay let's give him a comedy to do." So in a way, you get stuck in that ghetto, and then you have to ask yourself: Do I stop making films*

because I hate the limitations? Do I make them and try not to think about it? Or do I say to myself "For whatever reason, I'm in a position where I can make films of a particular sort . . . so what can I put into them that will be really interesting and different?" I realized that I could do my own version of these dark myths and fairy tales. Now I just had to figure out how to do it without getting too intellectual about it.[59]

First, he contemplated "a children's horror movie based around Hansel and Gretel"—an idea hinting at the direction his films would take in the 1980s and 1990s. Next, he filmed a Western-themed segment for a horror anthology called *Tales That Will Tear Your Heart Out*. (Outtakes from the latter project, featuring David Hess in a supporting role, appeared on the Anchor Bay DVD release of *Last House*.) Finally, while he was editing the sex comedy *Kitty Can't Help It* (a.k.a. *Car Hops*), he agreed to write another horror film for Peter Locke. The producer, who was at the time making regular trips between Los Angeles and Las Vegas, made a helpful suggestion. Craven remembers: "The desert was wide open [and] we didn't need permits to shoot out there."[60]

Craven's original script for *The Hills Have Eyes* began with an opening crawl that satirized his notorious reputation and acknowledged his reluctance to return to the horror genre. It read:

In 1973, following the release of Last House on the Left, *the writer/director of that film was committed for psychiatric observation. He was treated extensively with drugs, group therapies, electroshock programs and a final lobotomy. Despite these efforts at reform, Craven killed his nurse, Maura Heaphy, and escaped to the Mohave Desert. At the end of 1000 days of meditation he was taken up by a jet-black saucer and trained in Secondary Media Infiltration and parametaphysical survival on the Planet Jupiter. Upon his graduation he was returned to the planet earth at Exeter. This Film is his first since his return, and is respectfully dedicated to the memory of Maura Heaphy.*

Obviously, he knew that *The Hills Have Eyes* was unlikely to endear him to anyone who had not appreciated *Last House on the Left*, so

59 Interview with the author 3/12/10

60 Emery 103

in effect he was digging himself in. He would repeat his primal scream, this time with full awareness of what he was doing and how he would be perceived.

Much as he took his inspiration for *Last House* from medieval folklore, Craven drew inspiration for *The Hills Have Eyes* (1977) from a well-known British legend about a family of cannibals. The story first appeared in a periodical called *The Newgate Calendar* in the eighteenth century. According to that report, Sawney Beane was a runaway who bred a family of savages on the Scottish coast. The family made their living by robbing and murdering passersby. When dismembered body parts began washing up on nearby shores, the authorities sent spies into the region to track down the murderers. Eventually a would-be victim escaped the family's ambush and led the King's army in search of the family's hideout. Soldiers with bloodhounds found the cannibals living in a vast sea cave, filled with the dried and pickled remains of dozens of murdered travelers. They rounded up the cannibals and took them back to Edinburgh, where they were executed. Male family members were dismembered while their women watched; the women were burned alive. Craven says he was instantly intrigued by the implications of the tale:

> *In that nut of a story was everything I thought about civilization. Because on the one hand you have this wildness that can just run rampant and prey upon the civilization. But then the civilization, when they catch up with them, is completely uncivilized itself... and has its own macabre wildness to it. I just took that and translated it into the 20th century.*[61]

Interviewers Dennis Fischer and Christopher Sharrett each learned a bit more about the context for Craven's script when they interviewed the filmmaker in the mid-1980s. Craven told Fischer that he dreamed *The Hills Have Eyes* as a "Beauty and the Beast" story about a civilized family and an uncivilized family which function as mirror images of each other. The filmmaker went on to explain that his original draft of the script (titled *Blood Relations: The Sun Wars*) was set in 1984. By that time, the script speculated, states would have become territorial due to pollution and other social problems. As a result, passports would be required for interstate travel. As the

61 Craven: *Directors*

narrative unfolds, a civilized family leaves New York, headed for California, where the living is reputedly easy. Because they don't have the necessary passports, they have to sneak in through the Nevada desert. Along the way they meet a decidedly uncivilized family of cannibals.[62] Craven told Sharrett that he thought of the story as a variation on *The Grapes of Wrath*, a deconstruction of America's frontier myth. In effect, he added, *The Hills Have Eyes* is an apocalyptic anti-Western.

In the years following the Vietnam War, the Western film genre had all but died. In 1972, Westerns represented twelve percent of Hollywood's total output. That figure fell dramatically over the next few years: four Westerns were released in 1973; two in 1974; five in 1975; seven for the country's Bicentennial; and only two in 1977, the year *The Hills Have Eyes* was shot and released.[63] Craven insists that this decline in popularity was no accident: "American myth as previously conceived—John Wayne at Iwo Jima, the flag, good guys vs. bad guys—all this has to die, because as it is applied to the real world it clearly doesn't make it; it's failing every time."[64] In his estimation, the frontier myth—with its idyllic vision of American civilization—simply wasn't able to survive the Vietnam War and the Nixon presidency.

The Hills Have Eyes represents a transitional period in which the old ways were replaced by something new—or, more to the point, *consumed* by something older and more primal. The "civilized" father in the film, Big Bob Carter, is a gun-toting John Wayne type, an ex-cop full of piss and vinegar, but he doesn't stand a chance against the savagery of Papa Jupiter. Their encounter culminates with a scene in which Papa Jupe literally eats his nemesis while taunting Big Bob's disembodied head. Craven insists that he wasn't trying to comment on the weakness of "civilized" America, but on a more essential truth of human existence: "People just seem to grind up other people, in the same way that animals eat other animals to grow stronger."[65] In short: We are not nearly as civilized as we like to pretend we are. As the story progresses, the supposedly uncivilized family stalks and torments the supposedly civilized family until every character in the

62 Dennis Fischer 251
63 Hoberman 91
64 Sharrett 224
65 Sharrett 221

film is either dead or monstrously violent. Humanity is reduced to basic Darwinism—survival of the fittest. Craven calls it a "fairy tale for the apocalypse."[66]

To be fair, *The Hills Have Eyes* is not just a fairy tale. It is also a political allegory. When Papa Jupiter, a character right out of a Goya painting, tells Big Bob Carter "I'm in [and] you're out!", he's making a political statement in the crudest manner. Like so many of the European arthouse movies that Craven digested in the late 1960s, it is ultimately a film about revolution. Craven's film echoes the themes inherent in Jean-Luc Godard's *Weekend* (1967), a film about a bourgeoisie couple that gets trapped in a post-apocalyptic wasteland of abandoned cars and insane people. Both films suggest that "civilization" is a thin veneer on the essential truth of life: *Consume or be consumed.* Godard's film ends with a tribe of cannibal hippies munching on the remains of the contemptible "civilized" couple. Craven's film is actually a bit more optimistic.

In the midst of the anarchy, the filmmaker expresses hope for the future. The younger generation survives through a combination of intelligence and ingenuity—and, above all, an ability to work together. Bobby and his sister Brenda entrap and kill Papa Jupiter using a set of Rube Goldberg-type devices. At the same time, their friend Doug rescues his infant child with the help of one of the younger "savages." Ruby, the youngest member of the cannibal family, attacks her own brother (with a snake!) to save an innocent child.

What the survivors have in common is a willingness to fight for each other—like true family members. Without that sense of community, the filmmaker suggests, there's not much hope for any of us (especially in an environment as cruel and desolate as The Mojave Desert):

> *There's a scene where the baby is stolen and the father runs out into the desert, then realizes he's way out in the desert and has no way of knowing where anybody went. He screams, "Who are you and what do you want?" In my storyboards, I pulled all the way out until the earth is just this little dot [in outer space]. I was very much trying to touch on a feeling that I totally understand.*

66 Sharrett 220

> *On one hand there's a sense of awe, at the beauty and wonder of the world. On the other hand . . . how small and fragile we are.*[67]

The film conveys Wes Craven's search for meaning in a vast and complex world, and finds some solace in genuine human relationships. His original script for *The Hills Have Eyes* ended with a scene that symbolically unites the survivors from both families, signifying their triumph. The film, however, ends with the final savage murder, leaving things on a much more ambiguous note: *What comes after the primal scream?* Craven answers: "Both *Last House* and *Hills* contain characters who offer the possibility of change. Change is one thing I have a basic faith in."[68]

67 Interview with author 3/12/10
68 Sharrett 223

Roman Polanski, George Gurdjieff and *A Nightmare on Elm Street*

The commercial success of *The Hills Have Eyes* proved that Wes Craven was not a fluke, and quickly led to other job offers. In 1978, a producer named Max Keller hired him to direct the TV movie *Stranger in Our House* (a.k.a. *Summer of Fear*). The resulting film was a rather tepid thriller about a teenage witch, but *Stranger* gave the filmmaker his first opportunity to work outside the ultra-low budget world of exploitation cinema. It allowed him to direct an established cast (including *The Exorcist* star Linda Blair) in a real production studio with a real budget, and thereby legitimized his status as a filmmaker.

Emboldened by the experience, Craven worked hard to develop his next signature film. He wrote an adaptation of David Morrell's gut-wrenching novel *First Blood*, as well as an original script about Colombian drug smuggling, entitled *Marimba*. The former was not used for the Sylvester Stallone blockbuster; the latter eventually became the uncredited foundation of Ruggero Deodato's 1985 film *Inferno in Diretta* (a.k.a. *Cut and Run*), starring Richard Lynch and Michael Berryman. Before *Marimba* was unfairly repurposed, Craven also wrote "a screenplay based on the Jim Jones mass suicide" for the same producers. Later the filmmaker decided he was "thankful" that it was scrapped, because he didn't want to go from "being a director of horror films to a director of horrifying true incidents."[69] After a few years in development hell, Craven finally "latched onto the first thing I could," which turned out to be an adaptation of the DC comic book series *Swamp Thing*.[70]

Craven opines that this rather traditional monster movie—a cross between Universal's original *Frankenstein* movie and *The Incredible Hulk* TV series—lacks "the feeling of core Wes Craven films," because the story is not built around a family dynamic.[71] Nevertheless, his influence is apparent in the shooting script—in the symbolism of a deluged church transformed into a science lab,

69 Robb 45
70 Wooley 80
71 Szulkin 19

in the lead character's obsession with "an animal's aggressive power for survival," and in the "beauty and the beast" dichotomy between Swamp Thing and Cable (Adrienne Barbeau). Craven's voice is perhaps most apparent in a brief exchange between the unlikely lovers. After Swamp Thing allows himself to be captured in order to save Cable from ruthless mercenaries, she observes sadly, "You *knew* we'd be caught." Swamp Thing responds, like an enlightened mystic rather than a primitive creature, "The only way out is *through*." Craven's take on the DC Comic is that it's about a man shedding his baser instincts in order to become more human than the ordinary human. For the filmmaker, it would be the first of many stories about *spiritual* transformation.

Soon after he completed the screenplay for *Swamp Thing*, Craven received another call from producer Max Keller, offering him the director's chair on an indie horror feature called *Deadly Blessing* (1981).[72] In some ways, the project seemed tailor-made for Craven: a horror film about religious zealotry. The original story, conceived by Glenn M. Benest and Matthew Barr, begins with the mysterious death of John Schmidt, a farmer who was raised in a rural community of Hittites (a fictional cult conceived as an extreme variation on the Amish) and subsequently ostracized by the community when he decided to marry an outsider. John's widow Martha fears that members of the religious community may have killed her husband, but the leader of the Hittites insists that John's death was the work of a supernatural devil called the Incubus. The screenplay continues to cast suspicion on the Hittites by depicting them as close-minded and generally intolerant. Barr explains, "The Hittites as we portrayed them were very repressive on all levels—sexually repressive, very paternalistic and harsh. And so in a way we were kind of positing that the horror was coming out of that repression or in answer to that repression."[73] Benest adds: "It's about secrets that people push down and won't allow to come to the surface. And the more you repress something, the more you suppress the truth, the stronger it gets. Until finally it gets so powerful that it comes out in the horrific ways."[74]

72 Emery 104
73 Barr
74 Benest

Craven's take on the story was not quite as simple. The finished film explores the alternate (supernatural) explanation in a memorably seductive dream sequence featuring Martha's friend Lana. Almost as soon as she appears in the film, Lana begins reporting strange dreams, including one about a "man whose skin was all gray and ash" turning into a giant spider. Later, she has a dream in which an unseen devil holds her head and whispers in her ear while a spider falls into her open mouth. Craven has said that his own dreams inspired another memorable scene in the film—one where Martha is attacked in the bathtub by a snake. He remembers:

> *What was written was basically* Psycho, *where the girl's taking a shower... And I just said, "I can't do this." I kept trying to get the writers to give me something different, and they couldn't. That night I dreamed [the scene in the finished film]. I woke up in the morning, went to the set and said, "Get me a snake." And I basically shot the setup until some guy came in with a cottonmouth.*[75]

Snake imagery was nothing new in Craven's work. Ruby uses a Mojave Green as a weapon in *The Hills Have Eyes,* and Ferret (played by David Hess) uses a water moccasin as a weapon in *Swamp Thing*. A boa constrictor figures prominently within the Samson and Delilah sequence in *It Happened in Hollywood*, but perhaps we shouldn't blame "Abe Snake" for that one. Whatever the case, it doesn't take much imagination to speculate on why the serpent might figure prominently into the dreams and personal mythology of an ex-religious fundamentalist. The bathroom scene in *Deadly Blessing* is another suggestion that "devilish" forces are at work.

The final scene in *Deadly Blessing* confirms the supernatural theory. After everyone has accepted a rational explanation for the murder(s), the ghost of Martha's dead husband visits her. He tries to warn her that the Incubus is real, but he is too late. The devil rips through the floorboards beneath Martha and pulls her down into Hell. Paying off the ominous atmosphere of Lana's dream sequences, this scene is memorable because it is so unexpected, and also because it is so well executed. The way light and non-diegetic sound fade away with the arrival of the ghost, and then return after the Incubus

75 Interview with author 3/12/10

has magically disappeared, is genuinely unsettling. The scene suggests that the devil is ever-present, but never seen until it is too late. This might not have been the philosophical note that Craven wanted to end on—in fact, he says the shock ending was imposed by the studio—but the impressionistic style of the scene set the stage for Craven's future in the horror genre. Just as this scene introduced the supernatural into a mostly naturalistic story, so *Deadly Blessing* introduced surrealism into Craven's work.

After making *Deadly Blessing* and *Swamp Thing* back to back, Craven was once again eager to tackle a story of his own design. He didn't want to repeat the primal scream of *Last House* and *Hills*, so he drew inspiration for his next film from the European arthouse films that had lured him to filmmaking in the first place, aspiring to make something every bit as ambitious as the work of Bergson, Godard and Antonioni. In the early 1980s, he explained:

> *I'm interested in expanding the forms of consciousness within film because I think, with the exception of certain European directors, film is quite limited in the areas of consciousness it deals with. I think it's limiting of the art itself, because film is very dream-like. It's able to distort time, to contract it. It's able to go back and forth in time. It's not like a stage play—you can have optical tricks at your beck and call, you can have strange soundtracks, and everything else that you can do with film.*[76]

For as long as the medium has existed, filmmakers have been fascinated by the relationship between cinematic dreams and waking reality. Documentary-style films strive to capture objective reality while more stylized films create their own subjective reality. Early German Expressionist filmmakers used artificial landscapes to represent the psychological viewpoint of individual characters. In the famous case of *The Cabinet of Dr. Caligari* (1920), distorted sets convey the main character's madness. Even more unsettling was the use by early Surrealist filmmakers of free-association "dream logic" as a substitute for conventional narrative. Luis Buñuel's *Un Chien*

76 Robb 63

Andalou (1929) is a sequence of disconnected images culled from the dreams of Buñuel and his collaborator Salvador Dali. Buñuel adopted a more conventional narrative approach to his later films, but nearly all of his films contain at least one surreal dream sequence. "I find it impossible," the filmmaker confessed in his autobiography, "to explain a life without talking about the part that's underground—the imaginative, the unreal."[77]

Jean Cocteau's *Beauty and the Beast* (1946) likewise incorporates elements of "dream logic" into a romantic narrative. The goal, Cocteau says in his *Diary of a Film: La Belle et la Bete*, was to ground childhood fairy tales within the context of adult experience and beliefs, thereby presenting dreams as realities. The most evocative scenes in the film use simple movie magic to convey the illusion of supernatural forces at work: candelabras mounted on human arms extend from the hallway walls; statues move and breathe and blink; mirrors reflect times, places, and people that aren't "present." These subtle unrealities exist under the cover of just enough darkness, and within the context of a conventional narrative, to allow viewers to suspend their disbelief. Cocteau adjusts the unreal to the real, so that even the most skeptical viewers can allow themselves to *believe* in dreams.

In a 2009 article for *Entertainment Weekly*, Craven acknowledged the influence of Cocteau's *Beauty and the Beast* on his own work. He also noted Cocteau's influence on the films of Roman Polanski, his biggest filmmaking idol. "My model has always been Roman Polanski," Craven claims, noting that Polanski "has shown great mastery of the darker side of human nature, and yet has had the range that any artist should be allowed to have."[78] Although he envies the filmmaker's freedom to tell many different types of stories, Craven has been especially influenced by his horror films—including *Repulsion*, which Craven refers to as Polanski's "masterpiece."[79]

Repulsion is a harrowing depiction of one woman's descent into madness, combining the subjectivism of *Caligari* with Cocteau's technique of restraint. At the beginning of the film, Carole simply seems dazed and aloof. As the film progresses, her perception of the world becomes increasingly unreliable. First, she experiences audio

77 Buñuel 94

78 Wiater 56

79 Craven: "10 Movies"

hallucinations: the disproportionately loud sounds of a dripping faucet, a ticking clock, a barking dog. Then, she begins to suffer visual hallucinations: cracks opening suddenly in the walls of her apartment, and visions of a male attacker in her bedroom at night. Eventually, her entire world—which is to say, the apartment she has barricaded herself inside—becomes distorted to the point that she no longer has any coherent frame of reference for what's real. In his autobiography *Roman*, the director explains:

> *My aim was to show Carole's hallucinations through the eye of the camera, augmenting their impact by using wide-angle lenses of progressively increasing scope. But in itself, that wasn't sufficient for my purpose. I also wanted to alter the actual dimensions of the apartment—to expand the rooms and passages and push back the walls so that audiences could experience the full effect of Carole's distorted vision. Accordingly we designed the walls of the set so they could be moved outward and elongated by the insertion of extra panels. When "stretched" in this way, for example, the narrow passages leading to the bathroom assumed nightmarish proportions.*[80]

At the end of the film, Carole sees the walls literally come alive. A dozen hands reach across the hallway, in an apparent homage to *Beauty and the Beast*. Unlike the hands in Cocteau's film, however, these hands are not helping to light the way: they are *attacking* her. This moment underscores the philosophical differences between Cocteau and Polanski. Cocteau wants to lure us into a dream, Polanski is scaring us away.

Polanski's biggest fear, it would seem, is madness—which he defines as the inability to trust one's own senses. This fear underlies the narrative of his subsequent film, *Rosemary's Baby* (1967), in which a woman comes face to face with the Devil. Although many moviegoers interpreted the film as a debate over the existence of the Christian Devil, Polanski privately regarded it as the story of Rosemary's struggle to distinguish between reality and fantasy. In his mind, her vision of the Devil in the early part of the film does not prove anything—because there is always the possibility of hallucination and madness. Most movie-going audiences, however, were

80 Polanski 210

more willing to suspend their disbelief. Polanski explains the popular reaction by making reference to British psychologist R.L. Gregory's 1966 book *Eye and Brain: The Psychology of Seeing*:

> *One of Gregory's contentions is that our perceptions are shaped by the sum of our visual experiences. We see far less than we think we see because of past impressions already stored in our minds. This goes some way toward explaining what happened when the movie was finally released. Most people emerged from theaters convinced that they'd seen the baby, cloven hooves and all. In fact, all they'd really seen, for a split second, was a subliminal superimposition of the catlike eyes that glare down at Rosemary during her nightmare in the early part of the film.*[81]

Polanski personally discounts the supernatural explanation because Rosemary's vision of the Devil came to her while she was in a drug-induced altered state of consciousness. To the filmmaker's mind, that suggests "the possibility that Rosemary's experiences were figments of her imagination."[82] In general, the filmmaker shares Gregory's beliefs about the inherent limitations of altered states, which the neuropsychologist sums up as follows:

> *For the mystic, dreams and hallucinations are insights into another world. For them, the brain is seen as a hindrance to understanding; a filter between us and a supra-physical reality, seen only when the brain's normal functioning is disturbed by drugs, disease, or starvation. For the more down-to-earth empiricist philosophers the brain is to be trusted only in health. Although interesting and perhaps sometimes suggestive, for science hallucinations are seen as aberrant outputs of the brain, to be mistrusted and even feared, though of course Freud is an exception here. Aldous Huxley (in* Doors of Perception, *1954) describes most vividly the viewpoint of the mystic. But probably all neurologists and most philosophers hold that drugs distort and impair perception and thinking, with a danger to producing long-term effects, without revealing truths from any outside source.*[83]

81 Polanski 272
82 Polanski 265
83 Gregory 200

Polanski likewise defines himself as a down-to-earth empiricist. For him, Rosemary's drug-induced "nightmare" is interesting and perhaps suggestive, but no more "real" than Carole's waking hallucinations in *Repulsion*.

In a 1969 interview, Polanski remembers how his own personal experiments with mind-altering drugs led him to this conclusion:

> *Three years ago, I took some LSD, something that pulls you into a state that really is a kind of madness. It frightened me because I felt I was drowning and wasn't able to hold onto anything anymore. There's a piece of furniture over here. If I touch it I know it'll feel hard, and that telephone will be smooth. I also know that if I flick this switch, the light will go out. But when you're in this drug-induced state anything can change at any moment. The furniture can become fluid, the telephone feels rough, maybe even hot. The light might go on when I want to switch it off and vice versa. There's just nothing to hold onto anymore. You try—and fail—to focus on the little bit of reality that might still exist. I found this so frightening that it's impossible to describe.*[84]

He goes on, of course, trying to describe it:

> *All your life, thanks to your senses, you learn what reality is, at least as much as we can understand it. In any case, you learn to trust certain things, and even if you can't know absolutely everything, this gives you a basis upon which you're able to accept other certainties. Yet these are the same certainties you lose with LSD.*[85]

Unable to embrace such an experience, Polanski dismisses it as "madness." Wes Craven, however, seems more willing to embrace the kind of visionary experience that leaves one feeling as if there are no certainties in life. Even a dream, his films suggest, can profoundly and permanently change a person's understanding of reality—and sometimes for the better.

Craven's treatment of dreams in his films has slowly evolved over the years. In *Last House on the Left*, there is only one dream sequence, which occurs near the end of the film—when Weasel sees Mari's parents, dressed in hospital scrubs, preparing to perform

84 Delahaye 19
85 Delahaye 20

very rudimentary dental surgery on him. Mari's father places a metal spike on Weasel's teeth and prepares to strike it with a hammer. The dream, as it turns out, is prophetic. Mari's parents are indeed planning to murder him . . . and his death will be an equally painful scene involving teeth. The dream sequence was not included in the original screenplay. According to Craven, it was inspired by a conversation he had while the film was being shot:

> *At the time that I made* Last House, *I was living with a PhD candidate in anthropology. I was discussing the primal aspects of the film with her, and she told me that two of the most powerful male fears are of having your teeth broken off and the vagina dentata, the fear that the vagina is going to eat you, taking away your manhood. So Weasel's nightmare and his death actually touch on two basic fears.*[86]

It seems entirely appropriate that *Last House*, a film in which one character proclaims that "Sigmund Frood" perpetrated the sex crime of the century by making us all feel like sexual deviants, should climax with a Freudian dream.

A dream also inspired the basic plot of *The Hills Have Eyes*, though there are no dream sequences in the film itself. Craven says that the theme of the story, about two rival families, came to him in a dream that "ended with two dogs named Beauty and Beast, one very gentle and the other savage."[87] Likewise, the symbolic bathtub sequence in *Deadly Blessing* emerged from the filmmaker's subconscious, and Lana's dreams reveal the ultimate truth—the metaphysical reality—of the film.

In 1981, as Craven prepared to write his most personal screenplay, he turned again to his dreams. In contrast to Polanski, he did not intend to use dreams as a representation of delusional thinking. In his next film, dreams would instead represent hidden truths.

Wes Craven has said in many interviews over the years that the initial idea for *A Nightmare on Elm Street* came from three separate

86 Szulkin 91
87 Fischer 251

news articles in the *L.A. Times*, published between 1979 and 1981. He explained to fellow screenwriter John Russo that the articles were about "young men who were having severe nightmares and were not willing to sleep again. They would try to stay awake for a day or more, and when they finally fell asleep they would die in their sleep—apparently from suffering another, even more severe nightmare."[88] In fact, this story was appearing in newspapers across the country during those years—especially in cities with high populations of recent immigrants from the mountainous region of Laos. All of the victims were seemingly healthy young males from Southeast Asia.

In the spring of 1981, the national Center for Disease Control began conducting an investigation into the mysterious deaths, which numbered thirty-eight at the time. According to their report in December of that year, witnesses reported "abnormal breathing or brief groans" as the only precursors to sudden death. They interpreted those sounds "as signs of terror" supporting "the popular notion that deaths resulted from terrifying dreams." The CDC was a bit more cautious, noting that such sounds are "often heard following cardiac arrest," and they focused their investigation on the possibility of heart disease.[89] Contemporary studies theorized that the deaths might be related to chemical agents dropped on Hmong villages by Communist forces during the Vietnam War; others proposed "culture shock." Many researchers eventually embraced the Brugada Syndrome theory, which proposes that the underlying cause is a genetic disease that leads to lethal arrhythmia in the heart. This explanation, however, does not account for the fact that all of the victims were male, or explain why they all died in their sleep.

In 1982, an alternate theory was proposed that suggested a link between biology and belief. In *Hmong Sudden Unexpected Nocturnal Death Syndrome: A Cultural Study*, Bruce Thowpaou Bliatout shares evidence that the deaths were linked to stress "sometimes caused by beliefs in the powers of spirits, the inability to perform traditional religious ceremonies and rituals in Western countries, as well as a variety of other causes."[90] In a more recent study, Stella R. Adler compares Hmong beliefs to Western folklore. She points out that the

88 Russo 179

89 Kilman

90 Bliatout x

Old English term "night-mare" originally designated an evil spirit (usually female) that smothers and suffocates victims (usually male) in their sleep. Variations on this idea include the Christian Incubus and the Salem witches, as well as the Hmong nocturnal pressing spirit *dab tsong*. Adler concludes, "In the context of severe and ongoing stress related to cultural disruption and national resettlement (exacerbated by intense feelings of powerlessness about existence in the United States), and from the perspective of a belief system in which evil spirits have the power to kill men who do not fulfill their religious obligations, the solitary Hmong man confronted by the numinous terror of the night-mare (and aware of its murderous intent) can die of SUNDS."[91] In other words, personal *belief* makes the nightmares real; when the victims die in their dreams, they die in real life.

Craven apparently came to a similar conclusion on his own. He began to examine his own personal fears, and came up with an idea of a night-mare that would be more real and more deadly terrifying than the Incubus in *Deadly Blessing*. He called it Freddy Krueger. The name "Freddy," he says, was inspired by a childhood bully—"a boy that got his newspapers on the same corner I did, and used to try to beat me up."[92] "Krueger" was an extension of Krug, the villain in *Last House on the Left*, whose own name was inspired by Arthur Krupp, a munitions maker for Adolf Hitler.[93] Freddy's sadistic personality came from another real-life memory, as the filmmaker explained to Mick Garris in 2012:

> *The man himself was based on a man who frightened me as a child. Woke me from my sleep one night, tramping down the sidewalk in Cleveland. I got out of bed to see what it was, and I looked and there's this guy dressed very much like I made Freddy dress like. I think he was just a random drunk going down the sidewalk, but he had an uncanny ability somehow to realize this little kid was looking down on him from a second story apartment window. And he just stopped, and he just looked right up at me. Then I fell back and sat on the edge of my bed in the dark. My whole family was asleep. [I] counted to, I don't know,*

91 Adler 130
92 Robb 11
93 Sutherland

> *a thousand . . . [After a while I figured] he must have gone. He can't be waiting. I went back to the window and he was waiting. He just [glared at me, wide-eyed]. Then he turned and he walked down the sidewalk, looking at me. Then he walked around the corner, and that's where the entrance to our building is. I ran to the front of our apartment and I heard the door to the street open. I just went and pounded on the door of my brother, who was ten years older than I was, and I was, "There's a guy who's coming for me." My brother literally went down with a baseball bat and the guy ran away. But the essence of that man was that he enjoyed terrifying a child and enjoyed destroying the comfort of innocence. So that became Freddy.*[94]

In short, Craven envisioned Freddy as the worst kind of adult authority figure—one who uses his authority to corrupt the innocent. In a 1988 interview, the filmmaker described his dream demon as "the paradigm of the threatening adult," saying, "Freddy stood for the savage side of male adulthood. He was the ultimate bad father."[95]

In *A Nightmare on Elm Street*, Freddy Krueger wears distressed brown khakis, a dirty red and green striped sweater, work boots, and a fedora. Even more memorable is the villain's face and hand. Following the success of John Carpenter's *Halloween* (1978) and Sean Cunningham's *Friday the 13th* (1980), Craven believed that audiences would expect a horror movie villain to wear a mask and to wield a distinctive weapon. He did not, however, want to repeat the slasher movie formula: he wanted to reinvent it. He therefore decided that Freddy's mask would be his own face turned inside out . . . and that his weapon would be something that couldn't simply be purchased at the local hardware store. Craven explains:

> *I thought,* Okay, take yourself back to primal man, when he was not equipped with shields or weapons, what did he confront? *And it was "tooth and claw" . . . The reality of real life is that you have a huge spectrum of organisms all trying to rend each other open to get at their protein . . . One of the deepest fears of any critter, and certainly of human beings, is being opened up.*

94 Craven: *Postmortem.*
95 Gire 10

> *The skin is so thin and it takes so very little to spill us out into the world.*[96]

Special effects technician Jim Doyle crafted the steel claws that Freddy uses to "open up" his victims, and makeup artist David Miller designed the look of a man-made-monster who has been burned alive.

The sadistic personality of Freddy Krueger was realized by actor Robert Englund, who remembers that Craven pitched *A Nightmare on Elm Street* to him as "an uncensored Brothers Grimm story," and suggested that "the horror would be embodied not by Rumpelstiltskin, but by a disfigured boogeyman who haunts the dreams of his victims."[97] Englund thought that playing a monster sounded like fun, so he signed on to play Freddy. In his autobiography, he remembers that the character began to appear in his first meeting with costars Heather Langenkamp and Johnny Depp. In that meeting, Englund realized that he would be spending countless hours in the makeup chair to prepare for his role, and that neither one of these fresh-faced young stars would have to endure that kind of test for their roles. As the actor explains, an initial pang of jealousy provided him with the character motivation he needed:

> *I could take my jealousy and resentment of their youth, beauty, and potential and give it to my character. During the more gruesome scenes and difficult special FX sequences, that envy would be the perfect Lee Strasberg sense-memory substitute to call upon. In my new interpretation, Freddy hated kids because they represent the future, something he'd never have. This could help me understand why Freddy was the way he was, why he was compelled to torture and murder children.*[98]

To be fair, Englund's interpretation was not entirely his own. Craven's story was steeped in the traditional Gothic concept that "the sins of the father are visited on the children." There are some significant parallels between *A Nightmare on Elm Street* and early American Gothic literature—most notably Nathaniel Hawthorne's 1851 novel *The House of the Seven Gables*. Both are tales of urban gothic, set in seemingly "haunted" houses. One house is distinguished

96 Craven: *Directors*
97 Englund 107
98 Englund 116

by the presence of a giant old elm tree in the front yard, while the other is located on Elm Street. Both "haunted" houses belong to broken families, and the older generation in each family harbors a dark secret while the younger generation suffers for it.

The parallels don't end there. Freddy Krueger and Matthew Maule (the "pestilent wizard" who haunts the younger generation's dreams in *The House of the Seven Gables*) have both been persecuted by the ancestors of their present-day victims. Maule was condemned as a witch; Krueger was killed by a lynch mob. The main difference is that Maule was *unjustly* persecuted *within* the American legal system. Freddy was *justly* persecuted only after the American legal system failed to convict him . . . but just try telling him that.

At the heart of both stories is the coming-of-age of a young woman who must pay for "the sins of the father." In Hawthorne's story, that young woman is Phoebe, an innocent beauty with "a kind of natural magic" that enables her to "bring out the hidden capabilities of things" around her. Her naïveté is balanced out by the skepticism and tenacity of her beau Holgrave, who feels that "in this age, more than ever before, the moss-grown and rotten Past is to be torn down, and lifeless institutions to be thrust out of the way, and their dead corpses buried, and everything to begin anew."[99] Craven's heroine Nancy is much more self-sufficient than Phoebe, so she doesn't have to rely as much on her boyfriend Glen. (In fact, when she does rely on Glen, he fails her by falling asleep.) On her own, she awakens to the realization that her elders are liars and murderers, and that she can't expect to have a future until she confronts their past.

This metaphorical "awakening" is a central theme of much of Craven's work in the 1980s, and the filmmaker says that, on one level, "it's to do with my feeling that the next generation is getting short shrift."[100] In different interviews, he has referred to the breakup of the nuclear family, the breakdown of the environment, "the libertarian opening of the floodgates of morality in the seventies," and the policies of President Ronald Reagan as signs and symptoms that Generation X had been "discounted" by the Baby Boomer generation.[101] Accordingly, Nancy's biggest challenge in *A Nightmare on*

99 Hawthorne 124
100 Robb 10
101 Robb 10, Dennis Fischer 250, Sharrett 220

Elm Street is to wake up from that collective nightmare and start her own life. Craven explains the conflict in the simplest terms: "Who will be the most conscious, and insist on staying awake—that person will survive."[102]

It is possible that Craven partly derived his working metaphor from Arthur Janov's *The Primal Scream*, the central thesis of which is "unreality kills." Janov argues that nightmares are merely symbols of the growing need for a "primal scream," and concludes that the nightmares must be purged along with waking neuroses. Craven does not, however, subscribe to this dismissive theory about dreams. To his mind, which is more open to mystical experience, dreams can function as doors of perception, allowing the dreamer to see reality as it is.

When I interviewed Craven in 2010, he quietly and casually suggested that one of his main inspirations for *A Nightmare on Elm Street* was the writings of Russian mystic George Gurdjieff. "Around the time I wrote *A Nightmare on Elm Street*," he remembers, "I started equating God with what other religions might call 'in the moment' or Zen, and everything else is being asleep or not really looking at what's going on. That's the kind of spirituality I'm interested in."[103] In a 1924 lecture, Gurdjieff said:

> *A man who sleeps cannot "do." With him everything is done in sleep. Sleep is understood here not in the literal sense of our organic sleep, but in the sense of a state of associative existence. First of all he must awake. Having awakened, he will see that as he is he cannot "do."*[104]

In essence, this describes Nancy's character arc in *A Nightmare on Elm Street*: she has to permanently awaken from a metaphorical world of deadly delusions before she can assert control over her life.

Wes Craven spent two years pitching his story to every studio in Hollywood. The only major studio that expressed an interest was Disney. According to biographer Brian J. Robb, the Mouse requested a "toned down version of the tale which could have a short theatrical release and then run every Halloween on the Disney

102 Grey 117
103 Interview with author 3/12/10
104 Gurdjieff 70

Channel."[105] Craven decided to go his own way, and the only other studio that showed any interest was New Line Cinema. New Line CEO Robert Shaye had a history with horror—having re-released *Night of the Living Dead* and *The Texas Chainsaw Massacre*, as well as Sam Raimi's *The Evil Dead*—but the company was relatively untested as a production entity. Their only previous horror production was *Alone in the Dark* (1982), a tongue-in-cheek slasher movie that yielded respectable box office results.

While Bob Shaye attempted to raise the money for *Nightmare*, Craven continued to write (his latest project was an adaptation of the popular V.C. Andrews novel *Flowers in the Attic*), and he struggled to find work as a director. Eventually, he ran out of money. Broke and desperate, he consented to write and direct a sequel to *The Hills Have Eyes* in order to pay his mounting bills. *The Hills Have Eyes Part II* was shot in the fall of 1983 and released two years later in what Craven insists is an unfinished state. The filmmaker has effectively disowned the end result, which seems more like a cheapjack variation on *Race with the Devil* (1975) than a *Hills* sequel. Years later, Craven bluntly told interviewer Kim Newman, "I'm sorry about *The Hills Have Eyes Part II*. The reason I did that film was that I was dead broke and needed to do any film. I would have done *Godzilla Goes to Paris*."[106]

Craven is equally dismissive of the next film he made to pay the bills, calling *Invitation to Hell* "the most preposterous premise I've ever filmed."[107] The TV movie, about a father trying to save his wife and children from a soul-sucking country club diva/devil, at least revealed Craven's knack for satirical humor. In a way, it also set the stage for his much darker exploration of middle-class American life in *A Nightmare on Elm Street*. Desperate to move forward with his dream project, Craven signed an ill-advised contract with New Line Cinema that gave the studio full ownership of the intellectual property, and the cameras began rolling in the spring of 1984.

105 Robb 66
106 Newman
107 Wooley 97

A Nightmare on Elm Street is constructed around eight dream sequences, each more realistic than the last. The film begins with a scene in which a teenage girl named Tina wanders through a dark industrial labyrinth, pursued by some unseen, heavy-breathing monster. Toward the end of the sequence, she is startled by a bleating sheep, which runs terrified in front of her. In the laserdisc audio commentary for *Nightmare*, Craven claims that this detail was his "tribute" to director Luis Buñuel—presumably, the final scene in Buñuel's film *The Exterminating Angel* (1962), which depicts a herd of "sheep" taking refuge in a Catholic Church. For Tina, there is no refuge. When she wakes up, the first thing she does is reach for a crucifix hanging over her bed. It quickly becomes clear that her religion can't protect her from the monster.

Tina's friend Nancy learns this truth the following night, when the same crucifix falls on her while she is sleeping alone in Tina's bed. Soon after, a face and two arms emerge from the wall, looming over Nancy like some kind of dark angel. According to Craven, the inspiration for this scene was the surreal image of human arms protruding from the plaster walls in Roman Polanski's *Repulsion*.[108] The spectral blue light on the wall in *Nightmare* gives the scene an ethereal quality that suggests an overlap of the physical and spiritual worlds. Seeing it for the first time, one may wonder if the spandex wall is going to split open, spilling the dark angel into Nancy's reality like some kind of horrific newborn baby. Instead, Freddy pulls back—going elsewhere to seek out his first victim.

In a nearby room, Tina is awakened by the sound of a pebble hitting glass. She gets out of bed in time to see another pebble break the window in front of her—except Craven claims it wasn't a pebble at all, but rather a tooth. On the Elite laserdisc commentary, the director says this detail was intended as a homage to Roman Polanski's claustrophobic horror film *The Tenant* (1976), in which the main character finds a tooth in the wall of his apartment. Unaware of this macabre detail, Tina wanders outside to confront whoever woke her up, and finds herself face to face with Freddy. He appears in silhouette in a darkened alley, arms outstretched beyond the length of any *human* form. Craven says this particular image was inspired by Plastic Man, a DC Comics character who could stretch his body

108 Craven: "10 Movies"

into any imaginable form.[109] The bass-heavy sound of Freddy's voice is reminiscent of the Beast's voice in Cocteau's *Beauty and the Beast*, though the Beast never sounded so sardonic. Terrified, Tina pleads for help from the only source of protection she knows: "Please, God." Freddy quips, "*This*… is God."

In the ensuing chase, it becomes painfully clear that Tina has little chance of escaping. Freddy demonstrates his ability to teleport, defying the natural laws of space and time. He slices his own chest open, and feeds off of her fear as green blood and maggots pour out of his body. When Tina tries to push him away, his face falls off of his skull like a fleshy mask. And still he laughs. One thing is certain: Freddy does not play by any of the rules of conventional reality. This becomes even more apparent when Tina's boyfriend Rod wakes up and sees Tina thrashing in bed beside him. It's then that we realize Tina has been dreaming the entire time. That truth is reassuring only for a few seconds.

Tina's subsequent murder is a cinematic tour de force. Craven offers his own variation on Polanski's distorted set, literally turning Tina's world upside down. The effect was achieved with a 360-degree revolving room, creating the illusion that Freddy can defy even the laws of gravity. When the scene is over, one can only feel helpless in response to such an *unreasonable* display of power.

At this point, the narrative shifts focus to Nancy. Her first onscreen encounter with Freddy takes place at her high school. First, she sees a vision of her dead friend Tina in a body bag. She follows the ghost out into an empty hall and Tina leads her down into the school boiler room, where Freddy corners her. Nancy fearfully protests, "It's only a dream!" Freddy smiles, knowing that it doesn't matter. She narrowly escapes, by intentionally scalding her arm on one of the nearby pipes. There are, she now realizes, some rules to this game: What happens in the dream happens in real life.

The most memorable elements of Nancy's next two dream sequences were not in Craven's original script, but they further illustrate the formidable power of a monster who can manipulate reality. In a scene that initially plays out like a homage to *Deadly Blessing*, Freddy attacks Nancy in the bathtub. Instead of a snake, the child-killer's steel claw emerges from the water between the heroine's legs.

109 Biodrowski: "Wes Craven on Dreaming"

Moments later, Freddy tries to drown her in the suddenly bottomless bathtub. In a subsequent dream sequence, Nancy can't even trust the staircase in her house to remain solid. As she runs upstairs to get away from Freddy, her feet sink into gluey quicksand. Producer Bob Shaye reportedly suggested this detail.[110]

Nancy finally makes it up the stairs and barricades herself in her bedroom. She closes the door and stares at her reflection in the mirror, insisting, "This is just a dream. He isn't real . . . He isn't real!" No sooner than the words are out of her mouth, Freddy bursts through the mirror and attacks her. Nancy survives only because her alarm clock rings, fortuitously waking her up and saving her from the nightmare man. At this point, she overcomes her denial and carefully considers the only possible explanations for what is happening to her: (1) Freddy is real, (2) She is crazy.

Craven realized that he too had some explaining to do. Having defined the nightmares in his story as events that can inflict real physical damage on the dreamers, he now had to explain how his heroine could possibly hope to survive those nightmares. In the laserdisc commentary, the director acknowledges that "the philosophical underpinning of the film" is the idea that "sleep is equated with lack of knowledge of the truth." Accordingly, he says, "in order to survive you must know what the truth is and must face it and deal with it."

His conclusion is related to his many inspirations. In primal therapy, Arthur Janov encouraged his patients to acknowledge the "unreality" of their dreams *while they were dreaming*, and thereby recognize that dreams are only symbols of waking fears. Once they do this, Janov writes, the oblique symbolism of the dreams disappears and the dreams become a mirror reflection of the patient's "exact feelings about himself and his life"—real-world fears that must be conquered through the primal scream.[111] George Gurdjieff similarly advises that the sleeper must awaken into a higher state of consciousness, in which fear no longer exists. In his view, *the only way out is through.*

In *A Nightmare on Elm Street*, Nancy realizes that she has to confront Freddy not as a psychological illness or illusion, but as a real-world problem—by literally pulling him out of her dream

110 Cooper: *Nightmare* 28
111 Janov 269

and confronting him without fear. Once she stops running, she can finally wake up from her metaphorical nightmare. Craven explains: "*Nightmare on Elm Street* was very much about how do you stop some violence that's coming against you and not meet it with more violence, but to somehow turn your back on it."[112] Nancy does just that—literally turns her back on Freddy in their final fight. Robbed of his (illusory) power, Freddy disappears, screaming into oblivion.

As more than half a dozen sequels will attest, however, this was not the end of Freddy. In the coda of *A Nightmare on Elm Street*, Nancy and her mother emerge from their suburban house into a thick, luminescent fog. Nancy reacts, tellingly, "God… it's bright." Her mother, suddenly sober, suggests that the light is temporary. Her words prove prophetic. The spectral fog, combined with the apparent amnesia of the characters, conveys a lack of clarity and awareness, suggesting that this awakening is also an illusion. Is Nancy dreaming? *Is she dead?* Whatever the case, Freddy soon regains control of her.

Wes Craven says that he originally intended the scene to end with Nancy and her friends driving away into the mysterious fog. His goal was to show that "evil can be confronted and diminished," and also to suggest that "maybe life is sort of dream-like too."[113] New Line executive Bob Shaye, however, had a different agenda, which he explains in his forward to *The Nightmare Never Ends: The Official History of Freddy Krueger and the Nightmare on Elm Street Films*: "I wanted to have some menace at the end, not because I thought there was in a million years any chance for a sequel, but because the tradition of the genre always left the audience with that last heart-stopping 'jump.' I believed that fans would want that." Shaye's idea was to end with a shot of Freddy driving the car, and the kids screaming in back. The producer goes on to say that he and Craven haggled over the details of the ending right up until the day it was shot, with Craven continually arguing for "the morality of good vanquishing evil in the end" and Shaye preferring "the lesson that evil is, in fact, always with us, around every corner." The compromise was to shoot both endings, as well as a third scenario in which Freddy's steel claw pulls Nancy's mother back into the house through an impossibly small window. All three endings made it into the final cut.[114]

112 Grey 110
113 Robb 74, Clark 53
114 Schoell ix

Over the years, Craven has been very vocal about his dissatisfaction with this hodgepodge ending, noting that he felt a real philosophical attachment to his original ending because it supported his personal worldview. It's worth observing, however, that this scene is not the first scene in the film to defy the logic that Craven's narrative has set up. Just before Glen gets killed in his sleep, Nancy—who is still awake—receives an ominous phone call from Freddy, who taunts her, "I'm your boyfriend now, Nancy." Even before Nancy has pulled him out of her dream, Freddy has apparently crossed over into her waking reality. The viewer can regard that as a flaw in narrative logic, or as a suggestion that Freddy's power is greater than the logic of the film narrative. The ending reinforces the latter possibility—that the film cannot contain its monster. Time, and future sequels, would prove that to be the case.

Lucid Dreaming, The Uses of Enchantment and New Nightmares

A Nightmare on Elm Street was an overnight success, earning an instant cult following. Craven, who had set out to create a new kind of horror film, was not surprised. In interviews conducted soon after the release of the film, he distanced himself from the slasher subgenre and referred to *Nightmare* as "more of a fantasy, an impressionistic thriller," speculating that it might inspire a new breed of "hallucinatory horror films that are not restricted by day to day reality." In an interview with Randy Lofficier, he noted that, in films like *The Texas Chainsaw Massacre* the only "expansion of reality was in the madness of the antagonists," and proposed that "the new horror film will be expanding the boundary of reality in the minds of the protagonists, which is very different."[115] This is neglectful of films like Don Coscarelli's *Phantasm* (1979), another quasi-mystical tale about overcoming fear, but Craven was accurate in his prediction that *Nightmare* would inspire a rash of imitations—including *Dreamscape* (1984), *House* (1986), *Hello Mary Lou: Prom Night 2* (1987), *Slumber Party Massacre 2* (1987), and *Bad Dreams* (1988). In an interview with Stanley Wiater, Craven even offered a term for this new breed of horror film, coining the phrase "rubber reality."[116]

Foremost among the pretenders was *A Nightmare on Elm Street Part 2: Freddy's Revenge* (1985), a Jekyll & Hyde story livened up with surrealistic imagery. When Craven saw the script by New Line employee David Chaskin, he balked: "Freddy comes out of the hero, and, in effect, makes the hero do things. I felt that was a very dangerous violation of a basic dramatic rule. You should have a clearcut hero and villain and not mix the two together."[117] Citing creative differences, the director declined to helm the sequel, and the studio handed the reins to Jack Sholder, the writer/director of *Alone in the Dark*. Craven then turned his attention to more personal projects.

In early 1985, he told Glenn Lovell he was "talking to some people" about "an island castaway movie—a *Lord of the Flies* with

115 Lofficier 226, 237
116 Wiater 53
117 Schoell 31

girls."[118] Other projects in development around this time included a "futuristic" reworking of *Frankenstein*, an adaptation of John Wooley's novel *Old Fears*, an adaptation of Tom Ropelweski's novel *Haunted*, and a comedy called *Working Class Bride*. The first project that came to light was *Chiller* (1985), a TV movie about a man who returns to life after being cryogenically frozen for ten years. There's more than a bit of *Frankenstein* in this story as well, and it plays out as a tongue-in-cheek cautionary tale about the dangers of science and corporate greed in 1980s America. The soul of the story, however, is a priest's insight into the human condition. When he realizes what's happened, he reflects:

> *We believe that man is made up of body, mind and spirit. Now, the body is physical. You can see it. You can touch it. But the spirit . . . We believe that when someone dies, the soul goes off to paradise, to heaven, to some hereafter. Now suppose that a man died, really died (not one of those near-death experiences) and suppose that in fact he was buried for ten years, and after that time somehow he was reanimated, brought back to life. If the body and the mind functioned, then he would technically be alive. But what about the soul?*

Chiller encouraged Craven to tackle more humanistic stories, and he had ample opportunity thanks to an offer from producer Phil DeGuere, who was overseeing the revival of the classic TV series *The Twilight Zone*. Craven remembers, "He gave me a stack of scripts that they were planning on doing in the first year and said, 'Direct any ones you want.' I had time to do seven, so it was a great gift and a great entrustment."[119] *The Twilight Zone* proved to be a natural fit for the filmmaker, who was able to demonstrate his range as a storyteller.

Craven directed both segments of the series pilot, "Shatterday" and "A Little Peace and Quiet." The former is a doppelganger story by Harlan Ellison, about a man whose conscience literally takes custody of his soul. The latter is a timely update of the classic *Twilight Zone* episode "A Kind of Stopwatch," in which a character inherits the supernatural ability to stop time, yet still fails to "make time" to

118 Lovell
119 Robb 115

prevent a global nuclear disaster. Both stories are distinguished by their underlying moral message, as well as by the storyteller's sympathy for immoral characters.

Craven's most audacious episode of the *Twilight Zone* series is "Wordplay," which begins as a high-concept comedy and evolves into a tragedy that boldly affirms the strength of the human spirit. Equally contemplative, though not as nuanced, is "Chameleon," a classic *Stranger in a Strange Land* narrative. Craven rounded out his involvement in the first season with "Dealer's Choice," a dark comedy that depicts the devil as a poker-playing schlub, and "Her Pilgrim Soul." The latter was certainly his most heartfelt contribution to the series.

"Her Pilgrim Soul" revolves around a young scientist who invents a hologram device that channels the soul of an apparently deceased woman. Over the course of several days, the woman relives her entire life—from birth to death—inside the scientist's lab. At the same time, the young doctor learns the most important lesson of his life from her. As their bond grows, he reveals his deepest fears, confessing, "The moment that you start to feel happiness in this life, that's the moment that the rug's pulled out from under you." The visiting spirit responds, warmly and sympathetically, "And if you never have happiness, you don't know what it's like to lose it." Throughout his career, Wes Craven has repeatedly tackled the idea that a man must overcome his fear in order to live a full human life. "Her Pilgrim Soul" is his most humanistic treatment of the subject.

After his experience on *Twilight Zone*, it was understandably difficult for Craven to return to horror. Instead he chose to direct *Casebusters*, a short installment of The Disney Sunday Movie about two mischievous children who help their grandfather thwart a bank robbery. He was happy enough with the experience to pitch another idea to Disney—a children's comedy called *Circus Gang*—but the project was never developed. (Disney, meanwhile, developed its own family-friendly variation on Freddy Krueger for the Sunday night showcase, in the 1986 gothic comedy *Mr. Boogedy*.)

Craven's past continued to haunt him as he went to work for Warner Brothers on his first major studio film. In one respect, *Deadly Friend* (1986) was exactly what he'd been hoping for. He told *Cinefantastique* interviewer Lee Goldberg, "After 15 years of banging my head out there in the boondocks, I got my feet on the promised land."[120] By the time the film was completed, however, he had changed his tune. According to Craven, the film was initially conceived as a "love story with a twist"—*Bride of Frankenstein* (1935) meets *Short Circuit* (1986). After it was shot, the powers that be decided the film was "too soft."[121] At that point, the director told Stanley Wiater, everything changed:

> *When they test screened the film, they got in a heavy metal, hard-core audience who had been told they were going to see a "Wes Craven Film." So this horror audience was totally pissed off that there wasn't more blood and guts in it, and the studio did a 180-degree turn at the last moment, after the film was done. We were told to go out and "shoot some gory stuff," and so we shot those dream sequences, which we edited into the film . . . Nobody knew what the hell kind of film it was, including me.*[122]

In an attempt to rewrite the film after principal photography had been completed, the studio only succeeded in cobbling together their own Frankenstein monster. *Deadly Friend* is neither a light-hearted family comedy nor a Wes Craven horror film—it's simply a freak show, suggesting that the filmmaker's biggest problem was his own reputation.

Based on the success of *A Nightmare on Elm Street*, Craven had been permanently branded as a horror filmmaker—a reality that he could deny only at his own peril. But that was only a small part of his troubles, as he explained to Robert J. Emery:

> *I discovered, to put it discreetly, that my marriage was no longer anything but a sham. I was supposed to be directing* Beetlejuice, *and about two months into preparation for that, I was yanked from it. I was supposed to direct* Superman IV, *and I had an interview with Christopher Reeve, and he said, "Wes Craven will never direct my film." On top of that, someone who thought that I had copied a script that was so different from* Nightmare on Elm Street *that you can't believe it was suing me for about $30 million. All of that was going on at the time I*

120 Goldberg 52
121 Goldberg 52, 54
122 Wiater 52

> *was directing* Deadly Friend. *So, it was like the year from hell for me.*[123]

During the same year, Craven tackled one more story for the second season of *The Twilight Zone*. "The Road Less Traveled" begins teasingly with a series of nightmare visions, then turns into another doppelganger story, bringing Craven full circle to the themes of "Shatterday." This time, however, two versions of the same man are integrated into a new whole, with the more fortunate self agreeing to share the nightmares of the less fortunate self in order to become a more complete human being. The Jungian implications of that idea—integrating the Shadow self into a new whole—would bleed into several of Craven's subsequent films . . . but not until after he made his inevitable return to Elm Street, to confront the mythic monster he had created.

Wes Craven has said that his initial screenplay for *A Nightmare on Elm Street 3: Dream Warriors* was inspired by contemporary media coverage of a so-called "epidemic" of teenage suicides in middle-class America, which prompted President Ronald Reagan to designate June 1986 as "Youth Suicide Prevention Month." Reagan called on a coalition of "individuals, families, communities, churches, synagogues, private groups and government agencies" to "detect the early symptoms of suicidal tendencies and develop ways of helping those whose depression and despondency could lead to this terrible act." The President also offered his own cursory diagnosis of the problem, saying, "We must continue to combat those tendencies and influences such as the 'drug culture' that preach despair."[124]

Craven had his own ideas about the cause of the epidemic and how to combat it. The basic concept of *Nightmare 3*, he says, "was to show that it's not just some drug or something that's making them do it, it's a real perception of evil. A real teenager committing suicide doesn't want to do it, he wants somebody to know what's going on inside him, so he can be understood and not seen as sick."[125]

123 Emery 107
124 Reagan
125 Robb 100

The filmmaker then cobbled together his own coalition to fight the problem of evil at its source. He called them The Dream Warriors.

In the first draft of the *Dream Warriors* script by Craven and Bruce Wagner (dated June 16, 1986), Nancy Thompson—the heroine of *Nightmare 1*—is searching for her father, while her father is simultaneously searching for the childhood home of Freddy Krueger. Only Nancy and her father understand that Freddy is behind the a rash of teenage suicides haunting America's heartland. Lt. John Thompson is determined to put an end to the killings. Nancy, on the other hand, has spent the past five years clinging to a policy of avoidance, using an experimental drug called Hypnocyl to suppress dreaming and steer clear of Freddy. This policy works until she crosses paths with Neil Guiness, a psychiatrist at a hospital where several survivors of Freddy's nightmares are gathered. As Nancy earns their trust, she realizes that these teenagers have survived not by running away, but by harnessing their dream powers—individual strengths that allow them to fight back.

Craven's concept of dream powers is a significant departure from *Nightmare 1*, in which Nancy had to pull Freddy out of the dream world in order to fight him. In *Nightmare 3*, she becomes a friend and mentor to the "dream warriors," eventually leading them into battle on Freddy's turf. The basic concept bears some similarities to the concept of "lucid dreaming," as developed by psychophysiologist Stephen LaBerge.

LaBerge began studying dreams in 1977 and by the early 1980s he had become one of the foremost researchers in his field. With his 1985 book *Lucid Dreams*, he advanced the hotly debated idea that being aware of your dreams *while you're dreaming* is a learnable skill. By making a concerted effort to observe and remember dreams, he says, it is possible to exert greater willpower over the content of dreams. Taking this idea one step further, LaBerge encouraged people not to run from their nightmares, but to face their fears. He explains:

> *[W]hen we "escape" from a nightmare by awakening, we have not dealt with the problem of our fear or our frightening dream, but merely relieved the fear temporarily and repressed the fearful dream. Thus we are left with an unresolved conflict*

> *as well as negative and unhealthy feelings. On the other hand, staying with the nightmare and accepting its challenge, as lucidity makes possible, allows us to resolve the dream problem in a fashion that leaves us more healthy than before.*[126]

It is not difficult to imagine Freddy Krueger gleefully mocking this kind of psychobabble, but LaBerge's idea has practical applications that Craven's dream warriors put to good use. LaBerge writes: "Lucid dreamers are often overjoyed to discover they can seemingly do anything they wish. They have, for instance, but to declare the law of gravity repealed, and they float. They can visit the Himalayas and climb the highest peak without ropes or guides; they can even explore the solar system without a space suit!"[127]

In Craven and Wagner's script, the dream warriors represent "the next generation of the fight"—an "evolutionary leap" beyond the veteran Nancy. They are all capable of doing the impossible. Kirsten, Kincaid, Taryn, Joey, and Laredo ("Will" in the final film) all possess superhuman strength—not to mention the ability to materialize firebombs out of thin air! On top of this, Kirsten has the ability to summon other people into her dreams, bringing all of the warriors to the battlefield at the same time. In an interview with *Script*'s Rachel Wimberly, Wes Craven reveals that this particular idea emerged from his own childhood memory of asking his mother if she could come into his dreams and protect him.[128]

In the final act, the dream warriors collectively visit Freddy's childhood home in a dream, intending to burn it to the ground. According to Lt. Thompson, the house is a "doorway" between worlds: by destroying the doorway, they can destroy Freddy. Despite their strength in numbers, however, each individual suffers weakness stemming from unresolved feelings of guilt and frustration over real world problems—and Freddy knows his victims intimately enough to exploit those weaknesses. Taryn is lured to her death by her guilt-inducing grandmother. Joey is lured to his death by lust. Laredo is *almost* lured by his dead brother . . . but he gets wise to Freddy's game, and competes with the shape-shifter on his own terms. The result is a highly imaginative wizard's duel, like something out of

126 LaBerge: *Lucid* 102
127 LaBerge: *Lucid* 65
128 Wooley 101

Roger Corman's *The Raven* (1963) or Disney's *The Sword in the Stone* (1963). In the end, Freddy wins, leaving only three warriors. The nightmare man chases the survivors out of the dream world and into their reality, where Nancy and Kirsten try to rob him of his power by turning their backs on him. This ploy doesn't work any better than it did at the end of *A Nightmare on Elm Street*, but it does buy them enough time to burn Freddy's childhood home to the ground—magically reducing Freddy to a screaming mutant baby.

Craven and Wagner reportedly delivered multiple rewrites of the script, one of which provided the basis for Jeffrey Cooper's novelization of the film. The novelization places a much greater emphasis on Kirsten's story, beginning with her supposed suicide attempt rather than with Nancy's nightmares. This rewrite also eliminates the Lt. Thompson character and substitutes Nancy's childhood home (where the events of *Nightmare 1* took place) for Freddy's childhood home. The latter change apparently prompted the creators to dream up a new origin story for Freddy. Cooper's narrative tells us that Nancy's house on Elm Street was once an experimental sanitarium for psychotic women, including a teenager who was raped "a thousand times" and later gave birth to a "huge" child. According to local legend, the new mother accidentally knocked over a lamp, setting herself and her baby on fire. She died, but nobody knew for certain what happened to the baby. The patient's name was Amanda Krueger.[129]

The rewrite also modified the talents of the dream warriors. Instead of possessing the unlimited powers of a lucid dreamer, each character has a specific dream "gift"—not unlike mutant abilities in the *X-Men* comics. Kristen, in addition to being able to summon people into her dreams, is an Olympics-ready gymnast. Taryn can breathe fire. Laredo is a magician who works in "metal, rope and ectoplasm." Jennifer can make herself invisible. Joey, who is mute and frail in real life, is strong and virile in his dreams. Kincaid can float like a butterfly—and, given his size and strength, presumably sting like a bee. All of these talents become apparent very early in the story, and the dream warriors mount several united attacks on Freddy. In fact, the biggest dramatic problem with this version of the story is the overwhelming strength of the protagonists, who collectively kick Freddy's ass in their first battle royale. The nightmare man was

129 Cooper: *Nightmares* 181

starting to look a little weak. Perhaps that's why the producers at New Line brought in a new pair of writers.

Chuck Russell and Frank Darabont delivered the final shooting script, which mostly revolves around the individual *vulnerabilities* of the dream warriors. One by one, slasher-movie style, Freddy exploits their specific weaknesses in ingenious nightmare set-pieces. He turns amateur puppet-master Philip into a gruesome life-size puppet, then drops him off the roof of a building. He gives aspiring actress Jennifer a literal "big break in TV." He seduces Joey by growing breasts and employing a very unpleasant French kissing technique. All of these sequences appeared in Craven and Wagner's revision, but Freddy's tactics are clearer and cleverer in the final film. Russell and Darabont applied the same concept to a couple of new set pieces: Freddy haunts Will (a paraplegic in real life) with a demonic wheelchair, and taunts Taryn (a recovering drug addict) with a gleaming set of narcotic-filled syringes, protruding from the ends of his fingers.

Only Neil Guiness can effectively combat Freddy this time, by exploiting the dream master's own weakness. The ghost of Amanda Krueger—now identified as a nun who was raped (only "hundreds of times," instead of thousands) and gave birth to the "bastard son of a hundred maniacs"—tells Neil that he must bury Freddy's bones in hallowed ground. In the documentary film *Never Sleep Again*, director Chuck Russell says that it was his idea to relate the Freddy Krueger mythology to "an old school vampire movie." Just as Dracula is vulnerable to crosses and holy water, he theorized, so is Freddy. It's a somewhat problematic idea, given that one of the first things Craven did in the original *Nightmare* was to illustrate that religion cannot save Tina or Nancy from Freddy. (Craven and Wagner had also restated this idea in their drafts of *Nightmare 3*. In the first draft, Freddy mockingly crucifies Kirsten. In Cooper's novelization, he first appears to her through the glowing red eyes of her crucifix.) Nevertheless, it became part of New Line Cinema's official Freddy mythology.

In his initial response to the *Nightmare 3*, Wes Craven expressed disappointment with the transformation of his ultimate evil into a vaudeville vampire. At the same time, he acknowledged, "It's probably safer to deal with him that way."[130] Over the years, Craven has had plenty of time to think about the function of horror films and their influence on audiences, and he'd come to the conclusion that it was important to leave viewers feeling empowered—in much the same way that Stephen LaBerge's lucid dreaming techniques leave dreamers feeling empowered. In 1988, he explained his theory of horror filmmaking to *Cinefantastique* journalist Dan Gire:

> *I call them boot camp for the psyche, especially for young people. I think films process very powerful primal fears and trepidations. Teenagers see things very clearly, sometimes frighteningly clearly. They're going through a process of reevaluating their country, their mother and father, looking at their youth and seeing that they're about to be adults, deciding what to do about sex and drugs, what to do with lives and careers. It's a tremendous mine field in their lives . . . Horror films are playing out some of those things on a very primal level. It's life and death, blood and guts. But people come out of it at the end. There's a sense of exhilaration. They survive.*[131]

Subsequent sequels continued to riff on ideas in Craven and Wagner's original script for *Nightmare 3*, while pushing Freddy into more comfortable territory. New Line executive Sarah Risher claims that Craven wanted to break the mold by introducing a time-travel element in *Nightmare 4*, but (for better or worse) the studio parted ways with the series creator at this point.[132]

By the time *Nightmare 4* hit the big screen, Freddy had become (in the words of director Renny Harlin) "a James Bond kind of hero,"[133] marketable to the youngest audiences. Craven reflected on this strange turn of events in an interview with Stanley Wiater, once again suggesting that perhaps it wasn't such an unhealthy phenomenon: "The reason some of these kids walk around with Freddy Krueger dolls is the same reason that horror filmmakers are a little bit more relaxed about the terrors around us, because they are able to handle it, manipulate it, and call it their own for the moment.

130 Gire 10
131 Gire 10
132 Gire 101
133 Schoell 83

That's what a child does with a Freddy Krueger doll."[134] Even Stephen LaBerge recognized therapeutic potential in the series, as he explained to *Rolling Stone* magazine in October 1988. The following quote also appeared in the press kit for *A Nightmare on Elm Street 5: The Dream Child* (1989):

> *Freddy is an intriguing dream character. Ordinarily in our dreams, dream characters do not have more power over you than you have over them unless you give them that power. That was shown quite well in the third film, where Freddy overcomes each of his opponents by finding their own weakness, which is something they already know about themselves. They were trying to overcome this monster from the id, so they would fail for some reason having to do with failing in themselves. You see, you can't fool Freddy, because he knows what you know. And so Freddy just keeps coming back, no matter what. Actually, that's probably what he would do until you accepted him, or tried to love him. In my approach to nightmares, that is the whole key: you stop trying to get rid of these frightening characters; instead, you accept them as a part of yourself, and the moment that you love them, they transform.*[135]

Whether by accident or design, the creators of Freddy Krueger were transforming horror audiences into lucid dreamers. As a result, Freddy had become so wildly popular that everyone—including Wes Craven—was trying to repeat his success story.

Craven's idea for a new Freddy Krueger was initially part of a TV series concept called *Dreamstalker*. The filmmaker described the show as "a version of *The Thing* where a person is able to get into the body of another person, and you don't know who he is or who he is inside."[136] His concept combined the idea of "a killer who can get into people's bodies and take over their electro-magnetic field" with the idea of an empowered child, "a young kid that was a very unlikely psychic, able to dream whatever murders this man was committing, and so identify him and locate him."[137] According to Craven, *Dreamstalker* percolated at Fox for almost a year before the

134 Wiater 51
135 LaBerge: *Nightmare*
136 Wiater 53
137 Robb 138

network finally passed on it. In the meantime, producers David Ladd and Rob Cohn offered Craven a chance to direct a film that would explore the broader philosophical implications of lucid dreaming.

According to Stephen LaBerge, the practice of lucid dreaming originated with Tibetan Buddhists in the eighth century, who claimed that "all of our experiences are subjective and thus, by their very nature, no different in substance from what we call 'dreams.'"[138] By becoming conscious of our dreams, our minds may become more receptive to a higher level of waking consciousness. He concludes, "This capacity of lucid dreams, to prepare us for a fuller awakening, may prove to be lucid dreaming's most significant potential for helping us become more alive in our lives."[139] The same concept lies at the heart of Craven's film *The Serpent and the Rainbow* (1987).

The Serpent and the Rainbow mines an old Hollywood fascination with Haitian voodoo lore, going back to the publication of W.B. Seabrook's sensational study *The Magic Island* (1929) and its influence on genre films like *White Zombie* (1932) and *I Walked with a Zombie* (1943). As a result of such films, the popular American concept of voodoo is generally fearful and simplistic, but some Western scientists have been willing to dig a little deeper. Craven's film is based on a 1985 travelogue by ethnobiologist Wade Davis, who followed the voodoo lore to Haiti. Davis was not interested in horror stories, but in the possibility of finding a drug that could produce a temporary death-like state. He went looking for the drug, but he found much more: a new worldview.

Davis writes of Haiti as "a land where things are not what they seem,"[140] explaining:

> *The nation baffled me. Stunned by her multitudes, awed by her mysteries, dumbfounded by her contradictions, I paced. Only at dawn, when from sheer exhaustion or moved by the splendor of the city basking in such soft light, was I still. Sometimes with my eyes closed, and the silence broken only by the odd bird, I would*

138 LaBerge: *Lucid* 130

139 LaBerge: *Lucid* 155

140 Davis 47

hear whispered messages of the land that intuitively I understood, if only for a moment. Eventually I came to respect those moments, for the cycle of logical questions was getting me nowhere.[141]

If it sounds like Davis has been drugged by the landscape and the culture, it's worth noting that he was not the only one. Craven confessed to a similar enchantment with the place:

> *During rehearsals we realized the script was not up to the level of spirituality, beauty, and passion that we saw. We completely rewrote the script on the set and shot it to make it fit the reality of Haiti. We could never have guessed sitting in our offices in Hollywood when we were writing the screenplay what it was really like.*[142]

In his attempt to capture everything accurately, Craven elaborates, screenwriter Richard Maxwell got a little *too* close to the local culture. In the 2002 Showtime documentary *Masters of Horror*, the filmmaker explains:

> *Richard went down and interviewed this guy and Richard, who was interested in all sorts of spiritual things, said I'd love to be indoctrinated into voodoo sometime. And the guy, who was a very sly guy, said, "Well, then you will be." So somehow he must have dosed Richard in that visit, because Richard came back and just basically went mad in the course of a week. He locked himself into his room; he stopped wearing clothes; he was telling us he was writing but he couldn't concentrate. And finally, the day before we started shooting—actually the morning we started shooting—I woke up, like, five in the morning. Somebody was knocking on my door of my room [. . .] I opened the door and here's Richard, dazed and haggard, unshaven. I looked down and all around his feet are cigarette butts. He'd been there all night. He said, "I just want to wish you good luck because vodouns and the producers are in league against me and they're gonna kill me." And he was literally taken to a plane, flown from where we were, way out in the boondocks, to Port au Prince and then put on an airplane. His wife met the plane in Miami [and] took him back*

141 Davis 64
142 Szebin 121

to Los Angeles. And four days later he woke up, lucid, and the last thing he remembered was that guy saying, "Well, then you will be."[143]

For the storytellers and their onscreen surrogate, Dr. Dennis Alan, there are two journeys—one physical and one spiritual. The physical journey begins with a man who has allegedly returned from the dead. Davis writes that Clarivius Narcisse was poisoned, buried, dug up, and subsequently enslaved as a field hand. "He remembered being aware of his predicament [being dead and buried], of missing his family and friends and his land, of wanting to return," Davis writes. "But his life had the quality of a strange dream, with events, objects, and perceptions interacting in slow motion, and with everything completely out of his control."[144] Narcisse told Davis that a black magician, known as a *bokur,* had enslaved his body by capturing his soul at the moment of his death. Davis concluded that a poison was responsible for giving him the appearance of death, and that the man's pre-existing belief in zombies was responsible for his paralysis of will power.

Craven, whose film fictionalizes the story of Narcisse, approached the story from the same rational Western perspective, explaining in one interview that he regards zombies as "the chemical creation of people who have had their brains virtually erased," and belief in zombies as the same kind of transformative belief that killed dozens of Hmong refugees in their sleep.[145] Nevertheless, Craven has admitted that he saw the Haitians do things that filled him with a sense of wonder:

> *Their whole sense of reality is different, and that affects what they physically could do. One of the first times we location scouted, we went to this restaurant that featured a troupe that went into a trance when they danced. And something happened that I had to put into the movie. A woman who had gone into a trance came over to our table, picked up my glass—the glass that I had been drinking out of for the entire lunch—and ate it. Just bit off huge chunks of it and ate it right in front of me. And she was totally somebody else. She had been this kind of shy, demure woman,*

143 Mendez
144 Davis 80
145 Emery 108

> *and now she was very aggressive and sexual. Everything about her had changed.*[146]

In conversation with interviewer Stanley Wiater, he adds that he also saw people "leaning against very sharp machetes without them piercing the skin," and concluded that, "at a certain point, the line between belief and reality gets very, very cloudy."[147]

In the film, the glass-eating scene prompts Dr. Alan to question the nature of reality, and also serves as an introduction to the main villain—a *bokur* named Peytraud, who uses black magic to reinforce his power as the chief of the Tonton Macoute. Peytraud is a fictional character, but the Tonton Macoute was a real paramilitary organization that ruled Haiti by force from 1959 until 1986, under the dictatorship of Francois "Papa Doc" Duvalier and his son Jean-Claude "Baby Doc." Davis, who conducted research in Haiti under the Duvalier regime, observed that vodoun beliefs and political power were inseparable during that time. He explains:

> *Zombification was a social process unique to a particular culture reality. There had to be men and women actually creating this poison, deciding how, when, and to whom it should be administered, and completing the action by distributing and caring for the victims. Above all, if zombis actually existed, there had to be a reason, an explanation rooted in the structure and beliefs of the Haitian peasant society.*[148]

Accordingly, in Craven's film, Peytraud steals souls to maintain power within a culture of fear. When an American scientist naively threatens to expose that truth and unravel the delicate balance of order in Haitian society, Peytraud is compelled to show him that "death is only the beginning." That is the turning point of the film's spiritual journey.

Immersed in the exoticism of a strange world, Dr. Alan takes part in a religious procession involving hundreds of natives, and then makes love with a native woman who helps him to understand that in Haiti, "God is not just in our heaven... He's in our bodies, our flesh." The experience is his initiation into a new form of

146 Interview with author 3/12/10

147 Wiater 54

148 Davis 62

consciousness, where the line between belief and reality is very thin indeed. His response, like that of any new initiate, is fear. He wakes up to a nightmare—the first of many. Wes Craven says that this sequence also provided a rude "awakening" for the production crew:

> *That was a three-day shoot. On the first day, I said, "How much are we paying extras?" I was told, "Twenty-five cents a day." I said, "Are you kidding? Let's get a thousand extras." So we got a thousand extras for the second night. Then on the third night we got to the set and people were still coming. They were from villages throughout the country and they had walked all night and they all wanted to be employed. And they all wanted to be paid. At the same time, there were these kind of socialist provocateurs that were organizing them. Telling them they're being exploited by the white people. So we had to double their wages twice that night. And then they asked for more than we had to pay them. And they then picked up stones and threatened to kill us. Just like that. In the middle of the night, we were surrounded by two thousand angry people that are picking up stones and saying, "We are going to kill you." This was right after they had thrown Baby Doc out of office. So we got that night's footage in the can and left Haiti.*[149]

Dr. Alan, on the other hand, does not run. He is determined to get a sample of the zombie drug and return with it to America—which lands him in the torture chamber of Peytraud. The *bokur* administers "a little pain, a little terror," but warns the American that "the pain I can cause you in the room upstairs is nothing to the pain I can cause in your own mind." Dr. Alan finds out what he means when his waking nightmares follow him back to America. Having been initiated, he can no longer run from his fears. He must face them or become a slave to them, like Narcisse.

When Dr. Alan returns to Haiti, Peytraud poisons him and buries him. Then the fight for his soul begins. The final act, drawn mostly from the imagination of Craven himself, takes place entirely in the mind of the hero, who can "see things the living can't see." What he sees are nightmare visions that would not have been out of place in *A Nightmare on Elm Street*. Craven has conceded, apologetically, that

149 Interview with author 3/12/10

some of these scenes were added as an afterthought, and didn't mesh with the rest of the story: "We went back and did an extra shoot here in Los Angeles. The test screenings didn't score high enough, and the studio suddenly wanted to have horror-film scenes. I always regretted going back and doing that extra stuff."[150]

The good-versus-evil showdown diminishes the philosophical complexity of the film, but it does effectively fuse the cultural story of Haiti with the hero's spiritual journey. Importantly, the American initiate does not casually defeat Peytraud. Peytraud's power is diminished by the overthrow of "Baby Doc" Duvalier (which had happened in early 1986), making him vulnerable to attack at the precise moment when Dr. Alan returns. Within this context, the hero's victory is merely evidence of a larger change. And as Craven has said, "Change is one thing I have a basic faith in."

Craven has claimed that the experience of shooting *The Serpent and the Rainbow* in Haiti had a profound effect on his life. "Haiti really mellowed me out," he explains. "I almost died down there, and I experienced a lot of strange things. So, when I came through it all, not only alive, but healthy, I decided to begin taking my life a bit easier."[151] That doesn't mean that he stopped working so hard. Just the opposite, in fact. Over the next three years, he created two television series (*The People Next Door* in 1989 and *Nightmare Café* in 1991), directed a feature film about a psychic teenager pursuing a TV-obsessed serial killer (*Shocker*, 1989) and a TV movie about a psychic cop pursuing an occult-obsessed serial killer (*Night Visions*, 1990), and crafted an entirely new "fairy tale for the apocalypse" based on content from his own dreams (*The People Under the Stairs*, 1991).

The filmmaker was no doubt drawn to television during this period because the medium allowed him greater freedom in terms of subject matter. Ironically, it was also the preferred medium of his new Freddy Krueger. According to Craven, the *Dreamstalker* idea that he pitched to Fox was "was essentially the first and second acts of *Shocker*."[152] The network was unwilling to gamble on the series, but

150 Wooley 149
151 Robb 135
152 Wiater 53

Alive Films picked it up as part of a two-picture deal, hoping that the innovative slasher might duplicate the success of *A Nightmare on Elm Street*. Other filmmakers apparently had the same idea, as *Shocker* inspired nearly as many copycats as *Elm Street*—including Jack Sholder's *The Hidden* (1987), Renny Harlin's *Prison* (1988), and Sean Cunningham's *The Horror Show* (1989).

At the center of Craven's story is a super-villain every bit as nasty as Freddy Krueger. Horace Pinker works days as a TV repairman and moonlights as a serial killer, shredding entire families inside their own homes. After he has been captured and sentenced to death, Pinker uses "black magic" to transfer his spirit from his physical body into electromagnetic waves so that he can continue killing from beyond the grave. Craven explained his concept to *Cinefantastique* write Steve Biodrowski:

> *When I asked myself what else in our culture is as mysterious and as pervasive as dreams, the answer was the whole electromagnetic web of reality that envelops us now. So much of what we know—or think we know—comes through radio and especially television. According to scientists, the state of watching television is almost identical to dreaming. That's why it's such a powerful advertising medium—you're really being invaded from a very unprotected porthole.*[153]

In the filmmaker's mind, Horace Pinker was Freddy Krueger for the Information Age, a terrifying twist on Marshall McLuhan's notion that new media technologies have become extensions of human bodies and amplifications of human powers. After Pinker's transformation, static shock is enough to convey his spirit to new bodies.

Throughout the film, the only person who truly *sees* the killer is a slightly absent-minded college student named Jonathan Parker. He uses lucid dreaming to track Pinker in the dreamworld, and thereby helps police to capture him in the real world. Later we learn that Jonathan's connection to Pinker is not just in his head, it's in his blood. Horace Pinker is Jonathan's biological father. After that realization, the film becomes about Jonathan's journey to liberate himself from the dark influence of his bad dad.

---

153 Biodrowski: "Wes Craven, Shocker" 14

Unlike the characters in *Last House* and *The Hills Have Eyes*, the hero of *Shocker* doesn't succumb to violent revenge in the end. With an absurd chase sequence that surfs through four decades of soul-sucking American television (including a brief stopover in the holy temple of mock-televangelist Timothy Leary!), Jonathan simply turns on, tunes in, and drops out. The story ends, appropriately enough, with a power-outage that entraps Horace Pinker in TV Land, and prompts Jonathan and his neighbors to gather in the streets and look up at the stars—which are suddenly un-obscured by light pollution—as if for the first time. Craven explained to *Cineaste* interviewer Michael Banka that his intention was to "make people aware of the media," in much the same way that Stephen LaBerge made people aware of their dreams.[154] In both cases, the goal is an awakening.

The filmmaker later recycled some of the plot elements of *Shocker* in *Night Visions*, a pilot for a psychic cop show that also featured actor Mitch Pileggi and guru Timothy Leary in small roles, before teaming up with his own son Jonathan to develop an anthology series "with wraparound characters we thought would bookend the stories."[155] The elder Craven cowrote the *Nightmare Café* pilot with his *Night Visions* collaborator Thomas Baum, and NBC gave them a green light.

Craven sums up the series by describing its titular setting as "a way station between life and death, time and eternity":

> Nightmare Café *exists within our mind and hearts. It's a place where you go to review, to encounter the unexpected, to break through walls that are obscuring the truth, to go back and deal with things that you needed to deal with in your past that you've blocked for a while. It's a very real place, and it exists in all of us.*[156]

The title—as well as the casting of Robert Englund, fresh off of his "final" turn as Freddy Krueger—implied a connection to the horror genre and specifically to *A Nightmare on Elm Street*, but this was mainly a marketing gimmick. *Nightmare Café* was a show about wonder, universal mystery, and the human condition—certainly not the usual network TV fare. Craven's hope was that the series would

154 Banka
155 King
156 Keller

provide a home for all the different types of narratives that he had been telling for years, and the filmmaker put everything else aside in order to develop this new dream project. Unfortunately, the series premiere (on January 29, 1992) failed to draw a big enough audience. *Nightmare Café* lasted only six episodes, culminating with Craven's off-the-wall comedy episode "Aliens Ate My Lunch."

Different sources suggest that the filmmaker had a wide variety of film projects in development during this time period—including an adaptation of Giles Blunt's Faustian novel *Cold Eye*, a West Point ghost story called *Shades of Grey*, and feature film version of the old radio series *The Shadow.* All of them eventually gave way to *The People Under the Stairs*, Craven's second feature for Alive Films.[157] The filmmaker says that the origins of the story dated back to a series of newspaper articles he read in 1978, around the same time that he found the inspiration for *A Nightmare on Elm Street.* He explains:

> People Under the Stairs *was based on a story that happened in Santa Monica. There was this couple of upstanding citizens but were away at work and the police came to find the place broken into and found a place in the house that was barricaded. They broke down the doors and discovered these three kids who'd never been outside. Dressed in rags, they couldn't speak English.*[158]

In a 1992 interview, Craven told John Russo that he wrote the first act of the screenplay immediately after clipping the article, then put it in a drawer for twelve years.[159] Over a weekend at the Brussels Film Festival in 1989, he literally dreamed the rest of the story using lucid dreaming techniques. His subconscious mind delivered a "classic" Wes Craven horror narrative. Like *Last House on the Left* and *The Hills Have Eyes*, *The People Under the Stairs* is a primal, savage story rooted in everyday reality and revolving around family dynamics. Like *A Nightmare on Elm Street* and *The Serpent and the Rainbow*, it is also a parable of awakening—in this case, a coming-of-age.

The first act, drawing its inspiration from the 1978 newspaper article, introduces a thirteen-year-old black boy nicknamed Fool (a name that connotes innocence, not stupidity), who naively

157 Wooley 163, Dawidziak 46

158 Grey 118

159 Russo 180

accompanies a pair of burglars on a home invasion robbery. They have all heard rumors about the local slumlord's gold coin collection, and Fool goes after it like Jack up the beanstalk, hoping to save his dying mother and keep his family from being evicted. Like Jack, he gets caught. Booby traps kill Fool's partners in crime, and Fool gets stuck in the house of horrors. When the slumlords return, he quickly realizes that he's in way over his head.

In the second half of the film, a sadistic Mother and Father—inbred and insane, like the cannibals in *The Hills Have Eyes*—chase Fool throughout the house. He survives only with the help of Alice, their abused "daughter," and Roach, a "son" they banished to the basement, along with a host of other discarded (and dismembered) children. Fool repeatedly tries to summon help from the outside world, but the authorities fail to recognize anything wrong with the middle-class suburban couple. Mother and Father are, by all outward appearances, law-abiding and God-fearing citizens. This conflict between appearance and reality echoes the themes at the heart of Craven's most personal work: *Fear begins at home. The most horrific monsters are adults who prey on children. And the most dangerous darkness is the denial of reality.*

For the filmmaker, tapping into the truth of these themes meant tapping into memories of his own childhood fears—something he had tried to avoid while making *Shocker* but which he embraced on *The People Under the Stairs*. Like Craven himself, Fool has to face his fears in order to conclude his story in a healthy way. When cornered by Mother and Father, Alice advises him to hide in the walls. Fool argues, "I don't want *in*. I want *out*." Alice responds, casually and cryptically, "Sometimes out *is* in." Craven told Steve Biodrowski that he meant for the house itself to represent Fool's journey:

> *I was really fascinated with the idea of using a house as a material symbol of the human mind . . . In the sense that madness could be depicted as the spaces of the house. The outside seems quite normal, and the first floor seems luxurious and appropriate, and yet the further in you go, the more is unexplained or bizarre, so you have a feeling that any door could lead into an almost infinite labyrinth of places and meaning. [The People Under the Stairs] are down there howling and trying to crawl up through any crack*

in the foundation. In that sense, they're like the thoughts of people who are quite mad, who try to suppress the energies of life and youth and passion—those thoughts come out between the cracks, because they can never be fully contained.[160]

Once Fool goes deeper into his fear, he reemerges transformed. This gives him the strength to liberate the other children, who subsequently descend upon the sadistic parents like the beast-folk on Dr. Moreau. Reflecting on the meaning of the film, Craven says:

The boy and the girl escape from the house, but in a sense they also escape from the madness the house represents. The idea of children escaping the madness of parents, of the next generation liberating itself from the madness of a previous generation, is very old and powerful.[161]

Craven would explore this idea even further in his next film: a third and final trip to Elm Street.

In 1993, New Line CEO Robert Shaye approached Craven about writing and directing a new *Nightmare on Elm Street* sequel. The filmmaker was understandably reluctant, believing that the series had already run out of steam, but he was also intrigued by the possibility. "I went back and looked at all the previous Freddy films," he told Michael Emery, "and I couldn't see any pattern, anything that led to anything."[162] Soon after, he decided to drop the idea. Then he dreamed up an off-the-wall solution to his problem. He explained to Terry Lawson of the *Dayton Daily News*:

[I dreamed] I was at some sort of cocktail party, and Robert Englund was there in costume doing Freddy schtick. And I was standing off to the side, thinking, "This is exactly what's gone wrong with the films. Freddy has become this comedian." Then, off in the corner, I felt this presence, and I looked and there was a dark shape, moving with Robert, parallel to his movements,

160 Biodrowski: "People" 30
161 Biodrowski: "People" 31
162 Emery 110

> *but much more ominous and threatening. The next morning, I thought, "What the hell was that about?"' Then I realized that what it meant was that just because New Line had stopped making this series of films, that didn't mean that the essential thing out there that had inspired me to construct a figure like Freddy Krueger had stopped.*[163]

The dream suggested a meta-fiction narrative in which the essential Evil of Freddy would be separated from the fictional Freddy's creators—including Englund, Shaye, and Craven himself. For the sake of dramatic conflict, the filmmaker realized, this new story demanded an equally strong essential Good to counterbalance the threat. Accordingly, he reached out to Heather Langenkamp, the actress who portrayed Nancy Thompson in *Nightmares 1 & 3*.

At first, the actress was as reluctant to return to the series as Craven had been. Langenkamp was raising a young son at the time, and trying to maintain her privacy after an unsettling encounter with a celebrity stalker a few years earlier. Craven found that these real-life details perfectly suited his narrative, giving the heroine a more compelling reason to fight. The filmmaker says, "I was intrigued with the idea of doing a story based on events in her life as an actress who had made a horror film [. . .] What the influence of that was on her and also on her child."[164]

Inadvertently, Craven had also stumbled onto an idea that extended the natural progression of the *Nightmare* series. In *Nightmares 4 & 5*, the heroine Alice goes from being a mousy insecure teenager to a strong, confident mother. In part 5, her battle with Freddy escalates into a tug-of-war over her son Jacob—as Freddy exerts a corrupting influence through the unborn boy's dreams. *Wes Craven's Nightmare* examines the influence of the narrative itself on Heather's son.

In much the way that the previous *Nightmare* films blurred the line between dreams and reality, *New Nightmare* blurs the line between fiction and reality. It begins as a film-within-a-film—a test reel for a new *Nightmare on Elm Street* movie. Once this is revealed, the narrative shifts focus toward Heather Langenkamp, who is on the set with her son Dylan and her husband Chase Porter, a special

163 Lawson: "Cravin'"
164 Kutzera

effects designer. When Freddy's new animatronic glove comes to life and runs amok, this reality too is shattered. Heather awakens in her bed to the equally chaotic rumblings of an earthquake. On the DVD commentary for *New Nightmare*, Craven says that he always intended to open the film with the earthquake—playing off of a line in the first *Nightmare* ("Maybe we're about to have a big earthquake. They say things get really weird just before."). This is not, however, the real reason that Heather is rattled.

For weeks she's been receiving harassing phone calls, and the earthquake seems to have triggered a minor break with reality in her mind. Soon after, she sees four long gashes appear in her bedroom wall—Craven's homage to *Repulsion*, and a subtle suggestion that Nancy may be delusional. Her paranoia only increases when Bob Shaye contacts her about resurrecting his cash cow, explaining that Wes Craven is already working on the script for a sequel that will feature her in the lead role. Nancy turns down the job, mostly out of concern about the effect that the project will have on her son.

Dylan has already been having nightmares about Freddy Krueger, and in a pivotal scene he claims that the only thing saving him from the nightmare man is a stuffed animal named Rex. Later, Dylan attributes similar protective power to a particular bedtime story. With the introduction of "Hansel & Gretel" as a symbolic narrative within the narrative, Craven begins to illustrate his beliefs about bad dreams and horror stories. His insights reflect contemporary studies of child psychology and dreams.

In her 1984 book *Your Child's Dreams*, clinical psychologist Patricia Garfield proposes general principles for children dealing with nightmares. She suggests that parents should share stories that provide a model for successful confrontation and conquest of danger in dreams.[165] This is a lesson that Heather has to learn the hard way in *New Nightmare*. She is initially reticent about reading "Hansel and Gretel" to her son, fearing that it is too violent. When she stops short of the ending, Dylan pleads with his mother to tell him how Hansel and Gretel find their way home by following a trail of breadcrumbs. "It's important," he says solemnly, adding that he desperately needs to hear how the witch is killed and the children are saved. Child

165 Garfield 283-286

psychologist Bruno Bettelheim concurs, arguing that violent fairy tales are necessary for a child's healthy psychological development:

> *Morality is not the issue in these tales, but rather, assurance that one can succeed. Whether one meets life with a belief in the possibility of mastering its difficulties or with the expectation of defeat is also a very important existential problem. The deep inner conflicts originating in our primitive drives and our violent emotions are all denied in much of modern children's literature, and so the child is not helped in coping with them. But the child is subject to desperate feelings of loneliness and isolation, and he often experiences mortal anxiety. More often than not, he is unable to express these feelings in words, or he can do so only by indirection: fear of the dark, of some animal, anxiety about his body.*[166]

Bettelheim's perspective, outlined in his 1978 book *The Uses of Enchantment: The Meaning and Importance of Fairy Tales*, reinforces Craven's belief that adult rationality often fails to address the child's "real perception of evil." The psychologist observes, "Adults often think that the cruel punishment of an evil person in fairy tales upsets and scares children unnecessarily. Quite the opposite is true: such retribution reassures the child that the punishment fits the crime."[167] What's valuable for Dylan about "Hansel and Gretel," *New Nightmare* implies, may also be what's valuable about horror films for generations of young moviegoers. Answering his critics, Craven says, "My conclusion was that, as I never felt that these things were harmful, the good that they do and why they are so popular is that they somehow give shape and form and name to this unknowable, very frightening and very destructive thing. They somehow contain it, not to the extent that they stop it, but to the extent that they make it a bit more bearable."[168]

In *New Nightmare*, the biggest problem is that the fairy tale has been suppressed—on a pop cultural level by the demise of the *Nightmare* series and on a more personal level by Dylan's mother. If she fails to acknowledge the *reality* of Freddy Krueger, Dylan has to try to cope with the problem of Evil in his own. When Dylan

166 Bettelheim 10
167 Bettelheim 141
168 Robb 157

asks Heather, "Why does God let there be bad things?", she has no ready answer. When Dylan "reaches out" to God, he feels rejected. ("God wouldn't take me," he says solemnly.) A subsequent nightmare prompts him to shut down emotionally. While Dylan's doctor casually blames horror movies for the boy's nightmares, Nancy begins coming to terms with the importance of story. She visits Craven (the filmmaker within the film), who offers his perspective on Evil by outlining the plot of the new Freddy Krueger movie:

> *It's about this Entity. It's old, very old. It's existed in different forms in different times. About the only thing that stays the same is what it lives for: the murder of innocence. It can be captured sometimes, by storytellers. Every so often they imagine a story good enough to sort of catch its essence and then for a while it's held prisoner in the story. But the problem comes when the story dies. That can happen in a lot of ways. It can get too familiar to people. Or somebody waters it down to make it an easier sell. Or maybe it's so upsetting to society that it's banned outright. However it happens, when the story dies, the evil is set free.*

Craven proposes that the *Nightmare on Elm Street* films have served the function of *containing* that Evil, rather than spreading it. In order to keep Freddy from wreaking havoc in the real world, he suggests, it is necessary to make another film. Convinced by the filmmaker's rhetoric, Heather resolves to "play Nancy" one more time—recognizing that *the only way out is through.*

In the final act, Heather follows a trail of sleeping pills into the depths of a Greco-Roman Hell to save her son from the nightmare man, who now takes on the appearance of the Christian devil—sporting a forked tongue and even, in his final moment onscreen, horns. With his mother's help, Dylan defeats the serpentine Freddy by trapping him in a giant furnace, just like the witch at the end of "Hansel and Gretel." The resolution suggests that it is the fairy tale that has saved him. This idea is reiterated in the final scene, in which Heather reads the opening pages of the *New Nightmare* script as if it's a fairy tale.

Bettelheim writes that "an adult who has not achieved a satisfactory integration of the two worlds of reality and imagination is put off by such tales," and opines that those who are willing and able to share the experience of the darker fairy tales may be able to offer something of profound value to their children.[169] He explains:

> *If a parent tells his child fairy tales in the right spirit—that is, with feelings evoked in himself both through remembering the meaning the story had for him when he was a child, and through its different present meaning to him; and with sensitivity for the reason why his child may also derive some personal meaning from hearing the tale—then, as he listens, the child feels understood in his most tender longings, his most ardent wishes, his most severe anxieties and feelings of misery, as well as in his highest hopes. Since what the parent tells him in some way happens also to enlighten him about what goes on in the darker and irrational aspects of the mind, this shows the child that he is not alone in his fantasy life, that it is shared by the person he needs and loves most.*[170]

169 Bettelheim 66
170 Bettelheim 155

Post-Modern Screams, the Philosophy of Horror and the Soul of Wes Craven

After saying goodbye to Freddy Krueger in 1994, Wes Craven was at a crossroads. He had (somewhat accidentally) set a new standard for violent horror movies with *Last House on the Left*, reinvented the slasher movie with *A Nightmare on Elm Street*, and pushed the boundaries of genre storytelling with the self-reflexive *New Nightmare*. A few years later, he confessed that he had finally hit a wall: "I feel after almost thirty years in the genre that I can't just continue to do straight horror films. You don't see all these conventions and clichés without imitating yourself"[171] Perhaps that's why his follow-up to *New Nightmare* was a comedy.

Eddie Murphy and his brother cowrote the script for *Vampire in Brooklyn* (1995) because Murphy was also ready for a change. He wanted to play a villain—and, he figured, who better to oversee his transformation to an evil vampire than the master of horror Wes Craven? Unfortunately the studio brass wasn't particularly enthusiastic about the transformation, as Craven explains:

> *In* Vampire, *Eddie wanted to play a really dark and bad character. He didn't necessarily want to do comedy. The studio very much wanted him to do comedy. I think they sensed that they were just one* Nutty Professor *away from a lot of money. But Eddie both did and didn't want to go that way. So, he kind of played the comedy, but he also played the character quite dark, and not completely insanely funny, and not vulnerable, which is a way that we had suggested to him.*[172]

Craven found himself caught between a major studio (Paramount) and a major star. Clashing visions resulted in a toothless film that was neither scary nor particularly funny.

After this, the filmmaker tried to develop several psychological thrillers as an alternative to doing straight horror. Among the

171 Robb 178
172 Emery 111

projects he had in mind were *Original Sin*, a sexual thriller by Joe Eszterhas; *The Monster Butler*, which was based on the true crimes of serial killer Archibald Hall; and *The Cage*, the survival story of nature photographer Audrey Schulman. In the end, Craven could no more escape his horror label than Eddie Murphy could escape his comedic persona. Ultimately, he decided to simply embrace the role. He played a Jungian psychiatrist onscreen in the low-budget shockers *The Fear* (1995) and *Shadow Zone: The Undead Express* (1996), and loaned his name to his son's first feature film—a monster movie that began its life as *The Hills Have Eyes Part 3* and eventually morphed into *Wes Craven Presents: Mindripper* (1995).[173]

While the younger Craven worked on *Mindripper*, the elder Craven developed a remake of *The Haunting* (1963), emphasizing "the psychodynamics between the mother and daughter," for Miramax producers Bob and Harvey Weinstein.[174] The producers ultimately passed on the script, feeling that it wasn't edgy enough, but they offered Craven an opportunity to direct a hot new property called *Scream* (1996).[175] Written by newcomer Kevin Williamson, the script embodied a sly awareness of genre conventions and clichés that made it a natural companion piece to *Wes Craven's New Nightmare*.

In spite of its ironic humor, *Scream* was a brutal piece of work, opening with a scene in which a teenage girl gets eviscerated in her front yard. Dismayed by the intensity, Craven initially turned down the project, feeling that *Scream* was a little too similar to his earliest horror films. The more he thought about it, however, the more intrigued he became. The filmmaker remembers:

> *I thought about a lot of the interviews I did where kids would tell me that* Last House *was my best film because I really kicked ass [. . .] I started wondering if I was getting soft. So I decided to do one more to-the-wall horror film. I decided to really kick ass and do an opening scene that was really scary and really violent. I just turned into the old Wes and wasn't worried about offending people.*[176]

173 Robb 173
174 Robb 175
175 Grey 115
176 Emery 112

To be fair, however, he wasn't interested in simply repeating himself. When asked if he was tempted to incorporate some of his favorite themes—about family dynamics or spiritual self-awareness—into the script, he responded, "I felt like that would have been imposing too much of Wes Craven on the Kevin Williamson script. I didn't want to point back to the past. I wanted to do something new."[177]

Over the years, *Scream* has taken a lot of flak from horror fans for turning genre tropes into jokes. Based on its self-referential humor, some critics regard the film as a cynical parody rather than a serious horror film. But the filmmakers never intended to mock or parody the horror genre. Kevin Williamson simply wanted to make a horror movie that seemed *real*, and he figured the best way to do that was by creating believable characters that spoke and acted like real American teenagers in the mid-1990s—teenagers who have much more experience with slasher movies than with real-life horror. Williamson explained in a 1997 interview: "I finally had to ask myself what would scare me. 'I am a kid. I am a product of the VCR generation. I grew up next to a [video store]. What would scare me? . . .' If I watched a movie about myself and I was in this situation. *That* would be scary."[178]

To the victims and the killers in *Scream*, murder doesn't seem real. It's just something that happens in the movies. Even when it happens to people they know personally, most of the characters remain emotionally detached. When lead character Sidney Prescott comments that the first murder victim "sits next to me in English class," her friend Tatum coolly responds, "Not anymore." Their peers later respond to news of the murder by throwing a slasher-themed house party. At the conclusion of the party, when Sidney's boyfriend Billy reveals that he is one of the killers, he does so by quoting a line from *Psycho*—and then providing his own footnote. Craven told one interviewer that he found this kind of detached behavior to be hauntingly true to life:

> *The more kids I meet, especially in the current generation, the majority of their peak moments, their perception of the larger universe comes from films, rather than from experience. They're*

177 Interview with author 3/12/10
178 Mangels 50

> *incredibly aware and sophisticated when it comes to TV and movies, but in some ways it is quite superficial. When they have to face reality, you can see it surprises them.*[179]

This point is illustrated in the finale of the film, when Billy stabs his partner in crime and Stu crumbles in pain. "I'm feeling a little woozy here," Stu complains like a petulant child, genuinely surprised to learn that getting stabbed *hurts*.

Ironically, this scene—which treats violence as a cause of real suffering, not just a plot device—was the one that caused the most problems with the ratings boards at the Motion Picture Association of America. Craven remembers, "They said that the entire sequence had to come out." The only thing that saved the scene was a call from executive producer Bob Weinstein, who (according to Craven) told them, "I don't think you guys get it, but this is over-the-top comedy."[180] The scene *does* plays for laughs, but it also explicitly addresses a serious ongoing debate about horror movies: *Do they desensitize younger, more impressionable viewers?* More to the point: *Does media violence stimulate real-world violence?* The film offers its own answer. Billy insists, "Movies don't create psychos. Movies make psychos more creative."

One year later, *Scream 2* (1997) tackled the debate even more pointedly. In the opening scene, a copycat killer strikes at a theater where a fictional version of *Scream* is playing. Later, film school students debate the influence of the film on the true crime. A female student contends, "You can't blame real-life horror on entertainment . . . Movies are not responsible for our actions." Another student rebuts her, "The murderer was wearing a ghost mask, just like in the movie. It's directly responsible." This debate resurfaces in the climactic scene of *Scream 2*, when the killer tells Sidney that he plans to use the "movies made me do it" defense in court. "The Christian Coalition will pay my legal fees," he quips. The joke makes it clear which side of the debate the filmmaker falls on. For Craven, horror movies (at least, the responsible ones) are modern-day Greek tragedies, providing what Aristotle calls catharsis—a cinematic "primal scream." In Craven's words: "Kids today have fears and they need a way to process their terror in a positive and funny manner.

179 Mangels 67
180 Goldman

Scream accomplished this with scenarios of intense anxiety as well as playfulness."[181]

Less than a month after *Scream 2* was released into theaters, the debate was resurrected when a pair of Los Angeles teenagers blamed the *Scream* films for inspiring them to commit murder. In January 1998, sixteen-year-old Mario Salvador Padilla and his fourteen-year-old cousin Samuel Jeremias Ramiraz were arrested for the murder of Padilla's mother, thirty-seven-year-old Gina Castillo. According to the *Los Angeles Times*, "The boys had planned to buy a Grim Reaper mask and a voice-distorting box similar to those featured in the films, but couldn't afford them."[182] Inside the courtroom, no one bought the excuse; even the boys' defense lawyer argued that the movies could not be blamed for the killing, and the judge prohibited any mention of *Scream* during the trial. Ultimately, the killers—not the filmmakers—were held responsible for the murder of Gina Castillo.

Based on the overwhelming success of the *Scream* movies, Craven's name continued to be very valuable horror brand. In the following years, he began acting as a kind of godfather to a new generation of horror filmmakers, putting his name above the title of *Wishmaster* (1997), *Carnival of Souls* (1997), *Don't Look Down* (1998), *Dracula 2000* (2000), *They* (2002), and *The Breed* (2006), as well as the TV pilot *Hollyweird* (1997). All of these films were written, directed, or produced by people Craven had worked with on previous projects, but his personal involvement varied from project to project. As a result, the filmmaker had mixed feelings about his new role as "presenter":

> *It's kind of a mixture of fun with a very cautionary feeling about the danger of selling out. You know, How can I exploit this? I've worked so damned hard, how can I cash in on this legitimately? There's kind of [a] feeling of wanting to give back a little to the community of young filmmakers by shepherding something through that might give a young filmmaker a chance. It's kind of a mixture of all of those things. It's strange in a way because you don't have your hand on it the way you're so used to doing your own films, where you want every frame to kind of*

181 Robb 178
182 Krikorian

> *have your own initials on it someplace and you feel responsible for it and want to use every ounce of your strength to make it something that is completely your own. With this other kind of film we're talking about, you're kind of taking everything you've earned from that process and kind of lending it in a way to someone else. It's either a very good feeling or a queasy feeling depending on how you feel about the end product.*[183]

As the filmmaker himself suggests, not everything he loaned his name to was entirely successful.

The success of *Scream* also gave Craven the ability to expand his repertoire beyond horror. He remembers:

> *What happened is, after we had finished* Scream, *we had a test screening and it went through the roof in Secaucus. And the two brothers that run Miramax—who are Miramax—Bob and Harvey Weinstein sought us out. We were in a restaurant celebrating our test scores, and they came in, sort of elbowed everybody away and sat down next to me and my producer and said, "We want you to do three more [horror] pictures with us." And I said, "Well, jeez, I've been thinking of not doing that much more horror." And he said, "Okay, we'll sweeten the pot. We'll give you a non-genre film." This is something nobody has said to me in thirty years of trying to do something different.* [184]

It was an offer the filmmaker couldn't refuse. He looked through all of the intellectual properties that Miramax owned until he found the one that he wanted to adapt into a feature film. It was a documentary called *Small Wonders*, about a music teacher who teaches inner-city kids how to play the violin.

According to Craven, *Music of the Heart* (1999) was originally developed as a vehicle for Madonna, until the director and his star found themselves at odds about the focus of the story. According to Craven, Madonna wanted to emphasize her character's relationships with men; Craven thought the film should be about the inspirational power of music. When Madonna left the project just prior to filming, *Music of the Heart* nearly died a premature death.[185] Craven made

183 Rausch
184 Interview with author 3/12/14
185 Applebaum

a desperate Hail Mary pass, contacting Meryl Streep and asking her to take over the role. Streep declined, but the filmmaker followed up with a heartfelt letter, as he explained to journalist Terry Lawson: "I just sort of poured out my feelings about the project, and why Meryl would be ideal for the part of Guaspari. She called the next day and relented. Meryl later told me it was my passion she responded to."[186] The finished film was the first Wes Craven film that the filmmaker's mother was willing to watch, and Craven himself insists that it's "a lot closer to who I am than the other films I've made."[187]

For all of the obvious differences between *Music of the Heart* and Craven's horror films, there are some noteworthy parallels to his earlier films. Like *A Nightmare on Elm Street* and *Scream*, it is the story of a heroine's journey to overcome her personal fears. *Music* shows how Roberta Guaspari uses music recover from a life of dependency, and how she uses her own experiences to inspire scores of children to believe in themselves. Her character arc echoes that of *Elm Street*'s Nancy, who not only fought Freddy but also trained the next generation of "dream warriors." Sidney Prescott would traverse the same road from prospective victim to maternal mentor over the course of the ongoing *Scream* series.

In *Scream 3* (2000), Sidney doesn't just stop a sadistic killer, she stops allowing the existence of sadistic killers to control how she lives her life. The film as a whole is more lighthearted than its predecessors (due to extensive rewrites that followed in the wake of the Columbine High School massacre[188]) and it ends on a reassuring note that was important to Craven. In the final scene of the trilogy, the front door of Sidney's once-fortified home swings open for no apparent reason. In any other horror film, this would be a setup for one last scare. Sidney stares into the open doorway, knowingly. Instead of going to close the door, however, she decides to leave it open. Craven explains that this scene was, for him, the perfect note on which to end the series: "It's about moving past tragedy to a moment in your life where it seems there a chance for renewal and it's safe to leave the doors unlocked."[189] In a 2010 interview, he added:

---

186 Lawson: "Movie"
187 Wooley 207, Lawson: "Movie"
188 Bloody Disgusting
189 Portman

There's a t-shirt with the emblem "No Fear" that came out around 1990. It was associated with these new sports. It started with skydiving and surfing, then snowboarding and skating, BMX bicycles and motorcycles doing back flips over a 180 foot jump. Extraordinary stuff that you would never see a normal human being doing, and then suddenly kids are doing it. There's something about fear and overcoming fear that is one of the chief evolutionary mechanisms. I mean, think about how terrifying it would have been to sail out into the ocean when you'd been raised to believe that, sooner or later, you're going to hit the edge of the earth and fall over into perdition or whatever. Now think of all the benefits that came out of facing that fear . . . I think, in all of our lives, that facing our fears is a good thing. A lot of life just has to do with somehow putting fear aside. In that sense, making movies about people who confront their fears seems beneficial.[190]

As he was finishing the *Scream* trilogy, the aged eagle continued to stretch his wings by writing his first novel. At first glance, *Fountain Society* is not recognizable as a "typical" Wes Craven story. There is violence, certainly, and plenty of gruesome imagery, but there are no sadistic fathers or broken families. There are dreams and nightmares, but they exist mostly as straightforward reflections of psychological stress and buried intuitions. That said, the framework of the story must be familiar to any horror genre enthusiast. In the simplest terms, *Fountain Society* is a modern-day variation on *Frankenstein*—a story that Craven specifically sought to bring to the screen as early as 1985, and which undoubtedly provided inspiration for his films *Swamp Thing*, *Chiller* and *Deadly Friend*. In a 2009 article, the filmmaker summed up his fascination with the classic Gothic tale as follows:

Obviously, science, especially medical science, has brought an enormous amount of good to humanity. We live healthier and longer lives than any generation before us. But each step of science also brings a certain cold sense of how alone we are in the universe, how fragile our bodies are—and how utterly unprepared

190 Interview with author 3/12/10

> *our societies, laws, beliefs, or institutions are for whatever the geniuses among us are unleashing upon us next.*[191]

Fountain Society, like Mary Shelley's novel, is a cautionary tale about the potential dangers of scientific advancement without moral checks. It is also a brilliantly balanced character study.

The novel's "Frankenstein Monster" is Dr. Peter Jance, a weapons designer for the U.S. military whose brain is surgically transplanted into the younger, healthier body of his cloned self. Dr. Frederick Wolfe, the resident mad scientist (who the author compares to Nosferatu) carries out the surgical procedure, much to the chagrin of Jance's wife Beatrice. Afterward Jance finds himself drawn to a younger woman named Elizabeth—a character that may seem particularly familiar to Craven fans.

Although her name suggests a connection to Shelley's novel, Elizabeth has more in common with Nancy, the heroine of *A Nightmare on Elm Street*, and with Sidney, the heroine of *Scream*. Craven introduces her in the opening chapter as follows:

> *The fact was that Elizabeth liked risk—yearned for the taste and challenge of it. And deep inside she was even convinced that on the other side of such places and situations lay the reality she so desired. From the slopes of Switzerland to the runways of Paris, she had found everything she treasured most by threading passageways of fear to the other side.*[192]

At various points in the novel, the author also compares Elizabeth to the heroines of *Alice in Wonderland* and *The Wizard of Oz*—characters who must awaken from fearful realities.

Craven's twist on these archetypal stories is a unique fusion of the familiar elements. The resulting tale is an elaborate mystery that reveals the humanity of the would-be monster and allows the heroine to confront and overcome her fear of death. Despite Jance's fear that he has forfeited "some precious part" of his identity, the melding of two selves stimulates a new respect for life and nature. Elizabeth undergoes a comparable intellectual and spiritual transformation, and the story concludes on a transcendent note with the revelation that love is more powerful than death.

191 Craven: "10 Movies"

192 Craven: *Fountain* 8

Craven was pleased with the novel, and eager to turn it into a film. Unfortunately he spent the next two years in development before it became clear that the optioning studio, Dimension Films, wasn't interested in the philosophical elements of the story. The filmmaker remembers: "It kind of turned into a movie that was basically just a chase movie, and we were never really able to get to the point where we are all enthusiastic about it."[193]

Craven's name remained high profile during the early years of the new millennium, in spite of the fact that his next directorial effort didn't appear onscreen until 2005. During the time that he was working to develop *Fountain Society* at Dimension, he also worked on an adaptation of America McGee's video game *Alice* and wrote a prospective remake of the Japanese horror film *Kairo* (2001), entitled *Pulse*. The filmmaker remembers that he and his producing partner were five weeks away from shooting *Pulse* when Dimension pulled the plug and "made us an offer that we kind of had to accept."[194] Newcomers Ray Wright and Jim Sonzero later took over writing and directing responsibilities on *Pulse* while Craven reteamed with *Scream* scribe Kevin Williamson on a werewolf picture called *Cursed*.

Adding insult to injury, the Dimension execs eventually pulled the plug on *Cursed*—after eleven weeks of shooting—calling for extensive rewrites and a re-conceptualization of the special effects sequences.[195] The production delays necessitated the replacement of multiple actors, which prompted more rewrites. Craven's assistant (and future coproducer) Carly Feingold reports on the extent of the revisions: "I've been told there was 8 minutes of the first version that was shot that ended up in the final movie. They recast parts and rewrote the script entirely."[196] The results of the studio tampering speak for themselves. *Cursed* failed to capture the magic of *Scream*, and the director has been pretty blunt about his own disappointment over the project:

193 SciFi Wire
194 SciFi Wire
195 Faile
196 Feingold

> *It was two years of very difficult work and almost 100 days of shooting of various versions. Then at the very end, it was chopped up as the studio thought they could make more with a PG-13 movie, and trashed it. We were writing while we were shooting. It wasn't ready for film. We rewrote, recast and had two major reshoots... After a while, I regretted it was called* Cursed *because it was cursed.*[197]

Finally, the filmmaker decided it was time to part ways with Dimension Films. His next opportunity came from a small production company that offered him the reins on a Hitchcockian thriller called *Red Eye* (2005). Craven says, "I thought for years about making a thriller someday and there it was."[198] The screenplay by Carl Ellsworth treaded some familiar territory for Craven, revolving around a young woman struggling against the debilitating power of her own fears. The filmmaker was so pleased with the results that he agreed to do an extended press tour for the film instead of jumping into his next project right away. Midway through the tour, another non-horror project fell in his lap.

Craven remembers learning about *Paris Je T'aime*, an anthology of short films connected by setting, from an email inquiring whether he would like to write and direct a segment. As soon as he read filming would take place in Paris, he decided, "Okay, I'm there. What plane do I need to be on?"[199] At first, the filmmaker says, he wrote a story revolving around Jim Morrison's grave. Over the course of a few months it became clear that he would not be able to get the rights to use Morrison's name, let alone his grave, so Craven wrote another story revolving around Edith Piaf. The same problem arose. "And so," the filmmaker says, "in literally two hours, about two days before we were going to shoot, I wrote the one that we shot, and I think it turned out to be the nicest and the freshest of the three."[200] The filmed segment, "Pére Lachaise" features the ghost of Oscar Wilde playing matchmaker to a pair of young lovers. Although it is set in a cemetery, it is not a story about death or somber reflection but rather an idealistic expression of youthful optimism, suggesting new beginnings for the filmmaker.

197 Carolyn 102
198 Carolyn 102
199 Murray
200 Zingale

In 2006, Wes Craven turned sixty-seven years old. He was, by all accounts, the most successful horror director in the world, a living legend with no fewer than four modern horror classics to his name. At a time when many of the major Hollywood studios were remaking the iconic horror films of the 1970s and 1980s on big budgets, it was only natural for Craven to consider revisiting his most personal films. The rights to *A Nightmare on Elm Street, Shocker*, and *The People Under the Stairs* were out of his hands, but he and his producing partners had recently reacquired the rights to *Last House on the Left* and *The Hills Have Eyes*.

Craven recognized the business opportunity, but wasn't prepared to relive his "primal screams," as he explained to me in 2010:

> *I would never go back to that, personally.* Last House *was done at a time where I just burned all my bridges and didn't care what anybody thought about me, and it was painful. I feel like you have a right to do anything once, but to repeat it just because it might sell... I think that would be almost inexcusable.*[201]

He shared a similar sentiment with writer David Szulkin, saying, "I think if you spend too long working in that area, you brutalize your soul ... When you're making a film like that for a year, or a year and a half, it's not an easy place to live."[202] Having moved beyond his own youthful rage, Craven set out to find younger, angrier filmmakers to bring these tales to life again.

Craven and producer Peter Locke turned over *The Hills Have Eyes* to director Alexandre Aja and his writing partner Gregory Levasseur, the duo behind the French psycho-thriller *High Tension* (2003). *High Tension* was a homage to the savage American horror films of the 1970s—films like *Deliverance, The Texas Chainsaw Massacre* and *The Hills Have Eyes*—so it was natural for them to consider working again in this milieu. In fact, Aja says he was also approached about directing the Platinum Dunes remake of *Chainsaw*.[203] He turned that project down because he felt that it would be impossible

201 Interview with author 3/12/10

202 Szulkin 16

203 Rawshark

to improve on the original. When Craven approached him about a remake of *Hills*, however, Aja felt that he could add something worthwhile: "We brought this nuclear testing background forward as a way of developing the characters and making it more real and more brutal. Wes offered us his trust. From the beginning, he said, *'Look, I did my movie and I want you to do yours.'*"[204]

The resulting remake is both more monstrous and more politically subversive. By setting Craven's original story against the backdrop of America's first nuclear tests, the villains became horrific symbols of an unseen villain: the U.S. government. (It is not by accident that the American flag is used as a stabbing weapon in the film.) The significance wasn't lost on Craven, who told *Cinefantastique* journalist Steve Biodrowski that it was an appropriate time to revisit the films he made in the 1970s, considering certain parallels between then and now: "Let's see: a cynical era, an unpopular war, a corrupt administration. . . ."[205]

The political subtext of the *Hills* remake so intrigued Craven that he decided to play a more hands-on role in developing the sequel. The filmmaker cowrote *The Hills Have Eyes 2* (2007) with his son Jonathan, drawing on then-current events for inspiration. He explained to interviewer Justine Goodman:

> *I don't really have to have a morbid imagination these days—I just have to read the newspaper [. . .] Not that there's* Hills Have Eyes *people running around in the United States. But if you nudge that just a bit, you can understand what it's like, say, for an American soldier in Afghanistan, encountering people that will literally skin you alive or cut your head off in the middle of the mountains.* The Hills' *underlying concept is, "What do Westerners do when they confront people who would like to kill them, and follow none of the rules they were trained to fight by?" What does that do to your own sense of personal confidence and morality?*[206]

The sequel picks up right where the remake left off, with a group of National Guard soldiers investigating the disappearance of the Carter family. Craven's initial idea was for Brenda Carter to

204 Rawshark
205 Biodrowski: "Sense"
206 Goodman

return and lead the soldiers after the people that killed her parents. That scenario, reminiscent of *Aliens* (1986), was scrapped when it became clear that actress Emilie de Ravin would not available for the sequel.[207] After that, the elder Craven says, the writers decided to take a different approach:

> *At a certain point, we said, "You know what? It doesn't feel that scary if you send in a bunch of trained soldiers, but what if they were recruits and they're only halfway through their training. They were not sent in to do this at all, but they were just in there and just get swept up into it." So it kind of developed that way. It seemed interesting and it seemed to have parallels to things that are in the news, and we couldn't help making those comparisons.*[208]

Significantly, the only survivors in the film are the soldiers who question authority and voice confusion about the meaning and purpose of war. They are the only ones who are able to see the future clearly; the others never see their downfall coming.

Based on the success of *The Hills Have Eyes* remake, Craven's production company was quick to develop a remake of *The Last House on the Left* (2009). Once again, the veteran filmmaker sought new blood, as he explained to interviewer Scott Tobias:

> *With the help of a young man named Cody Zwieg in our office who just pored over all the emerging films and emerging filmmakers, we found [Dennis Iliadis']* Hardcore. *And we watched that and thought, "This is really a wonderful filmmaker." The material was very dark, very edgy, and yet at the core of it were magnificent performances and totally believable characters.*[209]

Working from a screenplay by Adam Alleca and Carl Ellsworth, Iliadis made a film that is faithful to the original story, but not without some significant modifications. The most obvious change is the survival of Mari, which profoundly affects the tone of the film. The narrative emphasis in this version is on protection rather than on

---

207 Horror-Movies
208 Douglas
209 Tobias

revenge, giving the story a sense of hope that is absent from Craven's original. Iliadis also counterbalances the savagery of the characters with the lyrical beauty of the visual storytelling, creating a much more nuanced and sophisticated film.

Craven's success with these remakes is doubly apparent when compared with the Platinum Dunes remake of *A Nightmare on Elm Street*. Despite moments of visual brilliance and an interesting twist on Freddy Krueger's origin story, that 2010 remake fails to develop its "dream warriors." All of the teenage characters sleepwalk through the film, looking despondent and failing to put up much of a fight against Freddy. In this revision of the heroine's journey, Nancy doesn't survive because of her personal strength, but because she's Freddy's "favorite." Thus, Craven's genuinely cathartic narrative is reduced to a depressing pastiche of music video imagery.

Craven has not spoken much about the remake, except to say that he is disappointed that he was not able to be involved with the attempted resurrection of his favorite creation. He has, however, commented on the general malaise that accompanies so many Hollywood remakes in the 2000s:

> *Somebody once wrote about jazz that guys Thelonius Monk, John Coltrane and Miles Davis kind of invented a whole new kind of music. Some new musicians are much better with the technique, but they're not inventing so much as trying to play better versions of what has come before. There's not as much of the actual person's soul [in their art].*[210]

After more than ten years of producing and directing other people's scripts, Craven resolved to put something of his own soul onscreen again.

In the spring of 2010, Wes Craven introduced his latest film as a story about a naive teenager's awakening from sheltered innocence into a darker world filled with violence and betrayal. He confessed that it was his most intimate film in years, explaining: "There's a ton of stuff that's happened in this kid's life that he's not aware of, or has blocked out. That felt more personal than anything I'd made in a long time. I felt like I was tapping into some things in my own

210 Interview with author 3/12/10

childhood." He concluded, "Bug is a kid who is very much the way I see myself in retrospect."[211]

The semi-autobiographical *My Soul to Take* (2010) is a philosophically complex film that attempts to draw together the essential elements of Craven's best work. The hero, Bug, is a teenager searching for a source of personal strength but haunted by the specter of his dead father, a notorious serial killer known as the Riverton Ripper. Just as the young Wes Craven was sheltered from darker truths about the world outside his door, so Bug has been sheltered from the truth about his biological father. Like Freddy Krueger, however, the Ripper won't be denied and forgotten. Craven originally made the parallels to *A Nightmare on Elm Street* explicit in the opening scene of the film, a dream sequence in which the supernatural killer slices through the wall above Bug's bed. The scene was accompanied by a solemn voiceover, intoning, "Sooner or later, every teenager has to ask the question: *How did I end up here?* You never know you're going to ask that question until you do... because you're still dreaming. This is a story of the day I woke up. I slept for sixteen years."

Bug's awakening is, naturally, a violent one. One by one, his friends fall under the Ripper's knife, and, with each death, Bug's personality seems to change. Craven explains that his idea was to suggest that the character is experiencing a unique kind of multiple personality disorder:

> *I've kind of developed this theory that, in a horror film, in a sense, you're kind of dealing with sort of an uber-personality, sort of a composite personality that is made up of the hero or heroine and all of his or her friends. They kind of all are aspects of sort of an overall personality, and the parts of that personality that don't work when faced with grim reality are killed off. It's kind of, in a strange way, a parallel with our own life, where the parts of ourselves that—at a certain point in your life where you said, "That was pretty stupid and I'm getting rid of it"—is the equivalent of what a character in a horror film dying [means]. That's how I look at it. So it's really in a way sort of honed by fate and fear and necessity to perform at the heroic level. With this film, I kind of consciously did that.*[212]

211 Interview with author 3/12/10

212 Craven and Thieriot

According to this theory, each victim represents an aspect of Bug's personality that he needs to discard in order to fully awaken. The first victim, Jay Chan, represents superstition. He tells Bug that he has kept the Ripper away for sixteen years by "spitting in the river" every time he crosses it. It quickly becomes clear that superstition is no longer effective. The second victim, Penelope, is a religious fundamentalist who talks to God. The Almighty warns her that the return of the Ripper is imminent, but that does not save her from the killer's wrath. Clearly, conventional religion is no solution either. Brandon, whose only apparent virtue is confidence (though this turns out to be a façade), is next to go, followed by Brittany, Bug's smart but spineless love interest—until the only ones left are Bug and his best friend Alex.

At this point in the story, it unclear if Bug is the hero of the story, absorbing the strengths of his friends like Alice did in the later *Elm Street* sequels, or if he is actually the killer, unknowingly consuming their souls like Freddy Krueger. Even Craven, it seems, is a bit uncertain about whether Bug is essentially good or evil. The original climax of the film (included among the Rogue DVD bonus features) reveals Bug as the carrier of the Ripper's evil spirit, prompting his sister to shoot him dead. In the aftermath of that climax, we see Bug's spirit walking the streets of Riverton alongside the ghosts of his dead comrades. The implication seems to be that death is the only certain escape from evil—an uncharacteristically defeatist ending for Craven. The theatrical ending, on the other hand, reveals that Alex is the one possessed by the Ripper. In this version, Bug heroically murders his best friend and dispels the evil spirit of the Ripper. Afterward, he tilts his head toward the sky, acknowledging God, and says, "I know you're up there and I know we're down here." Craven claims that this line sums up the hero's final insight: "By the end it's just Bug with a realization that if there is a God, He doesn't really intervene in the horrible things that happen on Earth very much at all, so we kind of have to embody it all ourselves.[213]

This is similar to the conclusion of Craven's *The Fireworks Woman*, and the conclusion that his cinematic idol Ingmar Bergman came to in *Winter Light*: *Good and Evil are what we make of them.* "I don't believe in God," Bergman explained, "but it isn't that simple.

213 Zimmerman

We all carry a god within us."[214] Soon after completing *My Soul to Take*, Craven summed up his own religious beliefs for biographer John Wooley:

> *I've reached a point in my life where I certainly don't believe in some God up in the sky dictating what we should do or not do. But it's not like I don't think there's some supreme essence to consciousness and to the world that is simply awe-inspiring. To me, it could simply be a bird. Things that I can actually experience are just so wondrous, as opposed to Jesus in my heart.*[215]

In an interview with me on the same day, he spoke of birds in a very different light:

> *You watch birds at a feeder and, if you're into birds, you start to realize that every second they're expecting to get wopped upside the head. They're just constantly looking over their shoulder, all the time. I live up in the hills and there's a hawk that's come into the area called a Cooper's Hawk. It's about three quarters the size of a Red-Tail Hawk. And they're ambushers. They'll sit up in the tree and watch the feeder, and just come in this low flight between the trees, hit a morning dove and the morning dove just explodes. The hawk flies off and all that's left behind is feathers . . .*[216]

It's worth adding that the director, a self-professed naturalist and avid bird-watcher, uses bird imagery to disturbing effect in *My Soul to Take*. One sequence presents the California Condor, a bird of prey with some particularly nasty hygienic habits, as the "keeper of souls" that "literally eats death." There's an ambiguity about Craven's depiction of this creature—as a protector and a predator watching us from above—that suggests a great deal of complexity in the filmmaker's worldview. In the end, he doesn't feel the need to offer a simple explanation for everything. To define things too decisively would be to rob them of power, and to rob the filmmaker of genuine awe. Michaelangelo Antonioni, another of Craven's cinematic idols, expressed the same hesitation: "When I see nature, when I look into the sky, the dawn, the sun, the colors of insects, snow crystals,

214 Bergman: *Magic* 174
215 Wooley 31
216 Interview with author 3/12/10

the night stars, I don't feel a need for God. Perhaps when I can no longer look and wonder, when I believe in nothing—then, perhaps, I might need something else. But I don't know what."[217]

In the forty-plus years since the release of *Last House on the Left*, Wes Craven has repeatedly expressed his misgivings about being identified mainly as a horror film director. At the same time he has become a defender of the genre, claiming that the best horror films offer moviegoers alike the possibility of escape from their fears. Reflecting on his recent fourth entry in the *Scream* franchise, Craven says:

> *There's a sense of pleasure to know that I've gotten to that place where [my work] hasn't so much bruised them but has allowed them to come out of the film happy. That's the majority experience. Coming out of a good scary film, the audience is bubbling. Something has been released in a way that scared the bejesus out of them, but also lifted something off them.*[218]

Reflecting on his fellow horror filmmakers, he adds: "I think there's a sort of exorcism that takes place with people who make horror films. They deal with things that were very frightful to them as children, or whatever. In the process of working it out in such a public way, they're made very happy. They're liberated, in a way."[219]

For Craven himself, that awakening is an ongoing process. In a 2011 interview with *New York Times* reporter Andrew Goldman, he admitted that he hasn't entirely exorcised the guilt and fear of his formative years. He told the interviewer that he still vividly remembers the terror that came with his rejection of the Church: "[I recently went] to a funeral at a very fundamentalist church, and I just had to get out of there. I went out in the parking lot and just sobbed. I think there was a sense of loss of that little boy not knowing if he was right or wrong. Everything I grew up with I had to walk away from."[220]

217 Billard 59
218 Craven: *Directors*
219 Persons 88
220 Goldman

All these years later, the filmmaker is still on his journey out of fear. And, like the strongest characters in his films, he recognizes that the only way to overcome fear is to keep going through it, all the way to the end. It's a journey perhaps best summed up by the poet T.S. Eliot, who wrote:

> *We shall not cease from exploration*
> *And the end of all our exploring*
> *Will be to arrive where we started*
> *And know the place for the first time.*[221]

As of 2014, Craven is developing a new film project. The working title is *Home.*

221 Eliot: *Little* 148

Bibliography

Adler, Stella R. *Sleep Paralysis: Night-mares, Nocebos, and the Mind-Body Connection.* Piscataway: Rutgers UP, 2010.

Applebaum, Stephen. "Satisfying a Craven." *The Scotsman* (Edinburgh). January 1, 2000.

Banka, Michael. "Interview on Elm Street." *Cineaste.* Vol. 17, No. 3. 1990.

Barr, Matthew. Interview. "So It Was Written, with Matthew Barr and Glenn M. Benest." *Deadly Blessing.* Shout! Factory: 2013. DVD.

Benest, Glenn M. Interview. "So It Was Written, with Matthew Barr and Glenn M. Benest." *Deadly Blessing.* Shout! Factory: 2013. DVD.

Bergman, Ingmar. Interview by *Vilgot Sjöman. Ingmar Bergman Makes a Movie.* 1963.

---. *Images: My Life in Film.* Trans. Marianne Ruuth. New York: Arcade, 1994.

---. *The Magic Lantern: An Autobiography.* Trans. Joan Tate. U of Chicago P, 1988.

Bettelheim, Bruno. *The Uses of Enchantment: The Meaning and Importance of Fairy Tales.* New York: Vintage, 1989.

Billard, Peter. "An Interview with Michaelangelo Antonioni." 1967. *Michaelangelo Antonioni Interviews.* Ed. Bert Cardullo. Jackson: UP of Mississippi, 2008.

Biodrowski, Steve. "The People Under the Stairs." *Cinefantastique.* Vol. 22, No. 3. December 1991.

---. "Sense of Wonder: Wes Craven on Building a new Last House on the Left." *Cinefantastiqueonline.com.* March 12, 2009.

---. "Wes Craven on Dreaming Up Nightmares." *Cinefantastiqueonline.com.* October 2008.

---. "Wes Craven, Shocker." *Cinefantastique.* Vol. 20, No. 1 & No. 2. November 1989.

Bliatout, Bruce Thowpaou. *Hmong Sudden Unexpected Nocturnal Death Syndrome: A Cultural Study.* Portland: Sparkle, 1982.

Bloody Disgusting Staff. "Wes Craven Talks 'Scream 4,' Blu-ray, Teens, Technology, Violence, and a Smidgen of 'Scream 5'!" *Bloody-Disgusting.com.* September 28, 2011.

Bracke, Peter M. *Crystal Lake Memories: The Complete History of Friday the 13th.* London: Titan, 2006.

Buñuel, Luis. *My Last Sigh: The Autobiography of Luis Buñuel.* Trans. Abigail Israel. New York: Knopf, 1983.

Carolyn, Axelle. *It Lives Again! Horror Movies in the New Millennium.* London: Telos, 2008

Clark, Jim. "A Nightmare on Elm Street—Part III." *Cinefantastique.* Vol. 17, No. 2. March 1987.

Cooper, Jeffrey. *The Nightmare on Elm Street Companion: The Official Guide to America's Favorite Fiend.* New York: St. Martin's, 1987.

---. *The Nightmares on Elm Street Parts 1, 2, 3: The Continuing Story*. New York: St. Martin's, 1987.

Craven, Wes. "10 Movies That Shook ME Up." *Entertainment Weekly*. October 26, 2009.

---. Commentary. *Wes Craven's New Nightmare*. New Line: 2000. DVD.

---. *Fountain Society*. New York: Pocket, 1999.

---. Interview. *Celluloid Crime of the Century*. Blue Underground: 2003. DVD.

---. Interview. *The Directors: The Films of Wes Craven*. AFI: 1999. DVD.

---. Interview. *Masters of Horror.* Sci-Fi Channel: 2002.

---. Interview. *Postmortem with Mick Garris*. FearNet: 2012.

---. Interview. *Still Standing: The Legacy of The Last House on the Left.* Red Shirt Pictures: 2003. DVD.

---. "*A Night* to Remember: *What the Living Dead Means to Me." Night of the Living Dead: Behind the Scenes of the Most Terrifying Zombie Movie Ever.* New York: Citadel, 2010.

Craven, Wes and Max Thieriot. "My Soul to Take." *Meet the Filmmaker* podcast. October 7, 2010.

Craven, Wes, Jacques Haitkin, Heather Langenkamp and John Saxon. Commentary. *A Nightmare on Elm Street.* Elite: 1995. DVD.

Cunningham, Sean. Interview. *Celluloid Crime of the Century.* Blue Underground: 2003. DVD.

Davis, Wade. *The Serpent and the Rainbow*. New York: Simon & Schuster, 1985.

Dawidziak, Mark. "Nightmare Café." *Cinefantastique*. Vol. 22, No. 6. June 1992.

Delahaye, Michel and Jean Narboni. "Interview with Roman Polanski." 1969. *Roman Polanski: Interviews.* Ed. Paul Cronin. Jackson: UP of Mississippi, 2005.

Douglas, Edward. "Exclusive Interview: Horror Master Wes Craven." *ComingSoon.net*. March 19, 2007.

Eliot, T.S. "Baudelaire." *Selected Essays of T.S. Eliot*. New York: Harcourt, 1964.

---. *Little Gidding. The Complete Poems and Plays, 1909-1950*. New York: Harcourt, 1967.

Emery, Robert J. *The Directors—Take Three*. New York: Allworth, 2003.

Englund, Robert with Alan Goldsher. *Hollywood Monster: A Walk Down Elm Street with the Man of Your Dreams*. New York: Pocket, 2009.

Faile, Chris. "Wes Craven & Company Are Back: 'Cursed' Will Re-Begin Filming November 17." *Filmjerk.com*. September 30, 2003.

Feingold, Carly. Interview. "Interview with *Scream 4* Co-Producer Carly Feingold." *The Bitter Script Reader.* May 2011. Online.

Fischer, Dennis. *Horror Film Directors, 1931—1990*. Jefferson: McFarland, 1991.

Freedman, James. "Director Wes Craven reflects on his time at Homewood." *Johns Hopkins News-Letter*. January 31, 2008.

Garfield, Patricia. *Your Child's Dreams*. New York: Ballantine, 1984.

Gire, Dan. "Bye Bye, Freddy!" *Cinefantastique*. Vol. 18, No. 5. July 1988.

Goldberg, Lee. "Visiting with a 'Deadly Friend.'" *Starlog* #109. August 1986.

Goldman, Andrew. "The Horror of Being Wes Craven." *The New York Times*. April 15, 2011.

Goodman, Justine. "Interview: Director Wes Craven." *YRB Magazine*. March 2, 2007.

Grey, Ian. Sex, *Stupidity and Greed: Inside the American Movie Industry*. New York: Juno, 1997.

Gregory, R.L. *Eye and Brain: The Psychology of Seeing*. Princeton: Princeton UP, 1997.

Gurdjieff, George. *Views from the Real World: Early Talks in Moscow, Essentuki, Tiflis, Berlin, London, Paris, New York and Chicago as Recollected by His Pupils*. New York: Dutton, 1975.

Hawthorne, Nathaniel. *The House of the Seven Gables*. New York: Dover, 1999.

Hoberman, J. "How the West Was Lost." *The Western Reader*. Ed. Jim Kitses and Gregg Rickman. New York: Limelight, 1998.

Horror-movies.ca. "Hills Have Eyes 2: The Team!" *Horrormovies.ca*. 2006.

Janov, Arthur. *The Primal Scream, Primal Therapy: The Cure for Neurosis*. New York: Perigee, 1970.

Keller, Julia. "Craven welcomes viewers to his 'nightmare'; 'Nightmare Café' airs at 10 tonight on WCMH-TV (Channel 4)." *Columbus Dispatch*. March 13, 1992.

Kilman, Lawrence. "Mystery disease killing Laotian refugees." *Associated Press*. December 2, 1981.

King, Susan. "Café Craven: NBC serves up tales of the weird from the horrormeister." *Los Angeles Times*. February 23, 1992.

Krikorian, Michael. "Son, Nephew Inspired by 'Scream' Movies to Kill Woman, Police Say." *Los Angeles Times*. January 15, 1998.

Kutzera, Dale. "Just When you Thought It Was Safe to Dream." *Imagi-Movies*. Vol. 2 No. 1. October 1994.

Leary, Timothy. *The Psychedelic Experience: A Manual Based on the Tibetan Book of the Dead*. New York: Citadel, 2000.

LaBerge, Stephen. *Lucid Dreaming*. New York: Ballantine, 1985. E-book.

---. Interview. *A Nightmare on Elm Street 5: The Dream Child—Terror's Newest Addition (press kit)*. New Line Cinema: 1989.

Landis, Bill and Michelle Clifford. *Sleazoid Express: A Mind-Twisting Tour Through the Grindhouse Cinema of Times Square*. New York: Fireside, 2002.

Lawson, Terry. "Movie reveals Craven's softer side." *The Cedartown Standard*. November 4, 1999.

---. "Cravin' a 'New Nightmare'; Director Allowed to Dig Up Freddy." *Dayton Daily News*. October 14, 1994.

Lofficier, Randy. Dreamweavers: *Interviews with Fantasy Filmmakers of the 1980s*. Jefferson: McFarland, 1995.

Lovell, Glenn. "The 'Professor' Who Makes Horror Movies." *The Philadelphia Inquirer*. January 21, 1985.

Mangels, Andy. *From Scream to Dawson's Creek: An Unauthorized Take on the Phenomenal Career of Kevin Williamson.* Los Angeles: Renaissance, 2000.

Murray, Rebecca. "Wes Craven Discusses the film 'Paris, je t'aime'." *About.com.* April 23, 2007.

Newman, Kim. "The Kim Newman Archive: *The Hills Have Eyes Part II* (1985)." *The Encyclopedia of Fantastic Film and Television.* Online.

Persons, Dan. "Horror! Wes Craven." *Cinefantastique.* Vol. 29, No. 4/5. 1997.

Polanski, Roman. *Roman by Polanski.* New York: William Morrow, 1984.

Portman, Jamie. "The Reality behind the Reality." *Ottawa Citizen.* February 4, 2000.

Rausch, Andrew J. "An Interview with Wes Craven." *Ain't It Cool News.* December 16, 1999. Online.

Rawshark. "Exclusive interview: Alexandre Aja—The Hills Have Eyes." *Eatmybrains.com.* February 24, 2006.

Reagan, Ronald. "Proclamation 5500 -- Youth Suicide Prevention Month." June 10, 1986. *Ronald Reagan Presidential Library and Museum.* Online.

Robb, Brian J. *Screams & Nightmares: The Films of Wes Craven.* Woodstock: Overlook, 1998.

Russo, John. *Scare Tactics.* New York: Dell, 1992.

Russell, Chuck. Interview. *Never Sleep Again.* 1428 Films: 2010.

Schoell, William and James Spencer. *The Nightmare Never Ends: The Official History of Freddy Krueger and the Nightmare on Elm Street Films.* New York: Citadel, 1992.

SciFi Wire. "Even Famous Film Directors Get the Blues (Studio Shuts Down Wes Craven)." *Freerepublic.com.* September 10, 2003.

Sharrett, Christopher. "Fairy Tales for the Apocalypse." July 1985. *Conversations with Directors: An Anthology of Interviews from Literature / Film Quarterly.* Ed. Elsie M. Walker and David T. Johnson. Lanham: Scarecrow, 2008.

Sklarew, Myra. "Eliott Coleman's seminary for writers." *The Fortnightly Review.* Online.

Sutherland, Claire. "Mr. Fright Guy." *Herald Sun* (Australia). April 19, 2007.

Szebin, Fred. "Serpent and the Rainbow." *Cinefantastique.* Vol. 18, No. 2. March 1988.

Szulkin, David A. *Wes Craven's Last House on the Left: The Making of a Cult Classic.* Surrey: FAB, 2000.

Tobias, Scott. "Interview: Wes Craven." *The A.V. Club.* March 11, 2009. Online.

Truffaut, Francois with Helen G. Scott. *Hitchcock.* New York: Touchstone, 1967.

Vahanian, Gabriel. *The Death of God: The Culture of Our Post-Christian Era.* New York: George Braziller, 1961.

Wiater, Stanley. *Dark Visions: Conversations with the Masters of the Horror Film.* New York: Avon, 1992.

Wood, Robin. *Hollywood from Vietnam to Reagan… and Beyond.* New York: Columbia UP, 2003.

Wooley, John. *Wes Craven: The Man and His Nightmares.* New York: Wiley, 2011.

Zimmerman, Samuel. "Exclusive Interview: Wes Craven on 'My Soul to Take.'" *Fangoria.com.* September 6, 2010.

Zingale, Jason. "A Chat with Wes Craven." *Bullz-Eye.com.* November 28, 2007.

Zinoman, Jason. *Shock Value: How a Few Eccentric Outsiders Gave Us Nightmares, Conquered Hollywood, and Invented Modern Horror.* New York: Penguin, 2011.

THE TELL-TALE HEART OF STEPHEN KING

How long has it been since you wrote a story where your real love or your real hatred somehow got onto the paper? When was the last time you dared release a cherished prejudice so it slammed the page like a lightning bolt? What are the best things and the worst things in your life, and when are you going to get around to whispering or shouting about them?
- Ray Bradbury

When I was eleven years old, my parents gave me a hardback copy of Stephen King's *The Eyes of the Dragon* for Christmas. I didn't ask for it. I didn't even know who Stephen King was. My dad later told me he had seen the book in the remainder bin at the local B. Dalton and decided to take a chance. (It *looked* age-appropriate.) I don't remember being the least bit interested in the medieval fantasy milieu of the book, but I do remember being captivated by the author's voice. King wrote about his main character, a boy named Thomas who was just beginning to see cracks in the artifice of the adult world, with complete sincerity. His unnamed narrator saw right into the heart of Thomas, which was filled with jealousy and resentment and, above all, fear. I remember one scene in particular, in which Thomas finds a place to spy on his father and watches the old man piss into the fireplace, recognizing his father's imperfect humanity for the first time. It was a revelatory moment for him, and for me too as I was beginning to understand that adults are not so different from children—at least, not all the time.

I finished *The Eyes of the Dragon* within a few days, and asked my dad to drive me to the bookstore so I could pick out another Stephen King title. I settled on *Four Past Midnight* because it was the newest, then moved on to *IT*, because it was the longest. I remember reading "The Langoliers," the first novella in *Four Past Midnight*, at my grandmother's house on New Year's Day. I lost track of the entire day because I was completely, helplessly immersed in King's twilight zone. By the time I started reading *IT*, the holidays were over. I was back at school, and promptly turned several of my friends on to my new favorite author. I remember one day when at least five students in a twenty-student class had their noses buried in a Stephen King novel. I don't remember what, if anything, the teacher said about that. My family moved to a new town a few months later, so I don't know how many of my friends kept reading King, but I spent the next four years reading everything the author had published up to that point. In 1994, the year of *Insomnia*, I finally caught up with the author, and heeded my favorite English teacher's suggestion that I should expand my literary horizons. I didn't read another Stephen King novel for about ten years, but I certainly didn't forget his voice. King had made me an avid reader and a dedicated short story writer. And, of course, a lifelong horror fan.

Non-horror fans always ask why we read "this stuff." It's a genuine question, based on general assumptions about the genre: mainly, that it caters to morbid or sadistic sensibilities. This assumption leads some people to the secondary assumption that horror fans are morbid or sadistic. I think both assumptions are naïve. I can't speak for all horror fans, of course, but I can say that the type of horror I am most drawn to usually espouses a complex philosophical or spiritual perspective on the world. Stephen King's best-known novel *The Stand* has a strong political and quasi-religious bent. That's not because the author consciously sets out to convey a political or religious "message," but because—like all serious writers—he has a unique and informed perspective on life, and his perspective inevitably comes through in his narrative voice. Stephen King believes in God, and in a relatively liberal social agenda. He is, at heart, a product of the Methodist Church and of the American Peace Movement of the 1960s. Above all, his work expresses faith in the redemptive power of storytelling. King insists that what's important is The Tale, not He Who Tells It.

Despite his misgivings about becoming a brand name author, King's voice has become more influential than any single one of his tales. Because of his decades-long popularity among readers and moviegoers across the globe, his beliefs have influenced the thoughts and ideas of multiple generations, and helped to define the horror genre as much more than a collection of dark fantasies. It is not too much to say that Stephen King is modern America's tell-tale heart, a modern day mythmaker who reveals to us our deepest cultural beliefs. He doesn't always tell us what we want to hear, but he tells the truth of his own experience, and that truth has become part of the fabric of our world.

Stephen King in the Twilight Zone

Stephen King was born in 1947, at the beginning of the post-World War II baby boom. For the first few years, he lived a nomadic life, drifting from town to town with his mother and stepbrother David. His father Donald King had abandoned the family when Steve was only two years old, so the trio's welfare depended entirely on Ruth King's ability to work long hours at odd jobs. Around the time Stephen King turned twelve, the family of three finally settled in the rural, working-class town of Durham, Maine, where the future novelist began writing.

For the next few years, King's entire world existed within a few miles of his childhood home on Hallowell Road. He attended church next door, at West Durham Methodist, and went to grammar school at a one-room schoolhouse on the other side of the church. His maternal aunt and uncle lived less than a mile away, across an open field in front of the house. His best friend, Chris Chesley, also lived down the road. Together Steve and Chris explored the secrets of the small town, testing their nerve against an allegedly haunted house on Deep Cut Road and, on another memorable occasion, viewing a dead body that had been dragged out of nearby Runaround Pond. Most importantly, they wrote stories together.

Stephen King has said that writers are not born, but *made*. His transformation may have begun as early as 1950, when he overheard an episode of the radio show *Dimension X*, featuring an adaptation of Ray Bradbury's short story "Mars is Heaven!" Bradbury's tale revolves around a group of American astronauts who set a course for Mars in the year 1987. When they land, they find themselves in the year 1928, in an idyllic American town populated by loving relatives who died many years ago. The astronauts are overwhelmed by nostalgic emotion, and quickly convince themselves that they have discovered Heaven. Later that night, while they sleep peacefully in their new beds, the dead relatives peel back their faces, and reveal themselves to be sinister, mind-reading Martians. King remembers: "I didn't sleep in my bed that night; that night I slept in the doorway, where the real and rational light of the bathroom bulb could shine on my face."[1]

The radio story terrified King, but it also attracted him. He quickly turned his attention to other horror tales, beginning with Victorian literature's "unholy trinity" of terror: Mary Shelley's *Frankenstein*, Bram Stoker's *Dracula*, and Robert Louis Stevenson's *The Strange Case of Dr. Jekyll and Mr. Hyde*.[2] King vividly remembers the day his mother came home from the library with the last of these. When her six-year-old son asked about it, Ruth King responded, knowingly, "Oh, you wouldn't like this one. This one's a really scary one." Naturally, he begged her to read it to him. The rest, as they say, is history. King remembers:

> *That was a happy summer for me. We sat out on the porch at night [. . .] and she read me* Dr. Jekyll and Mr. Hyde. *I lived and died with that story, with Mr. Utterson and with poor Dr. Jekyll, and particularly with Dr. Jekyll's other side, which was every vestige of pretense of civilization thrown away. I can remember lying in bed, wakeful after that night's reading was done, and what I usually thought of was how Mr. Hyde walked over the little girl, back and forth, breaking her bones; and it was such a terrible image and I thought,* I have to do that; *but I have to do worse, because it was the only way to get back to normal again.*[3]

The comment about "getting back to normal" suggests that, from a very young age, King understood storytelling as a kind of ritual. In *Danse Macabre*, the author defines Stevenson's story as a prescient variation on the timeless Werewolf myth, noting that *Jekyll & Hyde* illustrates Sigmund Freud's theory about the unconscious mind a good three decades before Freud articulated it. The young Stephen King was equally prescient in his understanding of the therapeutic effects of fiction writing. For him, storytelling was already a kind of psychotherapy, offering an opportunity to "get back to normal."

Soon after, King discovered Bram Stoker's *Dracula*. "I think I was about 11 when I first read it," he remembers. "I expected to be scared out of my wits, and I really wasn't [but] I was transported by

1 King: *Danse* 125
2 Pouncey 56
3 Beahm: *Story* 17

the excitement, by the adventure of it."[4] From *Dracula*, he learned about *suspension of disbelief.* Stoker's narrative assumes that superstition is as *real* as science, and tries to convince audiences of this idea by juxtaposing magic and modernism, arguing that the only difference between them is the matter of *belief.* Professor Van Helsing explains:

> *There are things old and new which must not be contemplated by men's eyes, because they know—or think they know—some things which other men have told them. Ah, it is the fault of our science that it wants to explain all; and if it explain not, then it says there is nothing to explain. But yet we see around us every day the growth of new beliefs, which think themselves new; and which are yet but the old, which pretend to be young—like the fine ladies at the opera."*[5]

For a reader willing to suspend their disbelief, guided by a writer willing to explore "things which must not be contemplated," the possibilities are endless.

King has not spoken quite as affectionately about *Frankenstein.* In his 1978 introduction to a Signet collection of the three classic horror novels, King refers to Shelley's novel as "the most notorious of the three" but also labels it the "worst written," noting that it frequently resembles "a college-dormitory bull session" more than a horror novel.[6] Nevertheless, the romantic sensibilities of Shelley's novel have found their way into King's work. Victor Frankenstein created his Monster out of a Faustian desire for knowledge and wisdom, "a fervent longing to penetrate the secrets of nature."[7] Instead of gaining knowledge, he ruined his health, his happiness, and the lives of those around him. Worse still, because he failed to teach his creation how to think and behave like a responsible human being, Frankenstein inadvertently unleashed a powerful destructive force into the world—and then couldn't take it back. King has offered similar techno-phobic variations on the Pandora's box myth in his science fiction stories "Trucks," *The Stand*, *Firestarter*, *The Tommyknockers*, *Cell* and *The Dark Tower* series.

4 Christian 37

5 Stoker 475

6 King: "Introduction," *Signet* vi-vii

7 Shelley 25

In *Danse Macabre*, King augments his examination of the "unholy trinity" with a slight acknowledgment of Henry James's *The Turn of the Screw*, a ghost story told from the first-person narrative. James adopted the first-person point of view because he was interested in more than simply telling a scary story; he wanted to examine the power of belief and imagination. The author sets up his narrator, Miss Jessel, as someone who is "young, untried, nervous."[8] After Miss Jessel has an experience that forces her to question her disbelief in the reality of ghosts, she becomes more frightened of what she can *imagine* than of what she might actually see. When a minor character asks if she is afraid of seeing ghosts, she responds: "Oh no; that's nothing—now! . . . It's of *not* seeing [them]."[9] In her mind, ghosts could be *anywhere* at *any time* doing *anything*. The possibility is maddening. Miss Jessel's confession underlines the truth that makes supernatural literature so powerful: We fear most what we can't see or know. We fear what we can only imagine, and what we *can't even* imagine.

During his early adolescent years, King was particularly attracted to this type of horror of the Unknown. The modern American master of the subgenre was H.P. Lovecraft, whose work King discovered in the fall of 1959 or 1960. Lovecraft introduced him to a longstanding tradition of horror literature that culminated with Victorian Gothic, and then continued to evolve in the first half of the twentieth century. In his 1927 essay *Supernatural Horror in Literature*, Lovecraft surveys the history of the "weird tale," contextualizing it as follows: "There is here involved a psychological pattern or tradition as real and as deeply grounded in mental experience as any other pattern or tradition of mankind; coeval with the religious feeling and closely related to many aspects of it."[10]

Lovecraft is careful to distinguish between what he calls the "literature of cosmic fear"—he cites *The Turn of the Screw*, along with Robert Browning's poem "Childe Roland to the Dark Tower Came" and W.W. Jacobs's "The Monkey's Paw" as examples—and the "literature of mere physical fear and the mundanely gruesome." The difference between the two, he writes, is atmosphere:

8 James 3
9 James 30
10 Lovecraft: *Supernatural*

> *The way one tells of the really weird is simply this—whether or not there be excited in the reader a profound sense of dread, and of contact with unknown spheres and powers; a subtle attitude of awed listening, as if for the beating of black wings or the scratching of outside shapes and entities on the known universe's utmost rim.*[11]

Lovecraft goes on to champion his favorite weird tales. He pays tribute to the originators of classic Gothic literature, acknowledging the "true touch of cosmic fear" in *Frankenstein* and the "justly assigned" fame of *Dracula*, as well as noting the "human element" in *Dr. Jekyll and Mr. Hyde*, which made the horror genre more palatable for a wider audience.[12] His survey begins in earnest, however, with an examination of the work of Edgar Allan Poe. He hails the psychological complexity of Poe's narratives (especially "Ligeia" and "The Fall of the House of Usher") and asserts, "To him we owe the modern horror-story in its final and perfected state."[13] He maintains that the spirit of Poe has inspired the best work of early-modern masters like Ambrose Bierce, Clark Ashton Smith, Robert W. Chambers, Arthur Machen, Algernon Blackwood and M.R. James. In praising these writers, Lovecraft was of course creating a context for his own weird tales. His peculiar horror stories, which transplant primitive religious beliefs and superstitions onto the landscape of his native New England, provided the next jumping-off point for future generations of American horror writers, including Stephen King.

King first discovered Lovecraft through a collection called *The Lurking Fear and Other Stories*, which included the short stories "Pickman's Model" and the often-anthologized "The Rats in the Walls." The latter tale, inspired by Poe's "The Fall of the House of Usher," revolves around a man named Delapore, the descendant of a reputedly cursed English family. When Delapore reconstructs the "accursed home" of his ancestors on the ruins of a prehistoric temple, he begins having vivid dreams of ancient rituals and subsequently awakens to the sound of rats scratching inside the walls. Delapore follows the sound deep into the bowels of the old structure, where

---

11 Lovecraft: *Supernatural*
12 Lovecraft: *Supernatural*
13 Lovecraft: *Supernatural*

he encounters a "pit of nameless fear" piled high with the bones of dead men and sub-human "quadrupeds."[14] Lurking within he senses the presence an unknown horror beyond the comprehension of mankind. Although he turns and runs before he can see it, or perhaps *because* he turns and runs before he can see it, the encounter drives him mad.

Lovecraft's tales made a big impression on King, who later wrote that "when Lovecraft was on the money—as in 'The Dunwich Horror,' 'The Rats in the Walls,' and best of all, 'The Colour Out of Space'—his stories packed an incredible wallop."[15] The influence of each of these tales is plainly visible in King's initial short stories "Graveyard Shift," "Gray Matter," and "Jerusalem's Lot," as well as the novel *'Salem's Lot* (an early draft of which featured a particularly nasty sequence involving a horde of carnivorous rats). King, however, did not set out to imitate Lovecraft or his literary ancestors. He recognized the limitations in the work of those older writers, as he explained to biographer Douglas Winter:

> *I had read Poe and I had read a lot of Gothic novelists, and even with Lovecraft I felt as though I were in Europe somewhere. I knew instinctively that I was trying to find a way to get back home, to where I belonged. And then I read Richard Matheson's* I Am Legend, *where this fellow is blockading himself in his house every night—and it wasn't a castle, it was a tract house in Los Angeles. [. . .] And I realized then that horror didn't have to happen in a haunted castle; it could happen in the suburbs, on your street, maybe right next door.*[16]

Richard Matheson has never claimed to be a horror writer—in fact, he detests the term "horror," believing that it suggested a visceral effect rather than the emotional effect he was aiming for—but he nevertheless became one of the most prolific and influential figures in the field. Matheson followed up his vampire novel *I Am Legend* with *The Shrinking Man,* a philosophical horror novel that quickly became a successful studio film. After that, Matheson wrote scripts for a host of seminal horror films, including *House of Usher* (1960), *The Pit and the Pendulum* (1961), *Burn, Witch, Burn!* (1963), *The*

14 Lovecraft: "Rats"
15 King: *Danse* 65
16 Winter: *Stephen* 20

Last Man on Earth (1964), *The Devil Rides Out* (1968), *Duel* (1971), *The Night Stalker* (1972), *The Night Strangler* (1973), *The Legend of Hell House* (1973), *Dracula* (1974), and *Trilogy of Terror* (1975). Matheson is best known, however, for his contributions to Rod Serling's TV series *The Twilight Zone*.

For Stephen King, the concept of *The Twilight Zone* represents a turning point in American horror fiction, superseding the work of H.P. Lovecraft and "opening a million entrancing possibilities."[17] Unlike most enthusiasts, King does not attribute the concept to series creator Rod Serling. He claims that Serling took most of his cues from Ray Bradbury and Jack Finney, and then wisely hired writers like Richard Matheson and Charles Beaumont to help enrich the concept. King suggests that the essential idea of "the twilight zone" can be found in its earliest form in Jack Finney's short story collection *The Third Level*, published in 1957. The title story in that collection relates an ordinary man's discovery of a magical gateway to the past, hiding beneath the floors of New York's Grand Central Station. The man discovers the gateway accidentally, and runs away in fear. Later, when he goes back to Grand Central with the intention of leaving the "real world" behind, he can't find the gateway. He tells his story to a psychiatrist, who thinks that the man is delusional—right up until the moment when the psychiatrist discovers the gateway for himself. According to King:

> *Finney's most important accomplishment, which the best episodes of the* Twilight Zone *echo (and which the best of the post-Zone writers of fantasy have also echoed), is that Daliesque ability to create the fantasy . . . and then not apologize for it or explain it. It simply hangs there, fascinating and a little sickening, a mirage too real to dismiss. [. . .] If the fantasy seems real enough, Finney insisted, and Serling after him, we don't need any wires or mirrors.*[18]

Serling defined the twilight zone, in the opening sequence of the series, as "the dimension of imagination." Obviously he understood that the most important special effect in the series was the illusion of everyday reality, because that was what helped audiences

17 King: *Danse* 259
18 King: *Danse* 259

to suspend their disbelief in the fantasy. "*The Twilight Zone* is about people," Serling once explained, "about human beings involved in extraordinary circumstances, in strange problems of their own or fate's making"[19] He understood that if the fictional characters were believable, then their experiences—however strange—would be believable. Matheson, whose early short stories and novels succeeded largely because they were built on the inner thoughts and feelings of the characters, understood this implicitly. He too approached *The Twilight Zone* with the idea of emphasizing reality over fantasy:

> *To me, fantasy at its best (strictly personal, of course) consists of putting in one drop of fantasy into a mixture which is, otherwise, completely factual, realistic. And, once that drop of fantasy has been put into the mixture, I try to forget that I am writing a fantasy and write as realistic a story as I can, recalling, of course, that the springboard has been some offbeat concept.*[20]

In this very simple—but frequently overlooked and underappreciated—storytelling formula, Stephen King found the secret of his future success as a storyteller. Many of the author's most popular stories take the otherworldly "what if" scenarios of a *Twilight Zone* episode and interweave them with the thoughts of ordinary, relatable people. In a 1998 lecture, King explained the formula with a very simple metaphor: "You try to bring those two pieces of cloth together and sew that hem so fine that the reader doesn't really know when he or she crosses over from the land of what's real to the land of what's unreal."[21]

The Twilight Zone series, which ran from 1959 to 1965, introduced American audiences to a wide variety of fantasy, science fiction and horror stories, the best of which were firmly grounded in human emotions. Rod Serling wrote the bulk of the scripts (ninety-two episodes over the course of a 156-episode run), and his contributions to the first two seasons largely defined the themes and the tone of the series. As King observes, "Those first two years—and they were the best—were the work of a man drunk on fantasy."[22]

---

19 Zicree 96
20 Zicree 57
21 King: "Night" 382
22 King: *Danse* 89

Serling's fantasy episodes are heartfelt, often wistful. The influence of Ray Bradbury's fiction, particularly his 1957 novel *Dandelion Wine*, is apparent in episodes like "Walking Distance" and "A Stop at Willoughby." The other series writers followed this lead, offering variations on the themes of lost youth and the power of childlike imagination. Matheson's "Young Man's Fancy," Charles Beaumont's "Miniature," George Clayton Johnson's "Kick the Can," and Reginald Rose's "The Incredible World of Horace Ford" are notable examples. Jerome Bixby contributed the most horrific variation on this theme with "It's a Good Life," an episode about a bratty child who literally holds an entire town hostage with the power of his mind. (Anyone who doubts the influence of this show on Stephen King need only compare "It's a Good Life" to King's novel *The Regulators*.)

Serling's science fiction episodes generally revolve around mysteries of space and time, parallel dimensions and purgatory, and almost always culminate with an ironic twist. In "Time Enough at Last," for example, a man is grateful to be the sole survivor of a nuclear holocaust, because the solitude will give him time to read. Then, just as he opens his first book, he breaks his only pair of reading glasses. In "Eye of the Beholder," a woman prepares to undergo plastic surgery to resolve what she perceives as a hideous deformity. In the final act, we see that she is beautiful by our standards...... but hideous to the pig-faced creatures all around her. In "To Serve Man," a super-intelligent alien arrives on earth, carrying a book whose eponymous title suggests that he is here to help. At the end of the episode, a human translator realizes that "To Serve Man" is actually a cookbook.

Twist endings were unnecessary in the best of the horror episodes. Serling, like H.P. Lovecraft, understood that humans fear the unknown and the unexplainable above all else, which is why episodes like "And When the Sky Was Opened"—about three astronauts who return from space, only to be erased from existence without any rhyme or reason—are particularly effective. The same can be said for Serling's "Mirror Image," a doppelganger story set in a bus depot, and "The After Hours," an uncanny exploration of one woman's existential crisis in a department store.

Richard Matheson and Charles Beaumont understood the horror genre even better, genuinely believing that there are more things in heaven and earth than can be understood by man. Although he wrote only fourteen scripts for the series, Matheson contributed some of the most frightening episodes: "Third from the Sun" (scripted by Serling, but based on Matheson's short story), "A World of Difference," "The Invaders," "Little Girl Lost," "Death Ship," "Night Call," and "Nightmare at 20,000 Feet." Beaumont's record is equally impressive, and Stephen King has cited many of his episodes—including "Perchance to Dream" and "The Printer's Devil"—as personal favorites.[23]

King has said, however, that he does not regard *The Twilight Zone* as the best horror series he grew up with: he grants that distinction to Boris Karloff's *Thriller* (1961-1963).[24] The short-lived program featured two episodes written by Charles Beaumont and a memorable contribution from Richard Matheson, but it mostly served as a showcase for Robert Bloch, another heavyweight in the annals of modern horror fiction. Bloch, a protégé of H.P. Lovecraft, was writing pulp fiction for the magazine *Weird Tales* as early as 1934, but his literary career began in earnest with the 1943 publication of his short story "Yours Truly, Jack the Ripper." Nearly two decades later, Bloch became a household name when Alfred Hitchcock's adapted his novel *Psycho*. By that time, Bloch had plenty of weird tales under his belt, and when the producers of *Thriller* came calling, he was ready.

Like Richard Matheson and Stephen King, Bloch admired Lovecraft's sense of "cosmic fear," but he recognized the need for a new kind of horror story, as he explained to Douglas Winter:

> *By the mid-1940s, I had pretty well mined the vein of ordinary supernatural themes until it had become varicose. I realized, as a result of what went on during World War Two and of reading the more widely disseminated work in psychology, that the real horror is not in the shadows, but in that little twisted world inside our own skulls. And that I determined to explore.*[25]

By the early sixties, Bloch was doing double duty on *Alfred Hitchcock Presents* and *Thriller*, contributing ten stories to each series

23 King: *Danse* 242
24 King: *Danse* 237
25 Winter: *Faces* 15

before Hitchcock convinced NBC to axe his competition.[26] Donald Sanford adapted Bloch's earliest weird tales "The Cheaters" and "The Hungry Glass," providing *Thriller* with its first major successes. Soon after, Bloch came on board as a screenwriter, contributing scripts for memorable episodes like "The Devil's Ticket," "The Grim Reaper," and "The Weird Tailor."[27] What all of these tales have in common is the combination of superstition and psychology. By transplanting ghosts into the human mind, like Robert Louis Stevenson and Henry James before him, Bloch made old-fashioned gothic horror seem *real* again.

Although King claims a preference for *Thriller*, and a great admiration for Robert Bloch, *The Twilight Zone* and its writers have exerted a more obvious influence on his most famous work. There is an element of gothic superstition in many of the author's stories, but it is easier to spot the speculative science fiction. In fact, many of King's best-known stories revolve around concepts that first appeared in episodes of *The Twilight Zone*. Before King wrote *Carrie*, *The Twilight Zone* tackled the subject of telekinesis in Charles Beaumont's "The Prime Mover." Before King created the dangerously "talented" kids in *The Shining* and *Firestarter*, *The Twilight Zone* presented equally "wild" children in Richard Matheson's "Mute" and Rod Serling's "It's a Good Life." Johnny Smith, King's psychic hero in *The Dead Zone*, is forecast by the psychic soldier in "The Purple Testament." Likewise, Thad Beaumont (*The Dark Half*) is predated by the magical realist in Matheson's "A World of His Own." There are also striking similarities between *Stephen King's Golden Years* and "Long Live Walter Jameson"; "Trucks" and "A Thing About Machines"; "The Langoliers" and "The Odyssey of Flight 33"; *Needful Things* and "What You Need"; "Low Men in Yellow Coats" and "The Fugitive"; *Christine* and "You Drive"; *11/22/63* and "Back There" (as well as "No Time Like The Past").

This is not to suggest that King hasn't come by his ideas honestly, only to point out that the type of stories told on *The Twilight Zone* made an indelible impression on him during the formative years 1959—1965, just as King's work has made an indelible impression on countless storytellers since the mid-1970s. No good story emerges from a vacuum. The basis of genre fiction, after all, is repeated tropes

26 Alan Warren 23
27 Alan Warren 16

and formulas. The vitality of *all* fiction, however, stems from the writer's ability to make us experience fictional stories as experiences relevant to our personal lives and the times in which we live.

Stephen King vs. the Flying Saucers

In *Danse Macabre*, Stephen King writes that the most effective horror films reveal "national phobic pressure points," reflecting the collective nightmares of a particular place and time.[28] In the early 1930s, Hollywood (particularly Universal Studios) made a killing off of classic Gothic monsters like Frankenstein, Dracula, and Mr. Hyde, and King suggests that this initial horror boom may have provided a nationwide catharsis for the "free-floating anxieties" of the Great Depression.[29] The formula for those early horror films, he points out, was simple enough:

> *There's an incursion into taboo lands, there's a place where you shouldn't go, but you do, the same way that your mother would tell you that the freak tent is a place you shouldn't go, but you do. And the same thing happens inside: you look at the guy with three eyes, or you look at the fat lady, or you look at the skeleton man or Mr. Electrical or whoever it happens to be. And when you come out, well, you say, "Hey, I'm not so bad. I'm all right. A lot better than I thought." It has that effect of reconfirming values, of reconfirming self-image and our good feelings about ourselves."*[30]

King concludes that classic Hollywood horror is essentially conservative: "as Republican as a banker in a three-piece suit."[31] Of course, that was merely the starting point for the American horror film.

In times when it is more difficult to convincingly reconfirm the status quo—times when real-life horror makes people question everything they hold dear—the popularity of cinematic horror declines. Such was the case in the 1940s, when World War II and the Holocaust made movie monsters seem quaint and silly. As if in direct response to this problem, King observes, RKO producer Val Lewton created a new type of horror picture, one that would rely on suspense and suggestion, and avoid showing the monster. King praises the producer's breakthrough film *Cat People* (1942),

28 King: *Danse* 4
29 King: *Danse* 29
30 King: "Evening" 9
31 King: "Evening" 9

calling it "the best horror film of the forties."[32] It is worth noting that the author also expresses strong admiration for *The Haunting* (1963), a later film by Lewton's protégé Robert Wise, who uses the same techniques to marvelous effect. Admiration aside, King regards the Lewton approach to horror as a cheat: "My own disapproval of this method—we'll let the door bulge but we'll never open it—comes from the belief that it is playing to tie rather than to win."[33] From King's perspective, *real* horror languished until the 1950s, when monsters returned to the screen in a big, bold way.

The first film that young Stephen King saw in the theater was *Creature from the Black Lagoon* (1954). He remembers the screening as a completely immersive experience, not unlike his initial reading of *Dracula*, defined by "total emotional involvement."[34] *Creature* marked Universal's return to the monster movie formula that defined the studio in the 1930s, but that legacy was soon dwarfed by a glut of Nuclear Age monster movies from independent studios like American International Pictures (AIP). In the mid-1950s, the minor studios produced a body of work that King regards as a kind of Rorschach test for his generation. The atomic monsters in *Them!* (1954), *Tarantula* (1955), *The Day the World Ended* (1955), and *The Beginning of the End* (1957) were not *consciously* allegorical or symbolic, he argues, but they nevertheless served as "an extraordinarily accurate barometer of those things which trouble[d] the night-thoughts of a whole society."[35] The films reflected contemporary fears that modern science might soon place the entire human race at the mercy of forces beyond human control, maybe even beyond human comprehension. The rising generation needed some kind of outlet for these overwhelming fears, King says, and so they turned to the twilight zone. Reflecting on the horror phenomenon many years later, the author explains:

> *We're the first generation to have grown up completely in the shadow of the atomic bomb. It seems to me that we are the first generation forced to live almost entirely without romance and forced to find some kind of supernatural outlet for the*

32 King: *Danse* 121
33 King: *Danse* 122
34 King: *Danse* 104
35 King: *Danse* 139

> *romantic impulses that are in all of us. This is really sad in a way. Everybody goes out to horror movies, reads horror novels—and it's almost as though we're trying to preview the end.*[36]

Ever since the end of World War II, he continues, new monsters have been arising steadily from the "dimension of imagination." *The Thing from Another World* (1951) was one of the first horror films about a potential alien menace. In its presentation of the monster as a bloodsucking Frankenstein Monster, and its depiction of the resident scientist as an impotent foreigner, *The Thing* is as fundamentally conservative as the Universal monster movies of the 1930s. Subsequent alien invasion movies like *The War of the Worlds* (1953) and *Invaders from Mars* (1953) adopted a similar perspective; they didn't always belittle the role of the scientist, but they certainly celebrated the might of the U.S. military and the authority of the U.S. government. Later films like *Invasion of the Body Snatchers* (1956) were more ambiguous, adding some philosophical complexity to the genre.

King reads *Invasion* as a reflection of McCarthy-era paranoia about communist takeover, but that was not the original storyteller's intention. Jack Finney's 1954 novel *The Body Snatchers* begins by explaining that the aliens have no ambition to take over the world: their only motive is survival. The pods are marvelous adapters who are simply looking for a place to carry on. Following a few failed attempts at mimicry, which include taking the form of slime at the bottom of a can of peaches (!), they begin morphing into exact physical copies of human beings. Finney implies, however, that the pods can only replicate what is *physically* present. They cannot duplicate the essential humanity that makes each of us more than the sum of our cells and synapses, and so they remain emotionally vacant. For Finney, that emotional vacancy is the locus of horror. He is not frightened of communist takeover, but of the dehumanizing effects of technological "progress" and increasing cultural conformity. At one point, early in the novel, the author reflects on the sudden redundancy of telephone operators and casually wonders if we aren't "refining all the humanity out of our lives."[37] To further convey his fears about the future, Finney establishes his main character, Miles, as an unusually quirky fellow—a doctor who literally keeps

36 Spitz 183
37 Finney 50

a skeleton in his closet, and who once showed up for a date with a confession of love stenciled on his forehead. These eccentricities demonstrate that Miles is deeply *human*. For the remainder of the story he will have to fight, against overwhelming odds, to remain so. At its core, Finney's novel is an ominous warning not just about America's future, but about humanity's future. It suggests that, soon, all of us will have to fight to retain our humanity.

We can forgive King for viewing *Invasion* through a reductive sociopolitical lens, because most critics of the film have done so since the time of the film's release. As the author points out in *Danse Macabre*, it has become increasingly difficult over the years to separate the monster movies of the 1950s from their cultural context. King himself remembers sitting in a movie theater in October 1957, when *Earth vs. the Flying Saucers* was interrupted by an announcement that the Russians had launched a satellite called Sputnik into outer space. He recalls it as a moment when fictional fears and real-life fears "vividly intersected with the reality of a potential nuclear holocaust."[38] Richard Matheson may have already taught him that horror fiction could be set in the everyday world, but that day in the movie theater taught King that horror fiction could be *prophecy*. The space race was on. The Cold War was on. The future looked grim. Stephen King got to work.

King's earliest extant story was written when he was only nine years old. The title, "Jhonathan and the Witches," suggests that he was predestined to work in a particular genre. Between 1960 and 1963, those pivotal years when *The Twilight Zone* series was at its best, King produced nearly a dozen tales of terror, which he and his friend Chris Chesley gathered into a self-published anthology entitled *People, Places and Things*. Stories like "The Hotel at the End of the Road" (about a museum of the dead), "I've Got to Get Away" (about a worker robot who thinks he's human), "The Cursed Expedition" (about a pair of astronauts on an ill-fated mission to Venus), "The Other Side of the Fog" (about a mysterious doorway to different time periods and dimensions), and "The Stranger" (about a murderer haunted by the Grim Reaper) illustrate the strong pull of *The Twilight Zone*.

38 Norden 39

At the same time, King was trying his hand at more overt, gothic horror. One of his short stories in *People, Places and Things* was called "The Thing at the Bottom of the Well." It revolved around a mischievous boy who likes to pull the wings off of flies. When he runs afoul of a "Thing" in the well, he finds out what it's like to be on the receiving end of that kind of treatment. King also wrote a "novelization" of *The Pit and the Pendulum* (1962), arguably the best of Roger Corman's adaptations of Edgar Allan Poe. The author cites the film as an "important moment in the post-1960s horror film, signaling a return to an all-out effort to terrify an audience . . . and a willingness to use any means at hand to do it."[39] Chris Chesley remembers that this was not the only time that King was influenced by the movies: "He would write the movie scenes down in words. And so even though he read a lot when he was young, and he learned from what he read, he also learned as much or more from the way scenes are written for television and the movies."[40]

This practice helped King to develop a strong visual storytelling style—a style that would eventually make his work very appealing to Hollywood producers. "My books are the movies I see in my head, that's all," King explains. "I write them down, and some producer says, 'Hey! This'd make a pretty good movie!' because in a way it already *is* one."[41]

King's penchant for visual storytelling was also influenced by his love of 1950s comics. His enthusiasm for the medium is apparent in his 1982 book *Creepshow*, in subsequent collaborations with comic book artist Bernie Wrightson (who provided illustrations for *Cycle of the Werewolf, The Stand: Complete and Uncut,* and *The Dark Tower V: Wolves of the Calla*), and in his twenty-first century forays into comic book writing (*American Vampire, Road Rage: Throttle, The Little Green God of Agony*). King says that the horror comics of his childhood also helped to shape his idea of what genre fiction should be. "Those horror comics of the fifties," he writes, "still sum up for me the epitome of horror, that emotion of fear that underlies terror, an emotion which is slightly less fine, because it is so entirely of the mind."[42] This confession helps to clarify his famous statement that

39 King: *Danse* 143
40 Spignesi: "Talk" 59
41 King: "Rita Hayworth" ix
42 King: *Danse* 22

he categorizes horror fiction in a three-tier system. The subtlest and longest-lasting type of fear, he says, is psychological terror. The next type is the more crude "horror." The lowest type is the gross-out, well known to readers of the E.C. Comics. King's first published story, "I Was a Teenage Grave Robber" (1965), falls into the third category, but the author doesn't apologize for that. When it comes to getting an emotional reaction out of a reader, he says, he'll do whatever *works.* To his credit, he quickly learned how to achieve the more subtle effects.

The Fate of Richard Bachman

In high school, King continued to expand his literary scope—devouring the crime novels of John D. MacDonald (the Travis McGee novels, *The Executioners, The End of the Night*) and Ed McBain (the *87th Precinct* series), as well as the suspense novels of Shirley Jackson (*The Haunting of Hill House*, *We Have Always Lived in the Castle*), the historical fiction of Don Robertson (*The River and the Wilderness*, *Paradise Falls*), and J.R.R. Tolkien's epic fantasy saga *The Lord of the Rings*. All of these authors exerted a recognizable influence on King's later work. In the immediate future, they prompted him to tackle a longer writing format.

According to some sources, King may have started his first novel, *The Aftermath*, as early as 1963. Biographer George Beahm proposes the more likely date of 1965—1966, contextualizing the work as a nexus between King's earliest fiction writing (the ending of *The Aftermath* features a Lovecraftian monster) and the themes of his later work: "technology out of control, plagues, the destruction of contemporary society, 'wild talents' (as King styles ordinary people with extraordinary mental capabilities), rite of passage, and [. . .] a downbeat ending."[43] Based on Beahm's description, it seems that *The Aftermath* was an ambitious effort—ultimately, *over*-ambitious. King was not happy with the finished product, and quickly moved on.

In the summer of 1966, he began writing his second novel, about a teenager who brings a gun into a high school classroom. The novel may have been inspired by an even earlier story, which is remembered by King's childhood friend Chris Chesley:

> *It was a mini-novel, and in the story he had us real kids—including him—take over the school. We stole our parents' guns, and everything else we could get, and we holed ourselves up in the elementary school. The whole story was basically like an Alamo kind of thing, where first the local cops, and then the National Guard come and try to get us out of the school and in the end we all die.*[44]

43 Beahm: *Companion* 305

44 Spignesi: "Talk" 60

This "mini-novel" bears some striking similarities to the eventual story of Charlie Decker, which King completed in 1971 and published in 1977 under the title *Rage*. Decker's tale proved to be the first fully-realized narrative of a future novelist. That novelist, however, was *not* Stephen King. By the time *Rage* was accepted for publication, King had already been branded as a supernatural horror writer—the creator of *Carrie, 'Salem's Lot* and *The Shining*. *Rage*, a comparatively literary novel, didn't seem to fit his brand, so the author decided to attribute the book to a fictional counterpart named Richard Bachman—a combination of Richard Stark (the pseudonym of crime writer Donald Westlake) and the rock group Bachman-Turner Overdrive.

For many years, "Bachman" took credit for King's youthful *Rage*. When it came time for the bestselling horror author to fess up to using a pseudonym, he claimed that he could barely remember the frame of mind from which the first Bachman book had emerged. In later years, King has come closest to explaining Charlie Decker's narrative when he talks about his own teenage fear of going crazy. "In those days," he says, "I was sure that you just went crazy all at once; you'd be walking down the street and—*pffft!*—you'd suddenly think you were a chicken or start chopping up the neighborhood kids with garden shears."[45] It is easy for the King to make light of this fear now, but his comic explanation is at odds with the grim intensity of the novel. Richard Bachman, it seems, never had Stephen King's sense of humor. Bachman was, in a very real sense, the manifestation of King's "darker half"—a man whose fears weren't offset by the glimmer of hope that appears in most "Stephen King" novels. Playing Mr. Hyde to King's Dr. Jekyll, Bachman was a wild and primitive version of his maker. He expressed a deep-rooted belief that life was cruel and unfair, and that it could only end in violence, suffering and death. We see that virulent belief played out in all of the early Bachman novels: *Rage, The Long Walk, The Running Man, Blaze,* and *Roadwork*. All are "last stand" narratives about angry young men fated for destruction.

In *Rage*, Charlie Decker takes his high school algebra class hostage for reasons that he can't fully articulate. The characters around him suggest that he has "gone berserk"; that he has become detached

45 Norden 40

from reality, irrational, maybe even schizophrenic. Charlie begins his own narrative by confessing to "madness," and quickly illustrates his point. He says he wants to kill his abusive father, but can't bring himself to do it, so he kills a pair of schoolteachers instead. Later, he realizes that he has misplaced his aggression, but by that point it doesn't matter. He has gone mad, and can't go back. He doesn't expect or desire any kind of salvation or redemption. "I didn't want salvation," Charlie says at the outset of the novel. "I was either past that point or never reached it. All I wanted was recognition."[46] His last stand is an attempt to be heard and perhaps understood by someone else, but his defeat is a foregone conclusion. Charlie may be pitiable, but Bachman's narrative suggests that neither he nor we can expect any kind of mercy. The story can end only one way.

Ray Garraty, the main character in King's third novel, *The Long Walk*, is comparatively sane but ultimately just as desperate as Charlie Decker. King wrote *The Long Walk* between the fall of 1966 and the spring of 1967, when he was a freshman at the University of Maine in Orono. Accordingly, the novel displays the intensity of a young man who is beginning to face his future as an adult—and feeling overwhelmed by it. Garraty's future looks especially bleak. He has volunteered to participate in an endurance contest that can have only one winner. To win, he must outlast a hundred other young volunteers, all healthy and supremely confident. If he doesn't win, he will be shot and killed like a dog in the street.

King told interviewer Michael R. Collings that he came up with the story idea while hitchhiking home from college one night. Specifically, he was thinking about the Kennedy March.[47] In 1962, President John F. Kennedy and his Council on Physical Fitness and Sports famously challenged U.S. servicemen to undertake a fifty-mile walk to prove that they were in ready military condition. Many average Americans also accepted the challenge as well, and the Kennedy March temporarily became a kind of patriotic obsession. Building on this idea, King imagined a future America in which fascist leaders parade America's promising young men down a nearly hopeless road, for *sheer sport*. The sadistic "long walk" is meant to boost the morale of America's citizens, who gamble on the march as if it's the Super Bowl. Spectators gather on the roadsides like

46 King: *Rage*
47 Beahm: *Story* 39

children at a Fourth of July parade, bloodlust in their eyes and, er, patriotism in their hearts.

Many critics have interpreted the story as a metaphor for the Vietnam War, but such a reading is too reductive. For the twenty-year-old novelist, "the long walk" expressed anxiety about the trial of becoming a successful and productive member of a world that seemed indifferent to him as an individual. Such anxiety is precisely why Ray Garraty volunteers. He means to make his mark, through sheer force of willpower, or die trying. For King, who grew up with a great many material disadvantages and was in no way predisposed to be a successful man of letters, the story may have been something of a spiritual autobiography. In a 1983 interview, he described his youthful drive as a product of living a "shirttail existence" for so many years.[48] His upbringing had taught him to endure hardship silently, but not to accept it. In another interview conducted around the same time, he noted that he was lucky to have found an outlet for his anger—one that would help him to face the future like Ray Garraty, literally spiting the odds, instead of self-destructing like Charlie Decker: "I could write, and that was the way I defined myself, even as a kid. Maybe I couldn't put one past the centerfielder, and maybe all I was good for in football was left tackle. You know, I used to get cleat marks up my back. But I could write. . . ."[49]

When King sat down to write, he engaged in a game of survival. He may have been afraid of where the road was leading him, but he kept going. He and Garraty had already come to the same conclusion: Life is an endurance contest.

When he finished *The Long Walk*, King submitted the manuscript to a first-novel contest. It didn't win, and the young author took the rejection so hard that he didn't submit the manuscript to a publisher for several more years. He did, however, show it to one of his college professors, who immediately recognized it as the work of a very talented writer. Burton Hatlen taught a course in American literature that King took during his sophomore year. Years later, Hatlen claimed that the course introduced King to the work of John Steinbeck (*In Dubious Battle, Of Mice and Men, The Grapes of Wrath*), William Faulkner (*Light in August*), and William Carlos Williams ("Paterson"), and he argued that these writers might have

48 Norden 34

49 Winter: *Stephen* 22

pushed King to become a mediator between traditional literature and pop culture.[50]

Around this same time King also discovered William Golding's *Lord of the Flies* and George Orwell's *1984.* He claims that these are the only two novels he ever read "where the fright actually raised itself to uncomfortable levels."[51] Equally noteworthy is the influence of certain Naturalist writers, beginning with Thomas Hardy and his novel *Tess of the d'Urbervilles*. In a 1990 essay, King writes:

> *I was told that* Tess *would introduce me to "the naturalistic school of writing." I didn't care a hang for the naturalistic school of writing or any other; what I cared for was Tess, a country girl who knew so little, tried so hard, and ended up with her neck in the hangman's noose. Tess, who was so naïve that she was raped without knowing it. My heart broke for her, and as I looked at the world through her eyes, I came to understand, for the first time, that ways of living and systems of morality are great, dangerous beasts, slow to wake but almost impossible to escape once they are on their feet.*[52]

No doubt "Richard Bachman" felt a certain kinship with Hardy's brand of determinism. King adds that Tess was his "introduction to women's lit,"[53] so it's natural to assume that Hardy might have offered some inspiration for the breakthrough novel *Carrie*.

After *Tess*, King moved on to the work of other naturalist writers like Jack London ("To Build a Fire"), Frank Norris (*McTeague*), and Theodore Dreiser (*Sister Carrie*). He told Douglas Winter:

> *Their stories would suggest to me that almost everything we do has a history. No matter where you come in on any situation, you are not coming in at the beginning. James Clavell says that the most difficult thing for him is to end a book, because the story always goes on. And the story always does go on. The hardest thing for me is to start a book, because the minute that I come in, I want to say, "But you don't understand, this is what her father was like, and his father, wait until I tell you about him—and look over*

50 Beahm: *Story* 40
51 King: "Evening" 15
52 King: "What" 356
53 Lehmann-Haupt

here, this is how things happened before World War Two." And how do you fit all of this history into a book?[54]

This may explain the trouble King had with his next writing project, a 500-page literary novel called *Sword in the Darkness*. The author says that the novel, written between 1967 and 1970, took much of its inspiration from Don Robertson (*The River and the Wilderness, Paradise Falls*) and from John Farris's novel *Harrison High*. It also reflected King's growing political awareness, as the novel revolves around "a race riot in a major (but fictional) American city."[55] Years later, the author reflected that he had undergone a significant transformation of values during his years at UMO: "While I began college with political leanings too far to the right to actually become radicalized, by 1968 my mind had been changed forever about a number of fundamental questions."[56] Hatlen recalls:

> *King himself, after some hesitation, voiced his opposition to the [Vietnam] war, and I have a vivid memory of him sitting on the edge of the stage in Hauck Auditorium, watching (along with hundreds of other students) as the Arts and Science faculty debated whether to support the student strike, and applauding wildly when the faculty "radical" carried the day.*[57]

The author apparently funneled his newfound political ideas into *Sword in the Darkness*. Carroll F. Terrell, another UMO professor who read the manuscript, suggests that the main character may have embodied King's personal feelings about civil rights and the war in Vietnam:

> *One of the things which bothered Steve most then as now is race prejudice, particularly anti-black demonstrations and behavior. He was also absorbed by the reaction-formations of guilt in students who escaped the draft by getting into college. They were also aware that over 50% of the draftees sent to Viet Nam were black even though only 10% of the population was black. Steve just did not and does not tolerate injustice very well, particularly programmed, deliberate injustice that victimizes*

54 Winter: *Stephen* 24
55 King: "On Becoming" 40
56 King: *Danse* 333
57 Hatlen 22

> *innocent, helpless people. The book had nothing to do directly with the war: it mainly concerned the effect of the war on a campus in the USA. Then the idea of a race riot in the making began to dominate the action.*[58]

The main problem with the novel, Terrell suggests, is that the central character did not fit into the climactic events of the story. Being neither "a born leader" nor a "blind follower," and believing that once the country had committed to the war in Vietnam, "only damage could be done and the war lengthened by violent protest movements in this country," the only thing he could do was to "take off" before the riots began.[59] That, apparently, was a dramatically unsatisfying conclusion. King himself eventually dismissed the novel as "a badly busted flush."[60] It has never been—and probably never will be—published.

Undeterred, King quickly moved on to his next novel, a variation on Steinbeck's *Of Mice and Men*, called *Blaze*. Hatlen dates this one around the time of King's college graduation, though King says he wrote most of it a few years later. Whatever the case, the novel didn't see publication until 2007, at least thirty years after it was written. The published version is attributed to Richard Bachman, and there are hints of "Bachman's" deterministic point of view, but the published novel lacks the raw intensity of *Rage* and *The Long Walk*. The title character's outbursts of anger and violence appear like the flicker of a match in a blinding snowstorm, and disappear just as fast. Rather than fight his cruel fate, the title character Blaze simply festers:

> *For years he had identified himself as a dummy, coming to accept it as just one more part of his life, like the dent in his forehead. Yet something continued to work away beneath the burnt-out surface. It worked with the deadly instinct of living things—moles, worms, microbes—beneath the surface of a burnt-over meadow. This was the part that remembered everything. Every hurt, every cruelty, every bad turn the world had done him.*[61]

58 Terrell 33
59 Terrell 35
60 King: "On Becoming" 41
61 King: *Blaze* 187

These impulses toward violence do not build to a satisfying catharsis, only to compounded sorrow and a rather depressing resolution. Perhaps that's why the novel remained unpublished for so long. There is no glory in *Blaze*.

While most of these early novels were initially relegated to an old trunk, King did manage to publish a few short stories during his college years. Eschewing literary pretensions, he wrote shorts that harkened back to his earliest genre-oriented writing experiments. "The Glass Floor" is a pastiche of Poe and Lovecraft. "Here There Be Tygers" recalls a similar story by Ray Bradbury. "Cain Rose Up" and "Strawberry Spring" are examples of psychological horror in the Robert Bloch mode. "Night Surf" suggests the post-apocalyptic world of a 1950s science fiction movie—and offers a brief glimpse of King's future opus *The Stand*. All of these stories were published in the University of Maine's literary magazine, with the exception of "The Glass Floor," which appeared in the pulp fiction magazine *Startling Mystery Stories*. Two other horror stories, "The Reaper's Image" and "The Float" (later revised and republished as "The Raft"), were also sold for publication in genre magazines. Bolstered by this modest success, King continued to write horror shorts. As it turned out, these stories—rather than the literary novels that he pinned his greatest hopes on—marked the beginning of his career as America's best-known writer.

Night Shift

Stephen King graduated from college in 1970. That summer, he holed up in an apartment on the banks of the Penobscot River in Orono, Maine, and started writing a story about a world-weary gunslinger and a mysterious man in black. As he had with his earlier novel *Sword in the Darkness*, King became overwhelmed by the scope of his story. He sensed that he was writing the beginning of a grand epic that might fuse the enigmatic mysteries of Robert Browning's poem "Childe Roland to the Dark Tower Came" with the violent panache of filmmaker Sergio Leone's spaghetti westerns.[62] For the time being, however, he decided to stick with horror shorts, figuring that he had a better chance of paying the bills with those. Years later, he reflected on the practicality of this decision: "I didn't exactly choose horror. If anything, horror chose me."[63]

The first short story he sold after college was a nasty little tale called "Graveyard Shift." On one level, it is a simple horror story about the fear of rats. King, however, personalized it by building on memories of a summer job he'd once had at the Worumbo Mill in Lisbon Falls, where he attended high school. He remembers:

> *During Fourth of July week, the mill closed. Employees with five years or more at Worumbo got the week off with pay. Those with fewer than five years were offered work on a crew that was going to clean the mill from top to bottom, including the basement, which hadn't been touched in forty or fifty years. I would probably have agreed to work on this crew—it was time and a half—but all the positions were filled long before the foreman got down to the high school kids, who'd be gone in September. When I got back to work the following week, one of the dyehouse guys told me I should have been there, it was wild. "The rats down in that basement were big as cats," he said. "Some of them, goddamn if they weren't as big as* dogs.*"*[64]

62 Winter: *Stephen* 27
63 Murari 238
64 King: *On Writing* 59-60

This dubious yarn set King's imagination to work. He had no trouble envisioning the dark, dank, oppressive environment, or imagining that the cleaning crew could have stumbled into a sub-basement full of monsters right out of H.P. Lovecraft's "The Rats in the Walls."

The same oppressive tone dominates King's subsequent short story "The Mangler," which is rooted in the author's experience at another blue-collar job—one that he took as a new husband and father. In 1971, just one year out of college, King married his girlfriend Tabitha Spruce and settled in the city of Bangor. By that time they already had one child and another on the way, and were struggling to make ends meet. Over the next few years, King managed to place ten short stories (beginning with "Graveyard Shift" and culminating with "Sometimes They Come Back") in the men's magazine *Cavalier*, but these publications were "just enough to create a rough sliding margin between us and the welfare office."[65] The family's main income came from minimum wage jobs. Tabitha worked in a doughnut shop; Stephen worked at a filling station and, later, took a job pressing sheets in an industrial laundry. He remembers how the latter found its way into his fiction:

> *There was a fellow there that had no hands or forearms. He simply had hooks. This is one of the things that they don't tell you about when you become management. You have to wear a tie. It was this fellow's tie that did him in. It was just after World War II and he was working around the machines. The steam ironer and folder is the machine the workers call the Mangler, because that is what it will do to you if you get too close to it or get caught in it. This fellow bent down to pick something up and his tie went into the machine. He reached down with his left hand to pull his tie out and his hand went into the machine. Then he put his right hand around his left wrist to try to pull it out and his right hand got caught. As a result, he lost both hands and forearms and was lucky not to have died. His hands were replaced by hooks. Thirty years later, when I worked there, he would go into the men's room, during the summer and turn on the hot and cold water and run it over the hooks. He would then come up behind you and lay the*

65 King: *On Writing* 70

> *hooks on the back of your neck. That's what gave me the inspiration for that particular story.*[66]

The hook-handed man wasn't the only reason King was haunted by his job. He had vivid memories of his mother working for a similar outfit in Stratford, Connecticut, when he was a young boy. She was, he wrote, "the only white lady on the mangle crew," and worked "pressing sheets in a laundry where the temperatures often soared to a hundred and ten in the summer and the foreman gave out salt pills at one and three every afternoon from July to the end of September."[67] While he was working for the laundry in Bangor, King came to the painful realization that he was essentially repeating his mother's life—a hard life that could easily mangle a person's spirit. He may not have encountered a demonically-possessed steam ironer at his day job, but the horror in his story was real enough.

Burton Hatlen has observed that in stories like "Graveyard Shift" and "The Mangler," King combined the "gritty social realism" of his own life with the supernatural elements of his favorite fiction, and produced a "unique contribution to American fiction."[68] In other words, he became "Stephen King" by writing about ordinary people in extraordinary circumstances. For the young writer, just out of college and struggling to pay the bills, "ordinary people" meant blue-collar workers with the odds stacked against them. King wrote from personal experience, as his friend Chris Chesley relates: "He was influenced by a working class, gritty little rural town. And in that sense it made him intellectually, and literarily, an outsider. And I think a lot of the push, a lot of the drive, a lot of the narrative force in his writing stems directly from that—his sense of himself as being outside the mainstream, outside the American suburban middle class ethos."[69]

The outsider mentality also extended to King's role as a new parent. The author first explored his paternal fears in the short story "The Boogeyman," about a man who finds his two children dead in their beds. Years later, King claimed that he started writing stories like that as a kind of "psychological protection," explaining:

---

66 Konstantin

67 King: *On Writing* 32, 37

68 Hatlen 20

69 Spignesi: "Talk" 50

> *It's like drawing a magic circle around myself and my family. My mother always used to say, "If you think the worst, it can't come true." I know that's only a superstition, but I've always believed that if you think the very worst, then, no matter how bad things get (and in my heart I've always been convinced that they can get pretty bad), they'll never get as bad as* that. *If you write a novel where the boogeyman gets somebody else's children, maybe they'll never get your own children.*[70]

This idea of the horror-tale-as-talisman was obviously a powerful one for King, and it gave him a solid formula for his future work, which he articulated as follows: "The story takes a childhood fear and saddles an adult with it; puts him back into that dreamlike world of childhood where the monsters *don't* go away when you change the channel, but crawl out and hide under the bed."[71]

Viewed in this light, "The Boogeyman" is the forerunner of all of King's domestic horror novels: *The Shining*, *Cujo*, and particularly *IT*. In a 1981 interview, the author claimed that he recognized those nascent novels in his early short stories, but "just wasn't ready" to write them yet.[72]

While he continued churning out horror shorts for *Cavalier*, King consciously pulled away from influences like Poe and Lovecraft, and found his horror stories getting longer and more confident. He recognized that "Sometimes They Come Back"—a dry run for *'Salem's Lot*, about a writer who returns to his hometown to confront childhood fears—represented "the absolute outer limit of what the men's magazine market could accept in terms of word count."[73] In 1973, the year he submitted the story for publication, King offered the following advice (ostensibly to other writers, but perhaps mostly to himself): "The men's magazines don't buy novelettes. The average length of accepted fiction is 2,500—4,000 words."[74] This recognition posed a particular problem while he was writing his first horror novel.

---

70 King: "Evening" 3
71 King: "On Becoming" 13
72 Munster 41
73 King: *On Writing* 76
74 King: "Horror" 16

Prom Night

Stephen King says that he started writing *Carrie* on a dare. In the summer of 1971, a college friend took him to task for writing "all of this macho crap" for men's magazines, and challenged him to write a story with a "feminine sensibility."[75] King accepted the challenge and began writing a short story about "an ugly duckling girl with the 'wild talent' of telekinesis, who finally uses her talent to get even with the bitches in her phys ed class who had been tormenting her."[76] He didn't get very far. After an hour or so of writing, he realized that he was in foreign territory: a women's high school locker room. All he had to draw on from his own experience was one brief memory from a summer job as a high school janitor. King remembers:

> *One day [a coworker named Harry] and I were supposed to scrub the rust-stains off the walls in the girls' shower. I looked around the locker room with the interest of a Muslim youth who for some reason finds himself deep within the women's quarters. It was the same as the boys' locker room, and yet completely different. There were no urinals, of course, and there were two extra metal boxes on the tile walls—unmarked, and the wrong size for paper towels. I asked what was in them. "Pussy-plugs," Harry said. "For them certain days of the month."*[77]

In the world of King's "ugly duckling," tampons become a weapon, used to torment the title character when she belatedly gets her first period. Carrie responds with a much more powerful weapon, which came to the author in a moment of inspiration:

> *I'd read an article in* Life *magazine some years before, suggesting that at least some reported poltergeist activity might actually be telekinetic phenomena—telekinesis being the ability to move objects just by thinking about them. There was some evidence to suggest that young people might have such powers, the article said, especially in girls in early adolescence, right around*

75 Grant: "Interview" 85

76 King: "On Becoming" 45

77 King: *On Writing* 74

the time of their first—Pow! Two unrelated ideas, adolescent cruelty and telekinesis came together, and I had an idea.[78]

What the author didn't have was a "feminine sensibility." Discouraged by his own lack of knowledge about the fairer sex, he threw the opening pages of his story in the trash and forgot about them . . . until his wife dug them out and urged him to continue. King has suggested that she did so not because she thought the pages were good, but because she was amused by his attempt to create a supernatural version of *The Feminine Mystique*.

In the fall of 1971, King took a job teaching English literature at Hampden Academy, just south of Bangor. The new job inspired him to return to his manuscript *Getting It On* (later published as *Rage*), and to revisit the "high school confidential" story of Carrie White. (It is no coincidence that the final version of *Carrie* suggests a thematic link between the two stories, when Billy Nolan says to Chris Hargensen: "We got it on, Charlie. We really got it on.") Eventually, despite his natural tendency toward "macho crap," the author came up with a satisfying vision of Carrie White. He took her name from Theodore Dreiser's novel *Sister Carrie*, and elements of her appearance and personality from as many as three different real-life inspirations: two girls he knew in high school, and one who was a student of his at Hampden Academy.

King writes that one of these girls was ostracized because she wore "the same stuff every day for the first year and a half of high school." (He hastens to add, "I am being literal when I say *every day*."[79]) In relating her sad tale, King remembers that when the girl finally came to school in a new outfit, looking "transformed," her peers only teased her more. He concluded: "Someone made a break for the fence and had to be knocked down, that was all."[80]

What he remembered most about the second girl was details from her home life:

One day her mother hired me to move some furniture. Dominating the trailer's living room was a nearly life-sized crucified Jesus, eyes turned up, mouth turned down, blood dribbling from beneath the crown of thorns on his head. He was

78 King: *On Writing* 75
79 King: *On Writing* 80
80 King: *On Writing* 81

> *naked except for a rag twisted around his hips and loins. Above this bit of breechcloth were the hollowed belly and the jutting ribs of a concentration-camp inmate. It occurred to me that [the girl I knew] had grown up under the agonal gaze of this dying god, and doing so had undoubtedly played a part in making her what she was when I knew her: a timid and homely outcast who went scuttling through the halls of Lisbon High like a frightened mouse.*[81]

This experience provided the inspiration for the character of Margaret White, Carrie's religious fundamentalist mother.

Journalist Charlotte Phelan has claimed that King also had another real-life inspiration for Margaret White; she says the author told her that he had based the character on a strange older woman who worked with him at the industrial laundry in Bangor.[82] In the novel, Margaret White works at the Blue Ribbon Laundry . . . the fictional home of the Mangler.

With these real-life details in mind, the writing of *Carrie* came more easily. Before long, King realized that he was no longer writing a short story. "It suddenly occurred to me that I wanted a longer fuse," he explains. "I wanted the reader to see that this girl was really being put upon, that what she did [in the end of the story] was not really evil, not even revenge, but just the way you strike out at somebody when you're badly hurt."[83] That meant more setup. More setup meant a longer word count. And a longer word count created a practical problem:

> *I saw immediately that it was going to be too long for the [magazine] market, but at the same time I didn't have time to write a novel. I couldn't invest that much time in a project that might not make money. I was getting $200 for the short stories, and that kept the phone in the house and bought medicine for the kids.*[84]

In 1971, King says, the prospects for publishing a horror novel were grim. William Peter Blatty's novel *The Exorcist* was not yet

81 King: *On Writing* 79
82 Phelan 9
83 Peck 94
84 Grant: "Interview" 85

the cause célèbre that it would become after the release of William Friedkin's film adaptation, and Thomas Tryon's paranormal bestseller *The Other* was still a year away from publication. In short, King saw no future as a horror novelist.

Out of desperation, he stopped writing *Carrie,* submitted *Rage* for publication, and began working on another, theoretically more marketable, novel. Between Christmas and New Year's 1971, King wrote the bulk of *The Running Man*. Like *The Long Walk*, *The Running Man* is the story of a man who has volunteered for a violent "game" that is almost certain to kill him. The setup is simple: For thirty days, Ben Richards will be on the run from an elite team of hunters who are expertly trained to kill him. As soon as the clock starts ticking, Richards runs while King writes. Neither the author nor the main character seems to harbor any real hope for survival, but both promise to go down fighting. In the end, through a series of convoluted plot twists, Richards manages to fly a plane into the Games Commission headquarters, killing his tormentors and becoming a martyr for the working class. In Bachman's world, King insists, this was a happy ending.[85] In King's world, it was a desperate last hope. He promptly submitted *The Running Man* for publication in early 1972. Like *Rage* before it, the novel was roundly rejected.

For the rest of the year, King suffered from debilitating self-doubt and writer's block. "I began to have long talks with myself at night," he confesses, "about whether or not I was chasing a fool's dream."[86] In December, he went back to work on *Carrie*, expanding the novella to novel-length by adding a series of epistolary interludes—not because he had any real faith in getting the novel published, but simply because he had nothing better to do.[87] When he completed the manuscript, he submitted it to Doubleday and quietly awaited its rejection. He had less faith in *Carrie* than in any of the novels he'd written over the past few years. This time, however, the time was right. In early 1973, the American publishing landscape changed. Horror was in.

Doubleday accepted *Carrie* for publication in the spring of 1973, and editor Bill Thompson sent his recommendations for changes to the final draft. First, Thompson asked King to revise the third act of

85 King: "Importance"
86 King: "On Becoming" 44
87 King: "On Becoming" 48

the book, to bring it "into line with the rather low-key development of what had gone before."[88] The author has since confessed that his original ending bore an unfortunate similarity to the 1957 B-movie *The Brain from Planet Arous*, in which a man becomes possessed by a free-floating alien brain named Gor. Under possession, the man carries out multiple demonstrations of telekinetic ability—exploding airplanes in the sky and replicating the destructive effects of an atom bomb on the ground through "the power of pure intellect." Every time he demonstrates his destructive power, his eyes turn to liquid mercury and he starts laughing maniacally. If King ever adopted such silly mannerisms, readers should be eternally grateful for Bill Thompson.

It seems unlikely, however, that the author could have vilified Carrie so casually. He had, after all, expanded his original story to novel length in an effort to show Carrie as a victim rather than a vengeful monster. In 1984 he reiterated his perspective on the character to Douglas Winter, saying, "I never viewed Carrie as evil. I saw her as good. When she pulls down the house at the end, she is not responsible."[89] There is only one moment in the novel—when a minor character reports that Carrie was smiling sadistically on her long walk home—that suggests otherwise. The reader can perhaps chalk that up to eyewitness bias.

One of Thompson's other significant suggestions was to change the setting of the novel. King had originally set *Carrie* in Massachusetts, in a suburb of Boston, but Thompson recommended that he move the action to his home state, opining that the characters were "a bit greasy" for Massachusetts.[90] Today it is hard to imagine Maine's best-known author starting his literary journey anywhere else. As soon as Thompson made the suggestion, King knew it was the right thing to do, "because Maine's home and I thought people up here would like it."[91] As a result, he set *Carrie* in the fictional town of Chamberlain, Maine, a rural community that the author locates near Lewiston and his hometown of Durham. The town is mentioned again in some of King's later work (most

---

88 King: "On Becoming" 49
89 Winter: *Stephen* 35
90 Bright 2
91 Chute 76

notably, "The Body"), even though it seems to be wiped off the map at the end of *Carrie*.

In the final act, after all hell breaks loose at the Ewen High senior prom, Carrie White physically destroys the town of Chamberlain and leaves a permanent psychological scar on the remaining landscape. Several local citizens even vicariously experience her destructive thoughts and feelings, like telepaths possessed by the brain from planet Arous; it is clear that they will never fully recover. When the dust settles, King writes, "It is not enough, these days, to say that Chamberlain will never be the same. It may be closer to the truth to say that Chamberlain will simply never be again."[92] It would not be the last time that the author created a small Maine town, only to violently wipe it off the map.

King's publication agreement for *Carrie* gave the author the validation he needed to keep writing horror novels, but it didn't give him overnight confidence, as he confessed to interviewer Charles Platt: "I was insecure inside, for a long time, saying 'Look, I don't trust this. Nobody can do this. You can't do this twice or three times.' My idea was, the success would never happen again."[93] Before the ink on his contract was dry, he tackled revisions on *Blaze* and went to work on a new horror novel called *'Salem's Lot*, ruthlessly determined to beat the odds again. This time, aware of the marketability of horror, he was more conscious about building on the time-honored tradition that he knew and loved.

92 King: *Carrie* 271
93 Platt 266

Vampires in Our Town

Stephen King says that the original idea for *'Salem's Lot* came out of a casual dinner conversation with his wife Tabitha and his friend Chris Chesley. This is how he remembers it:

> *I was teaching* Dracula *in high school; I taught it three or four times, and every time I taught it I got more interested in what a really strong novel it was. We were talking about it with a friend one night at supper and I said, "This is the magic question. What would happen if Dracula came back today?" And my wife said, "Well, he'd land at Port Authority in New York and get run over by a taxicab and that'd be the end of him." And then this friend of mine said, "But suppose he came back to a little town somewhere inland in Maine. You know, you go through some of these little towns and everybody could be dead and you'd never know it."*[94]

King confessed to interviewer Charles L. Grant that he had previously tried and failed to breathe life into the vampire myth, producing an early (and now presumably lost) short story about a vampire in a coal mine.[95] It may have been that failure that prompted him to write, in a 1973 essay, that modern-day horror writers should leave the classic monsters—vampires, werewolves and mummies—in their graves. "There are undoubtedly a few twists left in the Old Guard," he opined, "but not many."[96]

The idea of bringing Dracula to rural Maine, however, was too exciting to ignore. King became convinced that he could resurrect this old horror chestnut if he could "create a fictional town with enough prosaic reality about it to offset the comic book menace of a bunch of vampires."[97] Drawing inspiration from Thornton Wilder's play *Our Town*, he set out to create "a peculiar combination of *Peyton Place* and *Dracula*."[98] His main goal was to turn Stoker's theme on its head:

94 King: "Evening" 13
95 Grant: "I Like" 12
96 King: "Horror Market" 14
97 King: "On Becoming" 55
98 King: *On Writing* 85

It always seemed when I taught Dracula *that Stoker wanted to make science and rationalism triumphant over superstition. But Stoker wrote his book at the turn of the century. I started mine when I'd seen all the flies on modern science. It doesn't look so great anymore when you can see spray cans dissipating the ozone layer and modern biology bringing us such neat things as nerve gas and the neutron bomb. So I said, I'll change things around. In my novel, superstition will triumph. In this day and age, compared to what is really there, superstition seems almost comforting.*[99]

In his effort to speak directly to a generation that had grown up on the horror stories of the '50s and '60s—a generation that had always taken refuge in genre storytelling—he decided to root the novel in his own childhood experiences. The author would make Dracula relevant again by not only bringing the monster into his own backyard, but by fusing the vampire myth with personal memories.

King's counterpart in *'Salem's Lot* is Ben Mears, a novelist who returns to his hometown of Jerusalem's Lot, Maine, to write a book about a local haunted house. King had previously explored the town of Jerusalem's Lot in a college writing assignment for a course on Gothic literature. That piece eventually morphed into the short story "Jerusalem's Lot," which gives the history of an abandoned town in northern Maine, near the fictional village of Preacher's Corners. (In contrast, the novel *'Salem's Lot* places the fictional township further south, between Cumberland and Falmouth.) King has said that his primary inspiration was a town called Jeremiah's Lot in upstate Vermont, which he learned about when he was in college:

I was going through Vermont with a friend and he pointed out the town, just in passing, as we went by in the car. He said, "You know, they say that everybody in that town just simply disappeared in 1908." I said, "Aw, come on. What are you talking about?" He said, "That's the story. Haven't you heard of the Marie Celeste where everybody supposedly disappeared? This is the same thing. One day they were there and then one day a relative came over to look for someone that they hadn't heard from in awhile, and all of the houses were empty. Some of the houses

99 Allen 65

> *had dinner set on the table. Some of the stores still had money in them. It was covered in mold from the summer damp and it was starting to rot, but nobody had stolen it. The town was completely emptied out."*[100]

The name Preacher's Corners suggests that King was using his hometown of Durham as a point of reference; King grew up in an area of Durham known to the locals as Methodist Corners. The author also makes reference to Harmony Hill Cemetery, possibly inspired by the Harmony Grove Cemetery near his childhood home. It was just down the road from there, according to King's friend Chris Chesley, that he once explored a "real" haunted house. Chesley remembers:

> *We got in through a broken window. Steve showed me around the rooms. Some of them had picked-over junk in the corners, but most were empty, except for dust-motes and cobwebs and age. The house's past was almost a low sound whispering in the corners, a barely-heard mutter hiding away in the farthest room—the last room upstairs at the end of the hall.*[101]

King remembers the house as a "decrepit manse on the Deep Cut Road in my hometown." He also remembers getting scared away from the house by a group of kids who had also snuck inside and lain in wait for the perfect opportunity to make their presence known.[102]

In *'Salem's Lot*, Ben Mears remembers finding something much more frightening inside the Marsten House when he was a boy. When he went into the last room upstairs at the end of the hall, he saw the ghost of a notorious local gangster named Hubie Marsten hanging from the ceiling—face blue, eyes bulging. Years later, when Ben returns to the house as an adult, he wonders if what he saw was real. This becomes the central issue of the book-within-the-book: *Are ghosts real?* Ben isn't sure, but Stephen King's answer is yes. The author concedes that his fictional alter ego probably hallucinated the vision of Hubie Marsten, but he also concludes that "there may

---

100 Konstantin
101 Chesley: "Death" 584
102 King: *Danse* 278

be some truth in that idea that houses absorb the emotions that are spent in them, that they hold a kind of . . . dry charge."[103]

Anyone who has ever visited a significant setting from their youth has no doubt experienced the uncanny feeling that these settings are somehow *charged* by their memories of it. There's a perfectly natural reason for this, says King. Such places conjure powerful feelings because they were, at one time, *alive* for us. When we leave them, we surrender them to other imaginations. We let them die. When we return, we find that these places are no longer ours. Nevertheless they may still be alive, powered by other imaginations . . . or, if empty, by ghosts. "I'm not talking about ghosts, precisely," King writes. "I'm talking about a kind of psychic television in three dimensions."[104]

The author seems to be speculating about the objective existence of memories. Can we say that memories don't have an objective existence, apart from the mind of the individual that remembers them? We generally assume that when an individual dies, his or her memories die . . . but what, then, about collective memories? Collective memories—like the assassination of JFK or the 9/11 terrorist attacks—can obviously outlast the minds of the individuals who experience them firsthand, and have long-lasting influences on people who were not alive to experience them. Such memories shape the policies of nations and the beliefs of entire cultures. Can we then say that they do not have a life of their own? And if we define a ghost as a memory that has been granted such an objective existence, can't we say that ghosts are almost as "real" as we are?

Ben Mears returns to 'Salem's Lot because he wants to answer this question for himself. Unfortunately the ghosts of the Marsten House—collective memories, or psychic *impressions*, of the terrible things that Hubie Marsten did there—have attracted something to the town that is worse than anything Ben has imagined. The Marsten House is now home to a master vampire named Barlow. Over the course of the novel, the reluctant hero must join forces with a group of individuals who represent the collective conscience of the town, to defeat this incursion. His allies are a precocious boy named Mark Petrie, a world-weary priest named Callahan and a fiery high school English teacher named Burke.

---

103 King: *'Salem's* 58

104 King: *'Salem's* 59

King says that when he originally conceived the novel, he figured this motley crew of Mainers was running a fool's errand. He claims he did not expect any of them to survive Barlow's wrath. Perhaps horror writer Stephen King was living in the shadow of that notorious naturalist Richard Bachman, who had a habit of predetermining the fate of his protagonists. King has said he felt a similar compulsion in working out the fate of Carrie White: "I felt that I was her God, her fate, driving her down this cattle chute toward the end."[105] Carrie met her untimely death just as surely as Tess of the D'Urbervilles, but the characters in *'Salem's Lot* found a strength the author never knew they had. King reflects: "I was convinced that everybody was going to die. That's what I wanted to happen in that book. But it didn't. I didn't try to monkey with the fact because I knew in the end that it was right that they not all die."[106]

Although the fearless vampire killers lose everyone close to them, Ben Mears and Mark Petrie manage to escape (thanks, in large part, to Mark's memory of a mnemonic device from the 1953 movie *Donovan's Brain*!). Father Callahan likewise lives to fight another day (in *The Dark Tower V: Wolves of the Calla*). It may be glib to suggest that the publication of *Carrie* had given King enough hope for the future write a more optimistic horror novel; perhaps it would be more accurate to suggest that *'Salem's Lot* is the first real novel by the horror novelist who eventually won over the masses—a writer willing to confront the worst, who never stops fighting and hoping for the best.

The storyteller's vision reflects hope not only for his characters, and for himself, but also for a generation of Americans that seemed to be on an ill-fated path in 1973. King recalls that, while writing the novel, he felt less afraid of the vampires than of the culture of the town itself, with all of its dirty secrets. Ben Mears writes of Jerusalem's Lot: "There is not life here but the slow death of days, and so when the evil falls on the town, its coming seems almost preordained, sweet and morphic. It is almost as though the town knows the evil was coming and the shape it would take."[107] King saw 1973 America in similar terms:

---

105 Winter: *Stephen* 37
106 Wiater 164
107 King: *'Salem's* 324

All the time I was writing that, the Watergate hearings were pouring out of the TV. There were people saying "at that point in time." They were saying, "I can't recall." There was money showing up in bags. Howard Baker kept asking, "What I want to know is, what did you know and when did you know it?" That line haunts me, it stays in my mind. It may be the *classic line of the twentieth century: what did he know and when did he know it. During that time I was thinking about secrets, things that have been hidden and were dragged out into the light.*[108]

Elsewhere, King suggests that the novel is more closely related to *Invasion of the Body Snatchers* than to *Dracula* because "the fear behind *'Salem's Lot* seems to be that the Government has invaded everybody."[109] Viewed from that perspective, it is telling that the survivors in the novel are those characters who start out paranoid and afraid, but who ultimately resolve not to surrender to or run from their fears. The survivors are those who prepare for the worst, who see what's coming, and resolve to do something about it. They are the hope for the future.

With *Carrie* on a slow road to publication (it was released in April 1974), King prepared for his own future by continuing to write at a feverish pace. After completing *'Salem's Lot*, he produced a less horrific rumination on childhood fears in the novella "The Body," about four boys on a pilgrimage to see a corpse. The story takes place in more or less the same fictional landscape as *Rage*, *Carrie*, and *'Salem's Lot*—a rural town in southern Maine, somewhere between Portland and Lewiston. King named his new town Castle Rock, after the mountain fort in *Lord of the Flies*. Much like Jerusalem's Lot, Castle Rock seems to be a parallel universe's version of Durham, Maine, (although King's later narratives specifically place it a bit further south and west, in the Lakes Region). In fact, the event around which the entire story revolves may have been inspired by something that actually happened in Durham, when the author was growing up there. Chris Chesley remembers:

One night a friend of mine came by and asked Steve and I if we wanted to go see a dead body. He had heard about somebody

108 King: "Evening" 5

109 Winter: *Stephen* 46

who had gone down to the river one summer evening—a guy who had never learned to swim. When we got to the river it was already dark. We sat on some rocks set back from the scene, but close enough to see down to the low place where people usually put their boats in the water. [. . .] The body was inhuman; its sense of extreme difference and distance was subduing and forbidding. We looked and looked at its sunken mystery, but in some strange way it was in vain.[110]

Over the years, King has offered details about two other sources of possible real-life inspiration for scenes in "The Body." In *Danse Macabre*, published in 1981, he relates a story that his mother told to him:

According to Mom, I had gone off to play at a neighbor's house—a house that was near a railroad line. About an hour after I left I came back (she said), as white as a ghost. I would not speak for the rest of the day; I would not tell her why I'd not waited to be picked up or phoned that I wanted to come home; I would not tell her why my chum's mom hadn't walked me back but had allowed me to come alone. It turned out that the kid I had been playing with had been run over by a freight train while playing on or crossing the tracks (years later, my mother told me they had picked up the pieces in a wicker basket). My mom never knew if I had been near him when it happened, if it had occurred before I even arrived, or I had wandered away after it happened. Perhaps she had her own ideas on the subject. But as I've said, I have no memory of the incident at all; only of having been told about it some years after the fact.[111]

Critics have been quick to cite this story as proof that "The Body" is purely autobiographical, but King himself has refuted the claim. In 1983, he said that the novella was directly inspired by a story told to him in college, by his roommate George McCloud:

One day at their summer camp, or whatever it was, a story circulated that a dog had been hit by a train and the dead body was on the tracks. These guys are saying, "And you should see it,

110 Chesley: "Death" 583
111 King: *Danse* 86-87

> *man, it's all swelled up and its guts are falling out and it's* real *dead. I mean it's just as dead as you ever dreamed of anything ever being dead." And you could see it yourself just walk down these tracks and take a look at it, which they did. George said, "Someday I'd like to write a story about that," but he never did. [. . .] So about five years ago I went to him and said, "I took your idea and I wrote a story about these kids who walk down a railroad track to find the body of a boy." I didn't think anybody would be too interested in going to look at the body of a dog.*[112]

Since the novella is indeed dedicated to George McCloud, it seems possible that King's earlier story is apocryphal. But so what? What's the difference between a fiction writer making up a story for an interviewer and making up a story for a reader? In King's mind, there might not be much difference at all. Thomas Wolfe, one of King's literary idols, once proposed that "all serious creative work must be at bottom autobiographical, and that a man must use the material and experience of his own life if he is to create anything that has substantial value." In the same breath, he added, "In spite of this, it is impossible for a man who has the stuff of creation in him to make a literal transcription of his own experience. Everything in a work of art is changed and transfigured by the personality of the artist."[113] For a writer, the difference between fact and fiction may be as thin as the distinction between a ghost and a memory.

Whatever the main inspiration for King's fictional pilgrimage, it is clear that the author put a lot of himself into the novella. The main character, Gordie Lachance, is not Stephen King—even though both are anxious kids who grew up to "parlay all those childhood fears and night-sweats into about a million dollars."[114] Neither is Gordie's best friend, Chris Chambers, a fictionalized version of Chris Chesley. Chesley confirms this himself, saying, "None of the characters are based on specific people, yet there are salient characteristics of the individuals which are very reminiscent of people that he and I knew in common."[115] As for the central action in the novella, King insists that "almost every incident in the book actually

112 King: "Evening" 73
113 Wolfe 118
114 King: "Body" 350
115 Spignesi: "Talk" 49

happened," while stipulating that he "twisted everything around."[116] That is, of course, the magic of storytelling. As the stories are written, the memories may be transformed into something that seems even more real to the writer than what happened in real life. Or, to quote Wolfe again:

> *I wrote such things as this, not only the concrete, material record of man's ordered memory, but all the things he scarcely dares to think he has remembered; all the flicks and darts and haunting lights that flash across the mind of man that will return unbidden at an unexpected moment: a voice once heard; a face that vanished; the way the sunlight came and went; the rustling of a leaf upon a bough; a stone, a leaf, a door.*[117]

In much the way that Ray Bradbury riffed on word associations to produce *Dandelion Wine*, his classic novel of eternal summer, Gordie Lachance riffs on Stephen King's memories to produce his own fine wine. For Gordie, King writes, the word *summer* "is always going to mean running down the road to the Florida Market with change jingling in my pockets, the temperature in the gay nineties, my feet dressed in Keds."[118] The voice that comes through in this passage is clearly distinguishable from the voice of King's previous work. It has a remarkably transcendent quality about it. Gordie vividly remembers his early fears of personal failure, but more than that he remembers moments of profound peace and awe. Take, for example, these three short passages from "The Body":

> *Everything was there and around us. We knew exactly who we were and exactly where we were going.*[119]

> *My body felt warm, exercised, at peace with itself. Nothing in it was working crossgrain to anything else. I was alive and glad to be. Everything seemed to stand out with a special dearness.*[120]

> *What I was seeing was some sort of gift, something given with a carelessness that was appalling.*[121]

116 Beahm: *Story* 61
117 Wolfe 129
118 King: "Body" 337
119 King: "Body" 335
120 King: "Body" 359
121 King: "Body" 389

Gordie feels a need to preserve the wondrous spirit of these moments, and that is precisely what makes him a writer. Obviously this youthful optimism exists in the author's heart as well—at least enough to allow Gordie's voice to come through. King/Gordie sums up: "*The only reason anyone writes stories is so they can understand the past and get ready for some future mortality [. . .] The only two useful artforms are religion and stories.*"[122]

After the transcendent experience of "The Body," it is not surprising that Stephen King felt compelled to return to Castle Rock many times in the future, nor is it surprising the Castle Rock and its inhabitants took on an almost supernatural life of their own in his subsequent fiction. King had written "The Body" not to reclaim the past, but to confront it and let it go. There is every indication that the story had a liberating effect on him. It marks a dramatic shift in the writer's perception of reality, and in his presentation of *alternate* realities. After this, he knew: *Ghosts, both good and bad, are real.*

122 King: "Body" 395

Shine On

If *'Salem's Lot* is Stephen King's variation on *Dracula*, it is tempting to examine *The Shining* as his version of *The Turn of the Screw*. King, who opines that *The Turn of the Screw* "has had very little influence on the mainstream of the American mass cult," prefers to cite Shirley Jackson's 1959 novel *The Haunting of Hill House* as his main inspiration.[123] In fact, it may be fair to suggest that all of King's early novels owe a debt to *Hill House*. The poltergeist activity experienced by the main character in Jackson's novel could have been a source of inspiration for *Carrie*. Hill House, and the story of its former owner Hugh Crain, almost certainly inspired the Marsten House and its former owner Hubie Marsten in *'Salem's Lot*. *The Shining* seems to be constructed on Jackson's theory of haunted houses, as it is presented by one of the characters in her novel:

> *Certainly there are spots which inevitably attach themselves to an atmosphere of holiness and goodness; it might not be too fanciful to say that some houses are born bad. Hill House, whatever the cause, has been unfit for human habitation for upwards of twenty years. What it was like before then, whether its personality was molded by the people who lived here, or the things they did, or whether it was evil from the start are all questions I cannot answer.* [124]

King did not set out to mimic Shirley Jackson, of course. In fact, he didn't even set out to write a ghost story—at least, not a *conventional* ghost story.

King explained to Douglas Winter that his original inspiration for *The Shining* was Ray Bradbury's "The Veldt," a short story about a pair of children whose virtual reality nursery brings their thoughts and dreams to life.[125] He later told George Beahm that he came up with his own variation on that story while he was taking a shower one day in 1962:

---

123 King: *Danse* 51, Norden 48
124 Jackson 70
125 Winter: *Stephen* 51

I was wondering what would happen if you had a little boy who was sort of a psychic receptor, or maybe even a psychic amplifier. And I wanted to take a little kid with his family and put them off someplace, cut off, where spooky things would happen. I sort of wanted it to be Disney World—Goofy's coming to kill you . . . Anyway, I could never make it work. The thing is, you can't really cut a family off in an amusement park; they'll go next door and say, "We've got some problems here."[126]

The idea was still rolling around in the author's head in the fall of 1974, when he decided to temporarily relocate his family to Boulder, Colorado. King has said that he left Maine because he wanted to write a book with a different setting, but the move also may have been a symbolic attempt to put his own past behind him. King's mother had recently succumbed to cancer, and the author was simultaneously grieving for her and grappling with his new identity as a full-time novelist.

During his first few months in Boulder, King began writing a roman à clef based on the Patty Hearst kidnapping, entitled *The House on Value Street*. Hearst, the granddaughter of publishing magnate William Randolph Hearst, was kidnapped from her apartment on February 4, 1974, and held for ransom by a group of radical leftists calling themselves The Symbionese Liberation Army. Two months later, she was photographed as a participant in a violent San Francisco bank robbery. Thereafter, the SLA issued a series of communiqués in which Patty denounced her family and asserted that she was now "a soldier in the people's army." A warrant was issued for Hearst's arrest, and she remained a fugitive until her capture in September 1975, following a tragic shootout in Los Angeles. During that period, King felt an overwhelming empathy for the disillusioned teenager, as he explains:

One of the reasons I wanted to write a novel about Patty Hearst and the Symbionese Liberation Army was because I understood this upheaval they'd gone through. One of those little girls who was killed in the L.A. shoot-out worked for Goldwater in 1964. I worked for Goldwater in '64. I voted for Nixon in '68. I was convinced that people who burned their draft cards were

126 Beahm: *Story* 62

yellow-bellies. My idea was, "Let's bomb 'em into the Stone Age." I went to college from 1966 to 1970, and it was an accretion of the facts—teaching, seminars, and little by little I came around. It's like someone who converts.[127]

Despite his affinity for the subject matter, however, King couldn't make the novel work. He remembers:

> *I gathered my research materials, such as they were, to hand (Patty was still at large then, which was another attraction the idea had for me; I could make up my own ending), and then I attacked the novel. I attacked it from one side and nothing happened. I tried it from another side and felt it was going pretty well until I discovered all my characters sounded as if they had just stepped whole and sweaty from the dance marathon in Horace McCoy's* They Shoot Horses, Don't They? *I tried it in medias res. I tried to imagine it as a stage play, a trick that sometimes works for me when I'm badly stuck. It didn't work this time.*[128]

Around the time, a friend casually suggested that King should take a break and visit the nearby Stanley Hotel in Estes Park. The author and his wife arrived at the hotel the day before Halloween—the final day of tourist season. King remembers that the setting immediately captured his imagination:

> *We were the only guests in the hotel, and we could hear the wind screaming outside. When we went down to supper we went through these big bat-wing doors into a huge dining room. There were big plastic sheets over all the tables and the chairs were up on the tables. But there was a band, and they were playing. Everybody was duded up in tuxedos, and the place was empty. I stayed at the bar afterward and had a few beers, and Tabby went upstairs to read. When I went up later, I got lost. It was just a warren of corridors and doorways, with everything shut tight and dark and the wind howling outside. The carpet was ominous, with jungly things woven into a black-and-gold background. There were these old-fashioned fire extinguishers along*

127 Peck 99

128 King: *Danse* 424

the walls that were thick and serpentine. I thought, "There's got to be a story in here somewhere."[129]

Later that night, King dreamed that his three-year-old son Joe was being chased through the hallways of the Stanley Hotel. He woke up terrified, climbed out of bed and lit a cigarette. By the time he had finished the cigarette, he had an outline for a new horror novel.[130]

Although he planned *The Shining* as a five-act Shakespearean tragedy (a concept that inspired him to write a lengthy prologue and a lengthy epilogue for the completed three-act novel), the author says the story quickly took on a life of its own:

I discovered about halfway through that I wasn't writing a haunted-house story, that I was writing about a family coming apart. It was like a revelation. One of the things that nobody has ever mentioned to me—and it isn't something I generally bring up—is about Jack Torrance. People ask, "Is it a ghost story or is it just this guy's mind?" Of course it is a ghost story, because Jack Torrance himself is a haunted house. He's haunted by his father.[131]

In the opening scene of the novel, Jack interviews for the job of winter caretaker of the Overlook Hotel; right away, it is clear that the main character is troubled. He has an instinctive contempt for authority, and a rebellious nature that hides deep-rooted feelings of inadequacy and guilt. As the story progresses, we learn why: Jack is the son of an abusive alcoholic, and he's becoming uncomfortably like the father who damaged him. As soon as he's locked away in a secluded hotel with his wife Wendy and his telepathic son Danny, Jack's worst impulses become amplified.

On a conscious level, King was playing out the old Gothic idea that the sins of the fathers are revisited on their children. On a more subconscious level, the author says, he was writing about his own worst impulses:

I grew up without a father. I didn't have any experience in my own home, so when I got married and had kids, I had to

129 Allen 67
130 Winter: *Stephen* 51
131 Kilgore 105

fall back on the real role model of young American men, which is television. I thought I knew what a dad was. Fathers on TV were always cool. They had it together. Dad even wore a tie to the dinner table. The first time I realized that parents are not always good was when the kid wouldn't stop crying in the middle of the night. I was getting up to get the kid a bottle, and somewhere in the back of my mind, in some sewer back there, an alligator stirs . . . Make it stop crying. You know how to do it—use the pillow. *These were shocking, unpleasant emotions for me to discover in myself.*[132]

No one, apparently, was more surprised than the author himself when his haunted house story began morphing into a variation on *Dr. Jekyll and Mr. Hyde*. Jack Torrance slowly emerged as the embodiment of King's worst vision of himself—as a frustrated father, a failed writer, and a violent drunk. While writing *The Shining*, the author says he vividly reimagined the emotions of his life a few years prior, when he was living in a double-wide trailer in Hermon, Maine, teaching by day and struggling to write his breakout novel by night:

The more miserable and inadequate I felt about what I saw as my failure as a writer, the more I'd try to escape into a bottle, which would only exacerbate the domestic stress and make me even more depressed. Tabby was steamed about the booze, of course, but she told me she understood that the reason I drank too much was that I felt it was never going to happen, that I was never going to be a writer of any consequence. And, of course, I feared she was right. I'd lie awake at night seeing myself at fifty, my hair graying, my jowls thickening, a network of whiskey-ruptured capillaries spiderwebbing across my nose—"drinker's tattoos," we call them in Maine—with a dusty trunkful of unpublished novels rotting in the basement, teaching high school English for the rest of my life and getting off what few literary rocks I had by advising the student newspaper and maybe teaching a creative-writing course.[133]

132 Beahm: *Story* 71
133 Norden 32

King eventually came to think of *The Shining* as "a story about a miserable, damned man who is very slowly losing his grip on life, a man who is being driven to destroy all the things he loves."[134]

He might just as easily have been talking about *Roadwork*, the other novel he wrote in 1974, which was eventually published under the pseudonym Richard Bachman. In his original 1985 introduction to *The Bachman Books*, King dismisses *Roadwork* as the worst of the early Bachman novels, noting that it tries but fails "to find some answers to the conundrum of human pain."[135] In a later introduction to a second edition of the collection, he calls it his favorite of the Bachman books. It is difficult to account for the change of opinion, but it is certain that *Roadwork* is the most psychologically complex of the four Bachman books. Its hero, a forty-year-old blue-collar worker named George Barton Dawes, is a man overwhelmed by grief following the death of his mother (from cancer) and the death of his young son (from a brain tumor). In the wake of these natural disasters, Dawes seems to view everything in life with angry suspicion. When the local government announces that it is going to build a road through his neighborhood, demolishing both his house and his business in the process, Dawes comes unraveled. He slowly sabotages his job and his marriage, and all but drowns himself in a bottle while ruminating on his miserable future:

> *The March of Time, Freddy. That's what it is. Forty waiting for fifty waiting for sixty. Waiting for a nice hospital bed and a nice nurse to stick a nice catheter inside you. Freddy, forty is the end of being yourself. Well, actually thirty's the end of being young, forty is where you stop fooling yourself. I don't want to grow old in a strange place.*[136]

For Dawes, life has become too chaotic for comprehension. He sees symptoms of madness all around him—in Vietnam, in the energy crisis, and above all in the local *roadwork*. All of these things make him feel like he's suffering from "soul cancer," dying a slow death. Or like he's "a character in some bad writer's book [and the writer has] already decided how things are going to turn out and why." This line of thought shows King beginning to break away

134 King: "On Becoming" 62
135 King: "Why" xii
136 King: *Roadwork* 483

from the dour fatalism of Richard Bachman. King can't save George Dawes, any more than he can he save George's son, who was "cut down by writing in a brain tumor" before the story even started. He can and does, however, try to save Jack and Danny Torrance.

As with *'Salem's Lot*, King envisioned a very bleak ending for *The Shining*. He says, "The original plan was for them all to die up there and for Danny to become the controlling force of the hotel after he died."[137] When it came time to write the third act, however, he found that he couldn't bring himself to sacrifice Danny, or to completely give up on Jack. (Here I'm reminded of William Somerset Maugham's insight that an author giving up on his narrator is too much like an author giving up on himself.) Although Jack does not escape the corrupting influence of the Overlook and its ghosts, he does manage to resist them long enough to guarantee his wife and son's escape from the hotel. Despite his worst impulses, King assures us (and himself), Jack is not a bad man.

The looming question at the end of the novel is whether or not Danny will be able to psychologically recover from his experience in the Overlook. Will he eventually become a slave to the gothic nightmare, repeating the same cycle of alcoholism and violence that his father visited on him? King offers his hope for the future in the final pages of *The Shining*, speaking in the voice of a man named Dick Halloran, who shares Danny's telepathic abilities:

> *The world's a hard place, Danny. It don't care. It don't hate you and me, but it don't love us, either. Terrible things happen in the world, and they're things no one can explain. Good people die in bad, painful ways and leave the folks that love them all alone. Sometimes it seems like it's only the bad people who stay healthy and prosper. The world don't love you, but your momma does and so do I. You're a good boy. You grieve for your daddy, and when you feel you have to cry over what happened to him, you go into a closet or under your covers and cry until it's all out of you again. That's what a good son has to do. But see that you get on. That's your job in this hard world, to keep your love alive and see that you get on, no matter what. Pull your act together and just go on.*[138]

137 Ketchum 121
138 King: *Shining* 658

Even more than *Roadwork*, this seems to be the author's response to the painful and untimely death of his mother. It represents his conscious recognition that a man has only two options. He can choose to dwell on the past, and get trapped, or he can face the future, and embrace the unknown. He can surrender to his fear or he can pull himself together and "go on." By choosing the latter, King asserts a mature voice that is distinct from that of Richard Bachman.

Once he completed the first draft of *The Shining*, the author went to work on a novella that attempted to mediate between these two different worldviews. "Apt Pupil" is the story of a precocious teenager named Todd Bowden, who tests his own will against the dark influence of the past. When Todd discovers that his neighbor Kurt Dussander is a Nazi fugitive, he blackmails the old man into telling him *everything* about the atrocities of World War II. As Dussander fills his head with horrors, Todd gradually becomes corrupted. By the final scene, he is every bit as troubled as Charlie Decker, the main character in *Rage*. The difference between Charlie Decker's story and Todd Bowden's story is the narrator's voice.

Charlie tells his own story via first-person narrative, and he has already gone "mad" by the beginning of *Rage*. We, the readers, are asked to identify with him only *after* he has embraced murder as a solution to his problems. In contrast, "Apt Pupil" is a third-person narrative about a young man's *descent* into madness. At no point during the tale does the author take for granted that Todd Bowden is doomed. In fact, throughout most of the novella, he shows Todd actively resisting the negative influences in his life. Todd's fate, from the narrator's point of view, is a matter of free will. Unlike Jack Torrance, Todd is not a victim of supernatural forces beyond his control. He *chooses* to indulge his dark obsessions, and repeatedly makes bad choices until he has made so many mistakes that he cannot see himself as anything but a monster. Only once Todd admits defeat, and becomes like Charlie Decker, is King's story finished. Once that has happened, there is nothing more to say.

While serving as mediation between the voices of naturalist Richard Bachman and horror novelist Stephen King, "Apt Pupil" also echoes a real-life obsession that created both writers. King has told several interviewers over the years that, when he was a teenager, he kept a scrapbook on spree killer Charlie Starkweather. This understandably upset his mother, who couldn't comprehend why her son was obsessed with a madman. King admits that he "wavered between attraction and repulsion," like Todd Bowden as he listens to Dussander's tales of torture, but claims that "obsession is too strong a word" for his interest in Starkweather. He explained himself to *Playboy* interviewer Eric Norden:

> *It was more like trying to figure out a puzzle, because I wanted to know why somebody could do the things Starkweather did. I suppose I wanted to decipher the unspeakable, just as people try to make sense out of Auschwitz or Jonestown. I certainly didn't find evil seductive in any sick way—that would be pathological—but I did find it compelling. And I think most people do, or the bookstores wouldn't still be filled with biographies of Adolf Hitler more than thirty-five years after World War II.* [139]

In contrast to *The Shining*, which is rooted in the tradition of supernatural horror literature, "Apt Pupil" tackles a real-world fascination with real-world horror. It has all the gritty realism of a Richard Bachman story, but it transcends the hopeless determinism of *Rage*. The author of "Apt Pupil" is genuinely horrified by real-world madness and violence, not merely fascinated. He does not sympathize with the madman, nor does he allow him to "go on" in the end. With "Apt Pupil," King begins to assert himself as a moral writer. The horrors of the past are *real,* he says, but the future is unwritten. It will be what we make of it.

With the novels *Carrie*, *'Salem's Lot*, and *The Shining*, Stephen King created his own unholy trinity of horror literature: modern-day variations on *Frankenstein*, *Dracula*, and *Dr. Jekyll and Mr. Hyde*. With his subsequent novels—*The Stand*, *The Dead Zone*, *Firestarter*, *Cujo*, and *Pet Sematary*—he built on broader storytelling traditions, expanding into the realms of science fiction and literary Naturalism, and developing a narrative voice that would transcend any particular genre.

139 Norden 41

Despite his reputation as a horror writer, King says that he has never written with a particular genre in mind. In adolescence, his instincts simply led him to horror. Recalling some of his earliest (unpublished) short stories, he explains:

> *One of the few good ones was about an asteroid miner who discovered a pink cube, and all this stuff started to come out of the cube and drive him back further and further into his little space hut, breaching the airlocks one after another. And the thing got him in the end. All the science-fiction magazines sent it back, because they knew goddamn well there was no science in it, there were no aliens trying to communicate using psionic talents, or anything like that. There was just this big pink thing that was going to eat someone, and it ate him.*[140]

The publication of three horror novels did not discourage his inclination toward horror, but it did give him the confidence to write stories that moved beyond fear, to explore notions of quasi-religious transcendence and karmic justice. More and more, King's work counterbalanced supernatural horrors with relatively positive beliefs—particularly about Christianity and the future of America—while, at the same time, everyday horrors became increasingly threatening.

140 Platt 264

The End of the World as We Know It

In contrast to King's first three horror novels, which originated in personal memories, his fourth genre novel grew out of current events. The author explains:

> *The actual impetus to write* The Stand *came from a chemical-biological spill in Utah. This stuff got loose that was like Agent Orange, except more deadly, and it killed a bunch of sheep because the wind happened to be blowing away from Salt Lake City and into the barrens. But on another day, if the wind had come from a different direction, it very well could have blown over Salt Lake City and things might have been entirely different.*[141]

At first, King tried to imagine a way to incorporate this threat into *The House on Value Street* as an elaborate metaphor, "a plague of violence." Eventually, however, he settled on the idea of telling a story about a literal plague that decimates the world population within a matter of weeks.[142] The scenario reminded him of George R. Stewart's 1949 science fiction novel *Earth Abides*, and he started to write his own variation on the ideas in that novel.

In the first half of *Earth Abides*, a solitary ecologist named Ish Williams emerges from the wilderness near San Francisco to find that most of his fellow Americans have been killed by an outbreak of "super-measles." An old newspaper article offers only a vague explanation for the outbreak: "It might have emerged from some animal reservoir of disease; it might be caused by some new micro-organism. Most likely a virus, produced by mutation; it might be an escape, possibly even a vindictive release, from some laboratory of bacteriological warfare."[143] In search of more definitive answers, Ish embarks on a cross-country journey to see what's left of America. Along the way he encounters multiple survivors, but all of them have succumbed to fear and despair. Stewart writes:

> *These people were physically alive, but more and more he realized that they walked about in a kind of emotional death. He*

141 King: "Evening" 23
142 Kilgore 106
143 Stewart 14

> *had studied enough anthropology to realize that the same phenomenon had been observed on a smaller scale before. Destroy the culture pattern in which people lived, and often the shock was too great for the individuals. Take away family and job, friends and church, all customary amusements and routines, hope too—and life became walking death.*[144]

Only someone like Ish, with a relatively unemotional perspective on life, is able to cope with the loss of civilization. He casually returns to his home in central California, settles down with a fellow survivor named Emma and raises a family. Over the next twenty-one years, a tribe of thirty-six people springs up around him.

In the central section of the book, Stewart raises the subject of religion only once, and rather dismissively. During the eighth year after the outbreak, the tribe (then consisting of seven members) attempts to "go to church." The author characterizes this as a failed experiment. Ish, a rational skeptic, apparently "hated building on a foundation of insincerity," and found that the services "were cultivating disunion rather than a unity of feeling" by drawing too loosely on too many different religious traditions. Ultimately the tribe members agree to end the experiment and let "each one of us carry on in his heart as he wishes."[145] Stewart concludes that mutual respect is enough to bind the new society together.

The later part of the novel details the life of the tribe during their twenty-second year, mainly focusing on Ish's hopes for rebuilding civilization. In his mind, "civilization wasn't just only gadgets and how to make them and run them. It was all sorts of social organization too—all sorts of rules, and laws, and ways of life, among people and groups of people."[146] Ish comes to believe that the tribe cannot continue to grow without that kind of overarching structure, and he places his greatest hopes for the future on the shoulders of his precocious son Joey, who seems to share his intelligence and his sensibilities. When Joey dies, Ish loses hope for a return to the Old Times. On his deathbed he realizes that while the tribe will go on, civilization as he knows it is dead. He briefly considers the possibility

144 Stewart 78
145 Stewart 137
146 Stewart 157

that abandoning the church "experiment" may have been "a mistake," then resigns himself to his fate as "the last American."[147]

Stewart's thematic conclusions apparently did not appeal to King as strongly as the apocalyptic setup. "The first half of Stewart's long book is riveting," the author says, "[but] the second half is more of an uphill push—too much ecology, not enough story."[148] King had his own ideas about what kind of society would emerge from the ashes of such a disaster, and his novel *The Stand* places a much greater emphasis on the role of religion in the new order.

Like Stewart, King begins his story with the accidental release of a deadly "super-flu." Unlike Stewart, he depicts the collapse of civilization, offering rather unflattering predictions about the U.S. government's likely response to such a crisis. In the novel, the authorities are willing to sacrifice basic human rights to maintain law and order—or, perhaps more to the point, to maintain a system of power. The military gathers ordinary citizens into quarantine zones like cattle, prompting one minor character to plead, "*Isn't this America?*" Stu Redman, the novel's central figure, does not seem nearly as surprised by the turn of events. He is a member of a more cynical generation than Ish—a representative of post-Watergate America, who shares King's belief that the government "would rather kill us all than tell us the truth."[149]

After the eventual collapse of the U.S. government, the author contemplates a new type of civilization. The outbreak has produced a hauntingly empty world, but King optimistically proposes that beyond the overwhelming loss of life there is opportunity for a healthier, more peaceful, and more spiritually fulfilling kind of existence:

> *No more energy crisis, for one thing, no more famine, no more massacres in Uganda, no more acid rain or hole in the ozone layer.* Finito *as well to saber-rattling nuclear superpowers, and certainly no more overpopulation. Instead, there was a chance for humanity's remaining shred to start over again in a God-centered world to which miracles, magic, and prophecy had returned.*[150]

147 Stewart 223
148 King: *Danse* 425
149 Magistrale 7
150 King: *On Writing* 202

In Stewart's novel, the survivors don't seem to have much inclination to band together. In King's novel, by contrast, new societies begin forming immediately—not because human nature demands it, but because supernatural influences are at work in this post-apocalyptic world. Most of the survivors have visionary dreams that draw them into one of two tribes: a libertarian tribe in the mountains near Boulder, Colorado, and a more hedonistic tribe in the desert oasis of Las Vegas, Nevada. The differences between these groups create a new basis for conflict, which becomes the major focus of the novel.

King says that he did not want to define the two opposing groups as good and evil, or Christian and non-Christian, but rather as Apollonian and Dionysian.[151] Among the leaders of the Apollonian group, which gathers around an elderly Christian mystic named Mother Abigail, there is at least one atheist (Nick Andros), one agnostic (Ralph Brentner), and three rational skeptics (Stu Redman, Larry Underwood and Glen Bateman). These characters are freethinkers, like America's founding forefathers who advocated the separation of Church and State. The author has said that he wanted to present an "old fashioned frontier vision" of America, in which individuals must "master their own destiny and confront and overcome tremendous odds" in a world where "absolute values of good and evil [are] warring for supremacy."[152] King's vision supposes that good and evil are strong supernatural forces at work in the world, waging war via human decisions and actions. The symbols of those two opposing forces are Mother Abigail, the leader of the Boulder tribe, and Randall Flagg, the leader of the Las Vegas tribe.

It is impossible to overlook the fact that Mother Abigail is a Christian mystic, or that Randall Flagg exhibits characteristics commonly associated with the Christian devil, but it is necessary to reiterate that King does not view his characters purely in terms of good and evil. In interviews conducted in the late 1970s and early 1980s, the author described them in decidedly pagan terms, as expressions of "elemental forces—White and Black." He equates the White with the Christian God and the Black with the Christian Devil, but stipulates, "I don't see good as a completely Christian force."[153] Similarly, he does not define evil in theological terms, but

151 King: *Danse* 427
152 Norden 53
153 Ketchum 119

in vaguely ethical terms: "My definition of evil is 'the conscious will to do harm.'"[154] To clarify his position, he adds, "God and the devil—the White and Black forces—proceed from the *inside*."[155]

When King wrote *The Stand*, he was clearly not as interested in the *absolute values* of good and evil as in the *human capacity* for good and evil. In his vision, characters are never definitively good or definitively evil. They are redefined by every decision they make and every action they take. Flagg's followers succumb to his malicious influence not because they are evil, but because they are weak, lonely and vulnerable, like Todd Bowden in "Apt Pupil." Mother Abigail's followers are just as fallible, and they frequently stumble on their way to being good. Even Mother Abigail herself can commit a sin—because she is, after all, human.

Flagg, on the other hand, is not human. Nor is he the devil. "I didn't really want the devil!" King insists. "This guy's minor league compared to what I assume the devil to be in Christian theology, assuming that he really existed."[156] King presents his central villain as a supernatural instigator that has possessed infamous killers like Charles Starkweather, Lee Harvey Oswald, Charles Whitman, Charles Manson, Richard Speck, Donald DeFreeze (the leader of the Symbionese Liberation Army), and even Lyndon Johnson. More specifically, Flagg seems to be the embodiment of a floating curse on a particular generation of Americans. His power exists entirely in their corruptibility.

The author says that he initially conceived *The Stand* as "an American *Lord of the Rings*."[157] J.R.R. Tolkien's epic fantasy follows a diverse group of heroes on a quest to destroy an all-powerful weapon so that it won't fall into the hands of an evil magician named Sauron. None of Tolkien's heroes are definitively good—even the main protagonist Frodo turns out to be susceptible to the malicious influence of the ring. By the same token, no creature is inherently evil—as the priestly character Elrond explains, "Nothing is evil in the beginning. Even Sauron was not so."[158] Tolkien implies that evil is not an equal and opposite force of good, but rather a diminution of good. Following this logic, the battle between good and evil is

154 Perakos 66
155 Perakos 65
156 Kilgore 106
157 Peck 98
158 Tolkien: *Fellowship* 300

waged endlessly in the hearts and minds of the living, generation after generation. The White wins the day in *The Lord of the Rings*, but Tolkien (via the wizard Gandalf) advises that there will be many more trials ahead:

> *Other evils there are that may come. Yet it is not our part to master all the tides of the world, but to do what is in us for the succour of those years in which we are set, uprooting the evils in the fields that we know, so that those who live after may have clear earth to till. What weather they shall have is not ours to rule.*[159]

In King's story, "civilized" Americans in the late twentieth century face their own epic battle, and they seem to make particularly easy targets for the temptations of evil. According to survivor Glen Bateman their biggest weakness is not their lust for power, but their *rationalism*. Echoing the hero of *'Salem's Lot*, who champions superstition over science, Bateman explains:

> *If it hadn't been Captain Trips, it would have been something else. The fashion was to blame it on 'technology,' but 'technology' is the trunk of the tree, not the roots. The roots are rationalism, and I would define that word so: 'Rationalism is the idea we can ever understand anything about the state of being.' It's a deathtrip. It always has been. So you can charge the superflu off to rationalism if you want. But the other reason we're here is the dreams, and the dreams are irrational . . . We're here under the fiat of powers we don't understand. For me, that means we may be only beginning to accept—only subconsciously now, and with plenty of slips backward due to culture lag—a different definition of existence. The idea that we can never understand anything about the state of being. And if rationalism is a deathtrip, then irrationalism might very well be a lifetrip.*[160]

This expression of faith—in miracles, magic and prophecy—seems like a very personal confession on the part of the author. In the end, King hung the resolution of his epic battle between the elemental

159 Tolkien: *Return* 160
160 King: *Stand* 741

forces of White and Black on this vaguely mystical embrace of the Unknown.

In various interviews, King has explained that he reached a creative impasse about halfway through the writing of *The Stand*, when he suddenly realized that his characters had escaped from a deeply troubled civilization only to create new versions of the same problems. He realized that his would-be heroes had become engaged in a Cold War standoff with would-be villains; nothing had really changed. The author eventually solved this storytelling crisis by destroying civilization for a second time. A carefully placed bomb serves as "a stern message from the guy upstairs, a way of saying 'I didn't bring you all this way just so you could start up the same old shit.'"[161] As a result, Bateman presents his alternative to rationalism, suggesting that it is time for the survivors of the superflu to show a little faith in forces beyond their comprehension.

Just as *The Lord of the Rings* is rooted in the cultural beliefs of pre-Christian Britannia, the final act of *The Stand* is rooted in native American transcendentalism. Bateman proposes a traditional American Indian "vision quest" as a means to reboot humanity, explaining:

> *There were several American Indian tribes that used to make "having a vision" an integral part of their manhood rite. When it was your time to become a man, you were supposed to go out into the wilderness unarmed. You were supposed to make a kill, and two songs—one about the Great Spirit and one about your own prowess as a hunter and a rider and a warrior and a fucker—and have that vision. You weren't supposed to eat [. . .] The casting away of* things *is symbolic, you know. Talismanic. When you cast away* things, *you're also casting away the self-related others that are symbolically related to those things. You start a cleaning-out process.*[162]

Bateman's phrase "a cleaning-out process" surely would have resonated with Tolkien, who wrote in a 1939 essay that he regarded fantasy storytelling as a kind of spiritual recovery:

161 King: *On Writing* 206
162 King: *Stand* 1045

> *Recovery (which includes return and renewal of health) is a re-gaining—regaining of a clear view. I do not say "seeing things as they are" and involve myself with the philosophers, though I might venture to say "seeing things as we are (or were) meant to see them"—as things apart from ourselves. We need, in any case, to clean our windows; so that the things seen clearly may be freed from the drab blur of triteness or familiarity—from possessiveness.*[163]

The Stand seems to have provided that recovery process for King, counterbalancing his fears of the future with a renewed faith in humanity. King reflects: "Despite all the grisly scenes, the book is also a testament to the enduring human values of courage, kindness, friendship, and love."[164] Although it's usually categorized as a horror novel, *The Stand* is not primarily a book about fear. It's a book about overcoming fear and "going on."

In the final act, four of the central characters—Stu, Larry, Ralph and Glen—surrender their worldly lives, and travel on foot to Las Vegas. There, they confront Flagg with blind faith in the White. Their faith is rewarded by a vision of the "hand of God," King's *deus ex machina*. It is not the hand of God, however, that deposes Flagg. Instead, he is undermined by a human being. Just as the power-hungry Gollum inadvertently caused the destruction of the all-powerful ring in *The Lord of the Rings*, so Flagg's pyromaniac henchman Trash inadvertently destroys Flagg's empire with a nuclear weapon. In both stories, the pivotal characters that determine the fate of the world have been driven mad by the acute influence of evil. Through their madness, evil defeats itself.

King, like Tolkien, concludes his tale by reminding us that the battle between good and evil is never finished. The heroes of *The Stand* reclaim America's innocence on behalf of their generation, then sit back and wonder if the next generation will be able to maintain it. The implication of this finale is that every generation, like every individual, must go on its own vision quest.

---

163 Tolkien: *Tree* 57

164 Norden 30

Wild Talents

After three years of work, Stephen King had produced a 1,400-page manuscript that summed up his evolving worldview.[165] While his publisher tried to whittle the epic fantasy down to a more manageable length, Hollywood was making a killing off of the author's first novel. United Artists released Brian DePalma's film adaptation of *Carrie* in the fall of 1976, and it went on to become one of the most successful horror movies of all time—in large part because it was faithful to the source material.

A lesser screenwriter might have focused on the more sensational aspects of Stephen King's *Carrie*, but Lawrence D. Cohen understood that the novel worked precisely because it spent most of its time generating sympathy for the "monster." Cohen regarded Carrie's telekinetic ability merely as a "device" to reveal character, and focused his screenplay on the mother-daughter relationship between Carrie and Margaret White, and on the psychological effects of high school bullying.[166] Director Brian DePalma took the same approach, as he explained in a 1977 interview:

> *I wanted to use [telekinesis] as an extension of her emotions—her feelings that were completely translated into actions, that only erupted when she got terribly excited, terribly anxious and terribly sad. [. . .] I never wanted to use it arbitrarily, floating stuff around. In a movie that's kind of boring. Okay, she moves objects. As soon as you've established that, I don't think you can do anymore with it.*[167]

One of the highest grossing pictures of the year, the film solidified DePalma's reputation and earned Oscar nominations for actresses Sissy Spacek and Piper Laurie. It also raised Stephen King's profile significantly.

The author was not only grateful that the film retained the integrity of his characters, but also impressed that it turned out to be "more stylish" and more fun than his comparatively "sobersided"

165 Ketchum 119
166 Wood: "Stephen" 35
167 Childs 41

novel. Reflecting on the differences between the two, he said, "I was maybe too close to the subject, and DePalma's film is kind of light and frothy and he gets you at the end when you think it's over, and you're ready to go out."[168] *Carrie* certainly left audiences wanting more, and Hollywood filmmakers quickly snapped up the movie rights to *'Salem's Lot* and *The Shining*, while higher-profile periodicals like *Penthouse* and *Cosmopolitan* began publishing the author's short stories.

Amid this success, King struggled to write a follow-up to *The Stand*. In 1976, he started and abandoned two novels, one called *Welcome to Clearwater* and one called *The Corner*. Frustrated by their failures, he returned to familiar territory with the short stories "Children of the Corn" and "One for the Road." The former made use of the wide-open spaces of Nebraska, Mother Abigail's home in *The Stand*, and offered a darker vision of religious belief in America's heartland. The latter was a belated postscript to *'Salem's Lot*—or possibly a prologue to a sequel? (King later confessed that he had contemplated writing a sequel to *'Salem's Lot* for several years, but eventually decided not to return to the Lot. At least, not yet.)

In the fall of 1977, King moved his family to the south of England, where he planned to write a detective novel based on characters created by early twentieth century author Dorothy M. Sayers.[169] In the end, that project didn't pan out either. The only publication that emerged from his three-month stay in England was "Crouch End," a Lovecraftian tale inspired by the author's first meeting with fellow horror scribe Peter Straub. King didn't hit his stride again until he returned to small-town Maine in early 1978 and began writing *The Dead Zone*—a literal and figurative homecoming.

The Dead Zone begins with a skating accident on the black ice of Runaround Pond, just down the street from King's childhood home in Durham. The accident is a formative event (perhaps *the* formative event) in the life of Johnny Smith, who as of 1970 is a twenty-something schoolteacher living in the fictional Bangor suburb of Cleaves Mills, where he suffers an even more violent accident. King says that he invented the character because he wanted to draw on his own experiences as a teacher at Hampden Academy. He even

168 King: "Evening" 20, Norden 28

169 Spignesi: *Lost Work* 97

imagined the first pivotal scene in the novel taking place in a high school classroom:

> *I saw [Johnny] giving an examination to his class—it becomes very quiet, everyone's head is bent over their papers, and a girl comes up and hands him the test. Their hands touch, and he says into this quiet: "You must go home at once, your house is on fire." And I could see everyone in the room looking at him—all the eyes, staring.*[170]

As King developed the story, the locale of this scene moved to a hospital room, where Johnny miraculously awakens from a five-year coma with a psychic talent known as prolepsis. In much the way that King used psycho-kinesis as a device for exploring character in *Carrie*, he uses Johnny's coma and his wild talent in *The Dead Zone* to explore cultural changes in America. The author explains: "I wanted to talk about the seventies with *The Dead Zone*. But I didn't want to hit anybody over the head with it. So I thought, 'I'll do a Rip Van Winkle thing,' and we can see the seventies pass before us like a newsreel."[171] When the modern-day Rip Van Winkle wakes up from his five-year nap, he realizes that there has been "some great and fundamental upheaval in American politics."[172] Then, using his newfound talent, he begins looking into America's future.

King did not just want to explore politics. Like *The Stand*, *The Dead Zone* is dominated by larger concerns about faith, duty and destiny. The central symbol in the novel is a roulette wheel. Johnny first encounters the wheel in a carnival setting just prior to his fateful car accident. He finds that he is able to predict where the roulette ball will land with stunning accuracy. The author says he wanted the symbol to suggest that seemingly random events in our lives may not be random at all:

> *In the wheel I wanted to show that everything is fate—everything is chance; and that fate and chance are the same thing. That when we say that nothing is predestined, and when we*

170 Winter: *Stephen* 85
171 Peck 99
172 King: *Dead* 119

> *say that everything is predestined, we are really saying the same thing.*[173]

It's a perplexing idea, which may be why the author had to set aside the manuscript for a while and await more inspiration.

In the meantime he began another "wild talent" novel. The first act of *Firestarter* revolves around a father and daughter on the run from a secret government agency called The Shop. Andy McGee is telepathic, and his eight-year-old daughter Charlie is pyrokinetic; both owe their supernatural abilities to a genetic mutation experiment conducted by the agency in the late 1960s. On one level, *Firestarter* is a story about that decade's Human Potential Movement, as well as early warnings from the time period about the threat of America's military-industrial complex. More immediately, however, it is a story about the bond between a parent and a child.

Andy has brought up his daughter to believe that her power is BAD, and must be suppressed, but his influence over her begins to slip as she gets older and her power grows stronger. The author suggests a link between Charlie's wild talent and her budding sexuality; he tells us that Charlie willingly suppresses her ability because she fears that she won't be able to control it. At the same time, she is beginning to *like* the feeling of being out of control. When Charlie burns, King describes her as ecstatic—in the original sense of the word, *existing outside of oneself.* When she burns, she feels like she is literally inside of *other* people's bodies. This connection between female sexuality and supernatural empowerment is reminiscent of Carrie White's "coming of age"—a fact that almost made King abandon the story. He explained to biographer Douglas Winter:

> *I felt slightly desperate to finish something, and I think that, subconsciously, I returned to what I had written before. When I reached the scene of the shoot-out at Manders' farm [where Charlie displays her powers, prom night style], I realized how much of* Carrie *that I was reworking, so I fulminated for a while and went back to* The Dead Zone.[174]

Ironically, the specter of Carrie also hangs over the second half of *The Dead Zone*. After Johnny Smith correctly predicts that a local

173 Winter: *Stephen* 81

174 Winter: *Stephen* 85

fire will kill dozens of teenagers on the night of their high school graduation, one of the survivors blames him for the disaster, exclaiming, "It's his fault, that guy there! He made it happen! He set it on fire by his mind, just like that book *Carrie*." This is a rare instance of a Stephen King character acknowledging the fictional world of Stephen King, and it implies that the events taking place in *The Dead Zone* are more real to the author than the events in *Carrie*. It is not hard to understand why: *Carrie* relied on a gimmicky epistolary structure and adhered closely to its revenge story formula; *The Dead Zone* is a more confident narrative, and a much more accomplished novel.

Building on the worldview in *The Stand*, *The Dead Zone* considers the question of good and evil—or, at least, right and wrong—from a more troubling perspective. In *The Stand*, the main characters experience supernatural visions, and the narrative clearly indicates that these visions are produced by outside forces and intended to influence the actions of the characters for good or evil. In *The Dead Zone*, by contrast, Johnny Smith's visions come from *inside*; they are the products of his human mind—more specifically, the products of a human mind with a deadly brain tumor. Throughout the novel, Johnny wonders if his visions are proof of a higher purpose, or merely random events in a chaotic universe. Is it fate that he sees the things he sees, or merely chance? Is God communicating with him or not? Compared the characters in *The Stand*, Johnny Smith faces a much bigger leap of faith.

The initial question Johnny asks himself is whether his wild talent is a blessing or a curse. At first, it seems like the latter. His five-year coma has had the effect of crippling his body and alienating him from his fiancée, and his psychic ability turns him into a media circus sideshow. Even when he tries to use his ability for something good—by helping his doctor get in touch with his long lost mother, or helping his ex-fiancée find her lost wedding ring—it inevitably causes confusion and pain for everyone involved. Johnny's doctor, playing the role of moralist rather than scientist, advises him, "Some things are better not seen, and some things are better lost than found."[175] This is the voice of the traditional horror storyteller—a voice as conservative as a banker in a three-piece suit, which says that we must not gamble on the unknowable.

175 King: *Dead* 123

Johnny's mother, a fundamentalist Baptist, proposes an alternate explanation: "It's the power of God working in you. It's a great responsibility, Johnny. A great trust. You must be worthy."[176] Her words are more hopeful, but King avoids embracing this easy answer by characterizing Vera Smith as a superstitious zealot. He points out that her "deep religious feeling" is "strangely coupled" with esoteric beliefs about the lost city of Atlantis, visitors from outer space, and "races of 'pure Christians' who might live in the bowels of the earth."[177] She may not be as reprehensible as *Carrie*'s Margaret White, who used her religion as a weapon, but she is obviously delusional. The only question is whether or not she's delusional about Johnny's newfound talent. He chooses to test the theory. After using his psychic ability to save a little girl's life, Johnny ruminates: "Maybe some things should be told, or seen, or found again. It wasn't even so farfetched to think God *was* working through him, although his own concept of God was fuzzy and ill-defined."[178]

Johnny goes on to use his ability to help Castle Rock sheriff George Bannerman stop a serial killer named Frank Dodd, and then to identify "the political equivalent" of Frank Dodd. The psychic sees no darkness in Jimmy Carter or Ronald Reagan's futures (though King himself would later refer to President Reagan as "our American version of a vampire, of the living dead"[179]), but when Johnny crosses paths with a bitter, bigoted, sociopathic Congressman named Greg Stillson, he sees a vision of the man in the Oval Office, hastening a nuclear Armageddon. At this point, Johnny has seen enough proof that his visions are real to know that someone needs to prevent Stillson from becoming president . . . but who? And how? The only honest answer is also the most morally objectionable. Johnny theorizes that he has a responsibility to assassinate Stillson, but he resists this conclusion because he also believes that murder is inherently wrong. "*Killing only sows more dragon's teeth,*" he says. "*I believe that. I believe it with all my heart.*"[180]

Johnny continues to contemplate the assassination scenario from every angle, acknowledging the inevitable perception of him as a monster. He understands that assassinating Stillson will, in the

176 King: *Dead* 163
177 King: *Dead* 53
178 King: *Dead* 143
179 Pouncey 57
180 King: *Dead* 313

eyes of the public, put him in league with guys like Lee Harvey Oswald, Sirhan Sirhan, Arthur Bremmer, Charles Manson, et al. He recognizes that the world will inevitably view him as a villain on par with the disciples of Randall Flagg. Still he can't forget his mother's final plea for him to "do his duty," nor can he escape the ultimate nagging question: *"If you could jump into a time machine and go back to 1932, would you kill Hitler?"*[181] In a note of overwhelming frustration, Johnny rages against whatever Higher Power might have forced this decision on him:

> *If this talent was a gift from God, then God was a dangerous lunatic who ought to be stopped. If God wanted Greg Stillson dead, why hadn't he sent him down the birth canal with the umbilical cord wrapped around his throat? Or strangled him on a piece of meat? Or electrocuted him while he was changing the radio station? Drowned him in the old swimming hole? Why did God have to have Johnny Smith to do his dirty work?*[182]

King does not provide any reassuring answers to these questions, but his narrative does at least confirm that Johnny is targeting a genuine villain. King has shown us that Greg Stillson is already a two-faced, sadistic monster. *Is Johnny, then, justified in attempting to kill him?* The author leaves that question for the reader to answer. Johnny himself is unsure of the moral implications, but at a certain point he decides to act on faith—not necessarily faith in God, but faith in The Wheel. He rejects possibility that he has seen his dark vision of the future by accident, and concludes that he is meant to act on what he has seen. If such wild talents actually exist, King's narrative suggests, the author would have to come to the same conclusion. "I'd hate to think that life is all random," King says.[183]

---

181 King: *Dead* 327
182 King: *Dead* 365
183 Gagne 96

Dog Days

After completing *The Dead Zone*, Stephen King moved into a particularly productive phase that lasted through the end of the decade. He followed up *The Dead Zone* with the novella "Rita Hayworth and the Shawshank Redemption," a story about the "inner light" that is capable of sustaining a man in his darkest hours. He went on to complete *Firestarter*, and followed that up with another novella, an ode to drive-in monster movies called "The Mist." In a white heat, he wrote the novel *Cujo*, and followed it with a paean to the power of storytelling, called "The Breathing Method." Finally, in the closing months of the 1970s, he wrote *Pet Sematary*—arguably the darkest novel of his career, and one that turns the hopefulness of his earlier novels upside down.

King says that the idea for *Cujo* came from an experience he had in the spring of 1977, when he took his motorcycle to be serviced by a mechanic outside of Bridgton, Maine. When he arrived at the mechanic's shop, he was greeted by a huge, growling Saint Bernard. Luckily, the mechanic (a guy that King describes as looking "like one of those guys out of *Deliverance*"[184]) appeared and curbed his dog, but the author didn't forget his feeling of initial terror. He recalled the experience a few weeks later while thinking about a troublesome old Ford Pinto that he and his wife owned:

> *I was worried about my wife getting stuck in that Pinto, and I thought, What if she took that car to get fixed like I did my motorcycle and the needle valve stuck and she couldn't get it going—but instead of the dog just being a mean dog, what if the dog was really crazy? Then I thought, Maybe it's rabid. That's when something really fired over in my mind.*[185]

In order to make the fictional scenario work dramatically, he knew he would have to explain why the mechanic couldn't come to the rescue. He would also have to explain why the woman's husband wouldn't notice that his wife was missing. Most significantly, the

184 Winter: *Stephen* 109
185 Lehmann-Haupt

author felt the need to explain how the dog became rabid in the first place—*and why*.

Cujo is a non-supernatural horror story, with one major exception. At the outset, King invokes the spirit of Frank Dodd, the serial killer who took his own life in *The Dead Zone*, to suggest that natural horror may arise by supernatural means. The author doesn't say precisely how Dodd is connected to the rabid Saint Bernard in *Cujo*, but he suggests that there is some kind of significant connection. At the very least, Dodd is a symptom of a supernatural menace lurking in—or beneath—the town of Castle Rock. Accordingly, the dead killer's spirit hangs like a gothic curse over the lives of the characters in *Cujo*, from four-year-old Tad Trenton (who dreams of Dodd) to Sheriff George Bannerman (who recognizes Dodd in the face of the rabid dog). In that respect, King writes, "the monster never dies."[186] Even more terrifying is the author's suggestion that ordinary people must confront supernatural monsters without the aid of any kind of supernatural force for good. In *Cujo*, there are no religious visions, no wild talents, no divine interventions. There is only the deathless monster.

Tad believes wholeheartedly that the monster lives in his bedroom closet. His parents assure him that there is no such thing as real monsters, but they are wrong. Vic and Donna Trenton have a monster in their closet too. Donna has been having an affair with a local handyman because, like Jack Torrance, she can feel her youth slipping away from her and she believes that "the only place to run from the future is into the past."[187] By trying to escape her future as a middle-aged wife and mother, she inadvertently puts her life and her son's life at the mercy of Cujo. King says that he never intended to vilify Donna, or to present Cujo's wrath as some kind of karmic payback for her adultery. To him, Cujo represents cruel Fate. When Donna comes face to face with Cujo, she doesn't see a dog. She sees something that *knows* her, something that has been waiting for her all her life—a force of nature, single in purpose, inescapable. She sees Death, pure and simple.

Donna's tragic tale is offset by the story of Charity Chamber, a browbeaten housewife engaged in a tug-of-war with her crude, working-class husband over the future of their son Brett. Through a

186 King: *Cujo* 4
187 King: *Cujo* 91

miracle of chance, or perhaps kind Fate, Brett is spared the wrath of his dog Cujo. Charity wins the lottery and takes Brett away prior to the weekend when the dog goes mad. Chance or Fate—for Stephen King, remember, they are one and the same—spares Charity and Brett, and dooms Donna and Tad. Why? The narrator doesn't have a ready answer, but nevertheless the author had to field this question from countless readers and critics of his novel.

The simplest explanation, King says, is that life is not a fairy tale. That's why *Cujo* begins with the dreamy phrase "Once upon a time" and ends on a much more sobering note. At the end of the day, we—not just as readers, but as human beings—have to come to terms with inevitable loss, and with our lack of answers about the nature of the world we live in. If we don't, we run the risk of going mad. *Cujo* reminds us that it is not helpful to deny the existence of monsters, since monsters can attack us where we live. In response to readers who wanted a more reassuring ending, the author maintains that he did not "let" Tad die out of cruelty, but out of a need to honestly confront that inescapable truth:

> *Kids get run over, they get knocked out of their cowboy boots. People pick them up and take them away forever. Crib death. Leukemia. It isn't a large percentage—most of them do fine. But it has to be put into the equation: the possibility that there is no God and nothing works out for the best. I don't necessarily subscribe to that view, but I don't know what I do subscribe to. Why do I have to have a world view? I mean, when I wrote* Cujo, *I wasn't even old enough to be President. Maybe I will when I'm forty, or when I'm forty-five, but I don't know. I'm just trying on all these hats.*[188]

The young author, and father of three, wrote *Cujo* with his late mother's words in mind: "If you think the worst, it can't come true." Perhaps that's why he has called *Cujo* "the hardest thing I ever had to write in my life," and why he drank so heavily during the creative process that he can "barely remember writing [it] at all."[189] In the end, King could only hope against hope that his own words would

188 Winter: *Stephen* 115-116

189 Robertson 234, King: *On Writing* 99

have a stronger effect than Vic Trenton's "monster words," for the sake of his own children.

With *Cujo*, the author realized his worst fear: the death of a child. With his subsequent novel *Pet Sematary*, he examined the aftermath of that horrifying possibility. The idea for the new novel came in early 1979, shortly after King and his family moved into a big old New England colonial just off of Route Fifteen in Orrington, Maine. He remembers: "I got the idea when my daughter's cat died. It got run over."[190] King later told Douglas Winter that his two-year-old son was nearly killed on the same road as his daughter's cat.[191] This event became the inspiration for a pivotal scene in *Pet Sematary*, in which young father Louis Creed fails to save his two-year-old son from being run over by a truck. King says that writing the scene had an almost paralyzing effect on him:

> *I have always been aware of things that I didn't want to write about. The death of a child is one—and the death of Tad Trenton at the end of* Cujo *was bad enough, but there I didn't have to deal with the aftermath. And I have always shied away from the entire funeral process—the aftermath of death. The funeral parlors, the burial, the grief, and, particularly where you are dealing with the death of a healthy child, the guilt—the feeling that you are somehow at fault. And for me, it was like looking through a window into something that could be. I decided that, if I was going to write this book, perhaps it would be good for me—in the Calvinist sense—to go through with it, to find out everything, and to see what would happen.*[192]

In *Pet Sematary*, Louis Creed is not only tormented by the loss of his son Gage, but by the possibility that he could bring Gage back from the dead.

For a rational man of science, the notion of beating death is science fiction. Louis's sums up his initial skepticism in a speech to his daughter:

> *Faith is a great thing and really religious people would like us to believe that faith and knowing are the same thing, but I*

190 Peck 100
191 Winter: *Stephen* 146
192 Winter: *Stephen* 147

don't believe that myself. Because there are too many different ideas on the subject. What we know *is this: When we die, one of two things happens. Either our souls and thoughts somehow survive the existence of dying or they don't. If they do, that opens up every possibility you could think of. If we don't, it's just blotto. The end.*[193]

Later, after Louis's kindly old neighbor Jud Crandall shows him how to resurrect his daughter's cat, Louis concedes, "I believe that we go on."[194] The problem, he soon realizes, is that the dead don't come back "all the way." His daughter's cat, like George Romero's zombies, comes back slower and meaner. What's worse, the cat brings something else back with it—a dark supernatural force that Louis eventually dubs "Oz the Gweat and Tewwible, God of dead things left in the ground, God of rotting flowers in drainage ditches, God of the Mystery."[195]

Pet Sematary proposes that the power of resurrection no longer belongs to Christ. Louis's daughter makes reference to the Biblical story of Lazarus, but Louis himself senses "a much older God than the Christian one" at work.[196] "Oz" slowly corrupts Louis by tempting him with an opportunity to be God-like, and later by amplifying his grief until he can no longer think or act rationally. When Louis finally finds himself in the presence of a mythic monster, he prays: "Let there be God, let there be Sunday morning, let there be smiling Episcopalian ministers in shining white surplices . . . but let there not be these dark and dragging horrors on the nightside of the universe."[197] The Christian God—or, rather, the power of the White—does not answer. The only supernatural force that attempts to steer Louis away from his dark path is the human spirit of a man named Vic Pascow—and Pascow is no match for Oz.

When Gage returns from the dead, he is just as Jud has predicted he would be. Gage is *damned*—a mangled two-year-old corpse possessed by a malicious demon, more like Regan in *The Exorcist* than like Romero's zombies. This reality shatters Louis's sanity, leaving him in "total darkness." The author mourns:

193 King: *Pet* 200
194 King: *Pet* 201
195 King: *Pet* 344
196 King: *Pet* 344
197 King: *Pet* 364

> *It seems that some exponential effect begins to obtain as deeper and deeper darkness falls—as little as one may like to admit it, human experience tends, in a good many ways, to support the idea that when the nightmare grows black enough, horror spawns horror, one coincidental evil begets other, often more deliberate evils, until finally blackness seems to cover everything.*[198]

King, who had begun the novel with the vague hope that it would be "good for me," ended up feeling completely depressed and defeated, as he told biographer Douglas Winter: "In trying to cope with these things, the book ceased being a novel to me, and became instead a gloomy exercise, like an endless marathon run. It never left my mind; it never ceased to trouble me." When he completed the tale, he banished the manuscript to a drawer and resolved not to publish it.[199] It was, he told one interviewer in 1980, "too horrible."[200]

A few years later, King consented to let Doubleday publish *Pet Sematary* in order to fulfill a contractual obligation. In hindsight, he seems to be of two minds about the book. On one hand, he has defended it as a "very Christian" morality play, saying, "It is a book about what happens when you attempt miracles without informing them with any sense of real soul."[201] Elsewhere, he adds, "It's supposed to be a reflection on what happens when people in a materialistic society, people who live only for materialistic reasons, come into contact with questions of faith and death and outside forces."[202] In that sense, *Pet Sematary* bears strong similarities to the W.W. Jacob's story "The Monkey's Paw," and to Mary Shelley's *Frankenstein*, both of which are cautionary tales.

At other times, the author seems to regard the book as a kind of personal moral failure. "It's a terrible book," he told interviewer Craig Modderno in 1985, "not in terms of the writing, but it just spirals down into darkness. It seems to be saying nothing works and nothing is worth it, and I don't really believe that."[203] Despite King's overwhelming fear that he "couldn't handle" the death of one of his own children, *Pet Sematary* left him hoping that he would be able

198 King: *Pet* 229
199 Winter: *Stephen* 147
200 Peck 100
201 Winter: *Stephen* 151
202 Ewing 111
203 Modderno 144-145

to find solace in the vaguely Christian notion that "sometimes dead is better."[204]

204 Norden 43

The King of Hollywood

Building on momentum created by the film adaptation of *Carrie*, *The Shining* became Stephen King's first hardback bestseller. It was followed by a publishing frenzy. In early 1978, Doubleday collected the author's best short stories—spanning a ten-year period from college publications like "Strawberry Spring" and "Night Surf" to more recent unpublished pieces like "The Last Rung on the Ladder," "Quitters Inc.," and "The Woman in the Room"—to produce the collection *Night Shift*. That same year, Donald M. Grant published a piece of King juvenilia, "The Night of the Tiger," in his *Magazine of Fantasy and Science Fiction*, as well as "The Gunslinger," the first of five installments in what would eventually turn out to be King's longest story. Another short story, "Nona," appeared in Charles L. Grant's 1978 anthology *Shadows*, and King sold "Man with a Belly" to his loyal supporters at *Cavalier* magazine. According to a well-circulated rumor, the author also wrote a short story called "Squad D" for Harlan Ellison's *The Last Dangerous Visions* collection. The collection was scheduled for publication in 1979, but as of 2014 it remains unpublished.

As if a short story collection and five additional short story publications wasn't enough, 1978 was also the year that *The Stand* (in its truncated form) arrived in bookstores. The overwhelming success of the novel kicked off an annual tradition—a new Stephen King novel every fall. Viking Press released *The Dead Zone* in August 1979, *Firestarter* in September 1980, *Cujo* in September 1981, and *Different Seasons* (a collection of four novellas: "Rita Hayworth and the Shawshank Redemption," "Apt Pupil," "The Body," and "The Breathing Method") in August 1982. In addition to these high-profile releases, King released a few books through smaller publishers.

Unbeknownst to readers, the bestselling author was also leading a double life in publishing—his earliest novels finally appeared in print under the pseudonym Richard Bachman. *Rage* was published in September 1977, followed by *The Long Walk* in July 1979, *Roadwork* in March 1981 and *The Running Man* in May 1982. King has said that the main reason for using the Bachman pseudonym was that his publisher was concerned about over-saturating the market and diluting the author's brand. They need not have been concerned. Within a few years, Bachman would be dead and Stephen King would be the world's bestselling author. Readers simply couldn't get enough.

At the height of his newfound fame in the spring of 1979, Stephen King returned to the University of Maine at Orono to teach a master class in his favorite subject: "Themes in Supernatural Literature." The previous year, in his foreword to the *Night Shift* collection, he had begun laying the groundwork for a comprehensive statement about the value of horror fiction, theorizing that it is "like a central subway in the human psyche between the blue line of what we can safely internalize and the red line of what we need to get rid of in some way or another."[205] His time at UMO allowed him to flesh out his ideas, forming the basis of the non-fiction book *Danse Macabre* as well as his introduction to the 1981 collection *The Arbor House Treasury of Horror and the Supernatural.* In the latter he compares horror fiction to psychotherapy and religion, as "a way to stay sane in a mad universe":

> *Suffice it to say [. . .] that tales of horror and the supernatural have been one of the few channels (outside of attending the church of your choice) which people have had since those times in the cave in which to explore the great mysteries of mortality, memory and survival, and perhaps the only channel which we can explore without making up some particular badge of faith which blinds us to all the other possibilities.*[206]

In the author's mind, "all the other possibilities" are what drives a man to madness or faith. *How*, he asks, *can we ever become comfortable in a world that we understand so little about?* King's answer is that we can never fully understand, and we shouldn't expect to. Rather, we should learn to embrace life experience in its totality, like a child, and then to embrace the unknown and the unknowable, without fear. The best supernatural literature, he says, helps us do that—and over the course of the 1980s, King strived to create the kind of literature that would live up to his own prescription.

205 King: "Foreword," *Night* xxv
206 King: "Introduction," *Arbor* 18

Danse Macabre is an in-depth study of the twentieth century writers who, in King's opinion, represent the best tradition of the genre, from H.P. Lovecraft to Harlan Ellison. The author doesn't attempt to contextualize his own work, but the lionization of his main influences (Finney, Bradbury, Matheson, Bloch, Jackson) implies a place for his stories at the end of the tradition. It is worth noting that he heaps praise upon Robert Marasco's *Burnt Offerings*, a 1973 novel with strong similarities to *The Shining*, as well as the work of John Farris, whose 1976 novel *The Fury* bears strong similarities to *Firestarter*. King also comments on a kind of synergy between himself and novelist Peter Straub, and observes that Straub had cited *'Salem's Lot* as an inspiration for his 1979 novel *Ghost Story*. By the time *Danse Macabre* was published, King and Straub were also working together on a collaborative novel that would carry them both into new territory.

In addition to establishing his canon of horror literature, King proposed a horror movie canon for the years 1950–1980. His list is dominated by tales of murder and madness (*The Night of the Hunter*, *I Bury the Living*, *Macabre*, *Psycho*, *What Ever Happened to Baby Jane?*, *Dementia 13*, *The Haunting*, *Wait Until Dark*, *Deliverance*, *Night Watch*, *Looking for Mr. Goodbar*, *Halloween*), but his most telling selection is Roger Corman's visionary thriller *X: The Man with the X-Ray Eyes* (1963), a Lovecraftian story about a man who can literally see beyond the boundaries of space and time. Corman's tale is at once a Romantic warning about man's insatiable thirst for knowledge, and a mystical journey into the heart of faith and madness. By 1981, King was beginning to work on a horror novel with equally ambitious themes (though *IT* would take several years to come to fruition), as well as his first original screenplay.

As he prepared to tackle Hollywood, King did not hesitate to offer his opinion on the recent film and television adaptations of his work. While he regarded Hooper's transformation of the vampire Barlow into a mute Nosferatu clone as a "major boner," he said he was mostly "relieved" by how well the *'Salem's Lot* miniseries turned out.[207] He was not as enthusiastic about *The Shining*. Although he praised filmmaker Stanley Kubrick's technical ability to create atmosphere, King referred to the film as "a great big gorgeous car

207 Norden 28

with no engine in it."[208] In a 1983 interview with Philip Norden, he cited two basic problems with the movie. The first was the casting of Jack Nicholson as Jack Torrence. The novel, King explained, is about a man's "gradual descent into madness through the malign influence" of the supernatural, but Nicholson's performance—or perhaps just his larger-than-life screen persona—suggests that the character is mad from the very beginning.[209] King viewed the change as a conscious rewrite of his story, and speculated that Kubrick may have had a deeply personal reason to substitute domestic tragedy for supernatural horror:

> *Kubrick is a very cold man—pragmatic and rational—and he had great difficulty conceiving, even academically, of a supernatural world. He used to make transatlantic calls to me from England at odds hours of the day and night, and I remember once he rang up and asked, "Do you believe in God?" I thought a minute and said, "Yeah, I think so." Kubrick replied, "No, I don't think there is a God," and hung up. Not that religion has to be involved in horror, but a visceral skeptic such as Kubrick just couldn't grasp the sheer inhuman evil of the Overlook Hotel. So he looked, instead, for evil in the characters and made the film into a domestic tragedy with only vaguely supernatural overtones.*[210]

The result, King concluded, is a film that's not believable enough to be truly scary. Perhaps because of his personal bias about the material, he seems to discount the possibility that living with a madman can be just as terrifying as the threat of the supernatural. Although King regards *The Shining* as a horror film made by a director that doesn't understand horror, the reputation of the film suggests that Kubrick's film has scared plenty of viewers.

King expressed a much greater admiration for the sensibilities of filmmaker George Romero. As the creator of *Night of the Living Dead* (1968), Romero had built his entire career in the horror genre, and remained drawn to the genre for many of the same reasons as King. Romero's films—particularly *Martin* (1976), *Dawn of the Dead* (1978), and *Knightriders* (1981)—express the same Romantic temperament and humanistic values, as well as the dark humor, that

208 Peck 96, Modderno 143
209 Norden 29
210 Norden 29

inform King's early horror novels. When it came time for King to move into the new medium, it was only natural that he should collaborate with Romero.

Early discussions between the two men revolved around a feature film adaptation of *The Stand*, but King and Romero eventually developed a very different project together. They conceived *Creepshow* (1982) as a garish tribute to the E.C. Comics of the 1950s. The anthology film featured five original Stephen King stories (only two of which had been published in any form) and a wraparound segment inspired by the *Twilight Zone* episode "The Monsters Are Due on Maple Street." It also featured Stephen King in his least subtle writing mode—what the author himself refers to in *Danse Macabre* as the "gross-out" mode. Nothing could have been further from the slow-burn pacing and cold existentialism of Kubrick's *The Shining*—or from King's character-based novels. King once confessed that it was his editor who determined the direction of his career as a horror novelist, by prompting him to write for a broader readership than the "*Weird Tales* audience."[211] With *Creepshow*, King spoke directly to that niche audience. Perhaps for that reason, the film was only a marginal commercial success, and King and Romero were subsequently unable to raise the money to make their version of *The Stand*.

King, however, had every intention of working with Romero again. Accordingly, he dedicated his next novel to the filmmaker, and set the action in Romero's hometown of Pittsburgh, Pennsylvania. The idea for *Christine*, a novel about a teenage outcast named Arnie Cunningham who falls under the spell of a spiritually-infested Plymouth Fury named Christine, came to the author in 1978. King says it began as something of a lark:

> *I thought that I would write a really funny story about a kid and a car whose odometer ran backwards. The car would repair itself, and the kid would get younger and younger, and the kicker would be that, when the odometer returned to zero, the car, at the height of its beauty, would spontaneously fall into component parts. It would echo that Lewis Padgett story, "The Twonky" - really funny, but maybe a little sinister, too.*[212]

211 Kilgore 102
212 Winter: *Stephen* 135

As he wrote, the story became darker and more serious, and the author says he drew further inspiration from the 1977 horror movie *The Car* (which, coincidentally, uses Mozart's "Dies Irae," the theme from Stanley Kubrick's *The Shining*, as the soundtrack to its opening sequence). King writes, "There's something working in that opening sequence, something that calls up a deep, almost primitive unease about the cars we zip ourselves up in, thereby becoming anonymous . . . and perhaps homicidal."[213]

Unlike the black Lincoln in *The Car*, however, Christine is not "born" evil. Early in the novel, the author sets up the idea that the car's malevolence is related to her previous owner, a hellraiser named Roland LeBay. According to King, the spirit of LeBay has not exactly possessed or infested the car . . . but LeBay's actions nevertheless "haunt" her. From the author's perspective, the car—much like the Overlook Hotel—is a battery that has taken on a negative charge. In a promotional interview for the book, he articulated his theory of "hauntings" (borrowed from Shirley Jackson) as follows: "Places absorb the emotions of those individuals who have been there."[214] The Overlook exerts a pernicious influence on certain guests not because the place is filled with intelligent spirits acting out private agendas, but because bad things once happened in the Overlook, and bad things leave a kind of psychic residue that can infect subsequent visitors. In other words, it's the place—not the people—that is tainted. In *Christine*, it's the car—not the spirit of Roland LeBay—that corrupts Arnie Cunningham. This seems to be the author's way of suggesting that technology is dangerous not by its own nature, but based on its capacity to be misused and thereby transformed. LeBay used Christine as a killing machine; now she *is* a killing machine.

Arnie's story, like Jack Torrence's story, is about a personal struggle against overwhelming external *and* internal influences. Right up until the end of the novel, the narrator seems to hold out hope that maybe Arnie can escape those influences. King does not attribute independent will power to the car, nor to the dead Roland LeBay, so the final struggle is between Arnie and himself. Christine and LeBay can only be as powerful as Arnie allows them to be, and that is what makes the novel tragic. Like Todd Bowden in "Apt Pupil,"

213 King: *Danse* 173

214 Pouncey 60

Arnie allows himself to be crushed under the weight of his own bad decisions. Even the author says he was genuinely surprised by this dark turn of events:

> *When I began to see how badly everything would turn out [. . .] I really didn't like it very much because the whole thing started out to be a sort of a joke. It was like* Happy Days *gone mad: Boy gets car, boy loses car, boy finds car. I thought it was hilarious until the kid started to run people down. Because sometimes [stories] get out of control and they are like the car itself; they start to run by themselves and they don't always turn out the way you think they are going to turn out.*[215]

Although King has opined that *Christine* is "not my best book"—it is derivative of his earlier work and suffers from an overbearingly chatty narrative voice—it is nonetheless effective as a tragedy, because King makes Arnie and his friends so thoroughly human and sympathetic.[216] Tonally and thematically, *Christine* has much in common with George Romero's most personal film, *Martin*, and so one can imagine that the filmmaker might have made a film adaptation that emphasized the tragic aspects of the tale. In the end he didn't get that opportunity. Columbia Pictures hired director John Carpenter to bring *Christine* to the screen, Romero returned to his *Dead* series and King returned to his word processor.

It may be that the process of writing *Christine,* a book that draws heavily on King's memories of high school, prompted the author to reflect more deeply on his early life. His next project, a mini-novel called *Cycle of the Werewolf*, is colored by nostalgia for childhood and the simplicities of small-town life. King says that he contemplated writing a werewolf story for years, but the idea didn't really take hold until he adopted the perspective of a young boy named Marty, who dares to believe that werewolves are real. The resulting story has more in common with Ray Bradbury's *Dandelion Wine*—a coming-of-age novel about a young boy growing up in a town haunted by a serial killer—than it does with most werewolf stories. The nostalgic tone and themes about the loss of

215 Beahm: *Companion* 59
216 Cadigan 47

innocence soon found their way into King's subsequent novel, his "final exam" on monsters.[217]

217 Wiater 171

Final Exam?

Stephen King's *IT* originated in 1978, with a casual walk across a bridge at dusk. The author remembers:

> *I could hear my boots on the bridge. They made a very echoey sound, and then I got this "telephone call" from my childhood. I thought any second I'm going to hear a voice say, "Who's that walking on my bridge?" Then the troll would just jump out, grab me, and eat me up.* [218]

When he reached the other side of the bridge, a novel was already beginning to take shape. In King's mind, it was an adult version of the children's fairy tale "Three Billy Goats Gruff." He ruminated on the idea for over two years, and it began to take on shades of Ray Bradbury's masterpiece *Something Wicked This Way Comes.*

Something Wicked revolves around a thirteen-year-old boy named Will Holloway, growing up in Green Town, Illinois. In the beginning, Bradbury defines Will within the context of his friendship with Jim Nightshade. The two boys represent flip sides of the same coin—an inclination toward innocence and an inclination toward experience. Jim is fundamentally restless, eager to grow up and know more. Will remains grounded in the present, and advises his friend to take things as they come. "Everything in its time," he says.[219]

Bradbury also defines Will within the context of his relationship with his father Charles Holloway, a small town librarian who desperately envies his son's youth. Whereas the boy constantly gives himself over to new experiences, Charles recognizes that he is living his own life through books; he fears that he no longer has the child-like ability to take things as they come, or live a *real* life full of faith and magic. Seeing only death in his future, Charles yearns just as strongly for a return to innocence as his son's friend does for experience.

Everything changes for these three characters during one week in October, when a carnival rolls into town. The ringmaster, Mr. Dark, offers each of them an opportunity to cheat time, promising to

218 Grant: "Interview" 88
219 Bradbury 128

make them as young or as old as they wish with one quick ride on a magic carousel. Will intuitively understands that there is something "evil" about this offer. He prompts his father to do some research, and Charles learns that Mr. Dark's circus has been coming to Green Town every twenty or thirty years since at least 1846. He speculates that the "autumn people" have "learned to live off souls," and soon realizes that his own soul, along with his son's, is in danger.[220]

Will and Jim eventually fall victim to Mr. Dark. Only Charles can save them, and he does so by refusing to take Mr. Dark seriously—by laughing at him. Bradbury writes of the final confrontation: "Evil has only the power that we give it." Charles uses fearlessness as his weapon: "I give you nothing. I take back. Starve. Starve. Starve."[221] After the confrontation, the father understands that time, like dark magic, is an illusion that is subject to belief. A young mind can exist just as naturally in an older body as in a younger body. Once he understands that, he is no longer afraid of the future. He has learned to live outside of time.

Stephen King develops a variation on this theme in *IT*, his story of seven adults who reunite to face their worst childhood fears. Their main obstacle is the fact that, like Charles Holloway, they have grown up and forgotten the magic of childhood. For the author, that struggle represents a universal experience:

> *None of us adults remember childhood. We think we remember it, which is even more dangerous. Colors are brighter. The sky looks bigger. It's impossible to remember exactly how it was. Kids live in a constant state of shock. The input is so fresh and so strong that it's bound to be frightening. [. . .] They look at an escalator, and they really think that if they don't take a big step, they'll get sucked in.*[222]

As adults, King observes, we dispel our fears with the cold light of rationality. The author supposes, however, that this is only a form of *repressing* fear. If those childhood monsters resurface in adult life—and our rational understanding of the world fails to account for them—then we have only two ways forward. We can succumb

220 Bradbury 203
221 Bradbury 275
222 Peck 95

to insanity, or we can re-learn to embrace irrationality. King suggests that his function as a storyteller is to help stave off insanity:

> *The job of the fantasy writer, or the horror writer, is to bust the walk of that tunnel vision wide for a little while; to provide a single powerful spectacle for the third eye. The job of the fantasy-horror writer is to make you, for a little while, a child again.*[223]

Not coincidentally, the main hero of *IT* is a fantasy-horror novelist named Bill Denbrough, author of "one locked-room mystery tale, three science-fiction stories, and several horror tales which owe a great deal to Edgar Allan Poe, H.P. Lovecraft and Richard Matheson."[224] Bill's friend Mike Hanlon, a librarian like Charles Holloway, diagnoses the evil, but Bill is the one who is expected to destroy it—because Bill is the narrator's surrogate. As such, he controls the magic. Not coincidentally, King says he based "the actual physical character of Bill Denbrough," on fellow horror novelist Peter Straub, right down to the stutter and the male pattern baldness:

> *One of the reasons I think Peter stuttered, which is something that he's overcome now—was that when he was three years old [like] the character in* IT, *he was struck by a car and driven into the wall. He and his seven-year-old brother had been allowed to go down to the market to get ice cream cones. On their way back a car struck Peter, driven by a drunk driver, and drove him headfirst into a brick wall, at which point his older brother picked up his ice cream cone, walked back to the house, and said, "Peter's dead. He was a good brother." But Peter wasn't dead. . . .* [225]

It may be that Bill Denbrough—like Johnny Smith in *The Dead Zone*—has gained some kind of mysterious power from his early childhood trauma. In *The Dead Zone*, a childhood skating accident awakens Johnny's power; many years later, a near-fatal car accident quickens it. Bill Denbrough's stutter seems to be largely responsible for making him a writer; his experiences in Derry, Maine, in the summer of 1958 are responsible for the quickening, as Bill himself realizes:

223 King: *Danse* 434
224 King: *IT* 119
225 Beahm: *Story* 61

> *All those stories I wrote,* he thinks with a stupid kind of amusement. *All those novels. Derry is where they all came from; Derry was the wellspring. They came from what happened that summer, and from what happened to George the autumn before. All the interviewers that ever asked me THAT QUESTION . . . I gave them the wrong answer. [. . .] THAT QUESTION, of course, was "Where do you get your ideas?"*"[226]

Bill has been able to channel his childhood fears into an adult career—but, like all of his friends from that place and time, he is still living in a kind of arrested development, halfway between childhood and adulthood. None of the seven friends have been able to completely escape their childhood fears, only to *repress* them—and none, significantly, have had children. In a 1982 interview, King proposes that the two details are strongly related:

> *To me the real purpose of having kids has nothing to do with perpetuation of the race or the survival imperative. Rather, it's a way of finishing off your own childhood . . . By having children you're able to re-experience everything you experienced as a child, only from a more mature perspective. It's like completing the wheel. At that point, you can give your childhood up.*[227]

The characterizations in *Something Wicked This Way Comes* suggest that Ray Bradbury may have held a similar belief. Early in the novel, Jim Nightshade insists that he's never going to grow up and have children, because "people die," death causes pain, and "I'm never going to own anything [that] can hurt me."[228] Bradbury ultimately refutes this idea through his observations on the relationship between Charles and Will Holloway. He presents the father and son as mirror images, each reflecting something back to his "other self" that allows him to live in the present moment instead of clinging to the past or fearing the future. Likewise, each character in Stephen King's *IT* must forge a bond between childhood beliefs and adult faith in order to process their fears and become a healthy, fully integrated human being.

226 King: *IT* 210
227 Bandler 222
228 Bradbury 40

Early in the writing process, King stumbled upon another image that symbolized this concept—a correlative to the bridge experience that had sparked his initial idea for the story:

> *I started to remember Stratford, Connecticut, where I had lived as a kid. In Stratford there was a library where the adult section and the children's section was connected by a short corridor. The architecture of the adult section was Victorian; that of the children's library was 1950s modern. I decided that the corridor was also a bridge, one across which every goat of a child must risk trip-trapping to become an adult.*[229]

Accordingly, the public library and its "bridge" became a central location in King's tale, just as it had been in Bradbury's. In *Something Wicked*, Charles Holloway works in the library and it is there that Mr. Dark confronts him. In *IT*, Mike Hanlon works in the library and it is there that Pennywise confronts Mike's friend Ben Hanscom, both as a child and as an adult. In each case, the monster attacks the characters in a place where they are most impressionable, and therefore most vulnerable. Bradbury writes that, for Will Holloway, the library is the nexus of all possible realities:

> *Out in the world, not much happened. But here in the special night, a land bricked with paper and leather, anything might happen, always did. Listen! And you heard ten thousand people screaming so high only dogs feathered their ears. A million folk ran toting cannons, sharpening guillotines; Chinese, four abreast, marched on forever [. . .] This was a factory of spices from far countries. Here alien deserts slumbered. Up front was the desk where the nice old lady, Miss Watriss, purple-stamped your books, but down off away were Tibet and Antarctica, the Congo. There went Miss Mills, the other library, through Outer Mongolia, calmly toting fragments of Pieping and Yokohama and the Celebes. Way down the third book corridor, an oldish man whispered his broom along in the dark, mounding the fallen spices...*[230]

229 King: "How" 323
230 Bradbury 14

King writes with a comparable flavor of awe, on behalf of Ben Hanscom:

> *He would sometimes walk through the adult stacks, looking at the thousands of volumes and imagining a world of lives inside each one, the way he sometimes walked along his street in the burning smoke-hazed twilight of a late-October afternoon, the sun only a bitter orange line on the horizon, imagining the lives going on behind all the windows—people laughing or arguing or arranging flowers or feeding kids or pets or their own faces while they watched the boobtube.*[231]

In both stories, the library is a place where anything is possible. The problem is that the darkest stories are not safeguarded between bookends. The darkest stories exist outside, in an everyday world that children must learn to cope with.

When it came time to choose the larger setting for his novel, King didn't opt for his hometown of Stratford. He considered Portland, Maine, as a possibility, but decided that he wanted to set the particular story in more of a "hard-ass, working-class town."[232] (One of the characters in the novel is less diplomatic in his assessment of Derry as "a dead strumpet with maggots squirming out of her cooze."[233]) King found the place he was looking for in the summer of 1980, when he moved his family into a historic, and allegedly haunted, house in the city of Bangor, Maine. As he wrote, King grafted real landmarks in Bangor (The Kenduskeag Stream, The Standpipe, the Paul Bunyan statue, etc.) onto the fictional landscape of Derry. He later said, "Castle Rock is a lot more fictionalized than Derry. Derry *is* Bangor."[234]

King delved deep into the history and legends of his new community, and it didn't take long for him to get overwhelmed. "The problem isn't finding them or ferreting them out," he told one interviewer. "The problem is that old boozer's problem of knowing when to stop."[235] He completed a first draft of the novel in early 1982, but that didn't stop him. He kept returning to *IT* over the next several

231 King: *IT* 171
232 Magistrale 3
233 King: *IT* 26
234 Magistrale 4
235 Beahm: *Story* 92

years, expanding and refining the manuscript even as he tried to put the horror genre behind him.

In the summer of 1984, he ran across a local news story that inspired a new opening for the novel. During Bangor's annual Canal Days Festival that year, three teenagers had thrown a twenty-three-year-old gay man named Charlie Howard off of the State Street bridge, causing him to drown. In King's novel, a similar hate crime occurs. The only difference is that beneath the bridge in *IT*, an evil clown named Pennywise is awaiting his next meal. The incident initiates a new wave of mysterious deaths in Derry, and prompts Mike Hanlon to call his friends back for another battle with the monster that lurks in the sewers beneath the city. The details of the monster's lair also emerged from local lore. According to King, "the Bangor sewer system was built during the WPA and they lost track of what they were building under there. They had money from the federal government for sewers, so they built like crazy. A lot of the blueprints have now been lost, and it's easy to get lost down there."[236] In *IT*, the seven friends ultimately confront their worst fears in this labyrinthine underground city.

The setting is appropriate not merely because it pays homage the under-the-bridge setting of the "Three Billy Goats Gruff" fairy tale, but because it suggests the way that real evil can potentially use myths and legends to scare us. Throughout the novel, Pennywise has drawn his power from the fears of children, adopting the guise of whatever they fear the most. Bill Denbrough says that the clown is just one face of a "glamour," a supernatural being that can change shape at will and have "as many faces as Lon Chaney."[237] Over the course of the novel, It appears in the guise of all the famous boogeymen: Dracula, Frankenstein's Monster, The Mummy, The Golem, The Creature from the Black Lagoon, The Teenage Werewolf, The Fly, The Flying Leeches, The Crawling Eye, Rodan, and Jaws. In his "final form," It appears as a giant spider creature, similar to Shelob in *The Lord of the Rings*, lit from within by fearsome "dead-lights" (a description similar to the "corpse-light" of Sauron's eye in that same work). Despite allusions to Tolkien, however, King seems to draw much of his inspiration for the ending of *IT* from Bradbury.

236 Magistrale 3
237 King: *IT* 278

In *IT*, as in *Something Wicked This Way Comes*, only the adult who can acknowledge the *reality* of childhood monsters stands a chance of overcoming the monsters. Bill's friend Richie Tozier is able to vanquish It through the power of laughter, just as Charles Holloway vanquished the autumn people by mocking them. With this scene, King echoes Bradbury's sentiment that "belief has a second edge."[238] He explains: "The basic concept, and I've come to believe more and more in the validity of this over the years, is that you can laugh evil out of existence. Evil can only exist when it creates a feeling of awe and overmastering fear."[239] Thanks to Richie's insight, the seven friends manage to defeat It. In the process, they literally destroy their childhood home.

At one point in the story, Mike Hanlon advises his friends, "It has been here so long [. . .] that It's become a part of Derry, something as much a part of the town as the Standpipe, or the Canal, or Bassey Park, or the library. Only It's not a matter of outward geography, you understand. Maybe that was true once, but now It's . . . inside. Somehow It's gotten inside."[240] For that reason, there is no chance of destroying the monster without destroying Derry. King accomplishes the job in grand apocalyptic fashion, wreaking havoc on the town with an earthquake, a hurricane, a flood, and many fiery explosions. One senses that this is the author's personal resolution to put away all childish things, or at least to shake off the traditional Gothic novelist's obsession with the influence of the past in his own life. In interviews about *IT*, King says that the novel allowed him to reach the other side of the bridge between childhood and adulthood. When the story was finished, he was finally ready to grow up.

238 King: *IT* 1017
239 Gagne 95
240 King: *IT* 479

New Territories

King has said that, during the seven years "from inception to conclusion" of *IT*, he wrote five novels, six novellas, nine short stories and three movies (one of which he also directed).[241] Believe it or not, he might have been underestimating. Novels written at least in part during this time period include *The Dark Tower: The Gunslinger*, *The Talisman*, *The Eyes of the Dragon*, *Thinner* (attributed to Richard Bachman), *Misery*, *The Dark Tower II: The Drawing of the Three*, and *The Tommyknockers*. King also started and abandoned three other novels. Fragments of "Milkman" appear as short stories in the 1985 collection *Skeleton Crew*; King later self-published the opening chapters of "The Plant" and "The Cannibals" on his website. It is not clear exactly what distinction the author might be making between short stories and novellas, but is clear that—in addition to the publication of *Different Seasons* and *The Bachman Books*—King published fifteen new stories between 1980 and 1985, in a wide variety of periodicals and anthologies. During the same interval, the movie industry produced thirteen feature films based on his stories, including three that the author himself adapted for the screen. That number doesn't include short films or television adaptations. By mid-decade, King had become a one-man media firestorm.

Ironically, during the time he reached the peak of his fame, America's best-selling literary boogeyman was yearning to retire from horror. He told biographer Douglas Winter that the first draft of *IT* had taken too much out of him, and that he felt he'd said everything he had to say on the subject of monsters. After the failure of "The Cannibals," he managed to produce a handful of short stories that fit his name brand—from the remarkably sophisticated ghost story "The Reach" to the clinically gruesome "Survivor Type" (a story that the author later claimed "goes a little bit too far, even for me"[242])—but he was leaning more and more toward science fiction and fantasy. "The Word Processor of the Gods," "Mrs. Todd's Shortcut," and "The Ballad of the Flexible Bullet" represent a point in King's career when the line between fiction and reality became

241 King: "How" 321

242 Grant: "Interview" 80

so blurry that the author's characters were getting irretrievably lost in alternate universes.

For years, King had been making short trips into one particular fantasy realm to tell the tale of a mysterious gunslinger named Roland Deschain. He came up with the idea while still in college, and slowly expanded it into a series of short stories. *The Magazine of Fantasy & Science Fiction* published the first one, "The Gunslinger," in 1978, and followed up with "The Way Station" in 1980, then "The Oracle and the Mutants," "The Slow Mutants," and "The Gunslinger and the Dark Man" in 1981. In the summer of 1982, publisher Donald M. Grant collected the five stories into a limited edition novel called *The Dark Tower: The Gunslinger*. The publication escaped the notice of Stephen King's fan base, which suited the author just fine because he wasn't exactly sure what Roland's story meant, or where it was headed. Although he had already sketched out sections of a follow-up book, *The Dark Tower* remained a complete mystery to him.[243]

At first glance, *The Gunslinger* is a traditional western about an archetypal hero, Roland, pursuing an enigmatic Man in Black across the desert. What distinguishes it from other westerns is the fact that it takes place in a parallel universe where magic is real and technology is taboo. In the vernacular of the story, Roland's world has "moved on." There are hints that the place called Mid-World was once very much like our own world, before it was robbed of its vitality and overrun by mutants. Now an advanced stage of entropy has set in, and Roland's pursuit of the Man in Black is related to a desperate final hope to reverse the process.

Unlike the heroes of *The Stand* and *IT*, King's other early epics, Roland is a relatively coldhearted loner. He sacrifices his surrogate son, a boy named Jake who hails from 1970s New York, in order to continue his quest. When he finally catches up to his quarry, the Man in Black suggests that Roland's quest is a meaningless riddle—only so much fear in a handful of dust. He offers no answers, because King did not know the answers yet and had no inkling that he ever would. He tried, in vain, to forget the riddle.

King and his co-author Peter Straub created a comparable parallel universe in their joint novel *The Talisman*, a story that likewise

243 Vincent

originated in King's college years, as he explained to biographer Douglas Winter:

> *I must have been nineteen or twenty, originally, when it occurred to me to write a story about a woman who is a failed actress and her young son, living in a deserted resort area on the Atlantic coast while she waited to die, and what it would be like. And it occurred to me that the kid would try to find something that would save her.*[244]

As with *The Gunslinger*, King initially felt overwhelmed by the scope of the story and quickly abandoned it. He returned to it in 1981 only with Straub's help. King told Winter that his co-author's modifications were what really brought the story to life, prompting him to claim that "it's probably more his book than it is mine."[245] Straub himself says that he may have contributed the central idea that *The Talisman* is set in two parallel universes, late twentieth century America and The Territories, and that its main character, twelve-year-old Jack Sawyer, is magically able to "flip" back and forth between those two universes.[246] Whatever the case, *The Talisman* became a project through which King expanded on his core beliefs about the dangers of rationalism and the necessity for magic.

The first half of the novel is a coming-of-age story with shades of Charles Dickens's *Oliver Twist* and Mark Twain's *The Adventures of Huckleberry Finn*, two of King's favorite novels. Jack sets out like Roland Deschain on a quest toward a mysterious destination; his Dark Tower is the Alhambra, or Black Hotel, in northern California. To get there, he has to cross the continent from east to west, like the nineteenth century American pioneers. That means passing beyond The Outposts, the western frontier of The Territories, and through The Blasted Lands, a radiation fallout zone where the hills have eyes. Along the way Jack gets exploited by the owner of a sleazy roadhouse, enslaved by the sadistic headmaster of an evangelistic orphanage, and hunted by the ruthless businessman who murdered his father. Luckily, he also befriends a teenage werewolf who is willing to die for Jack's sake.

---

244 Winter: *Stephen* 158
245 Winter: *Stephen* 158
246 Wiater 171

The second half of the novel reads like a trial run for the ongoing *Dark Tower* saga. Jack continues his quest after joining up with his childhood friend Richard Sloat, taking a train—a demon, in the eyes of the Territory's inhabitants—through the Blasted Lands. When the boys finally reach the Black Hotel, Jack finds the magic talisman that he hopes will cure his mother. He soon learns, however, that the talisman has a will of its own. It tests Jack's resolve the way that the One Ring tests Frodo in *The Lord of the Rings*, and Jack quickly realizes that he has not simply found a source of healing magic; he has found the source of *everything*. The authors refer to the talisman as the axle or nexus of all possible worlds. When the boy approaches it, he experiences "light and heat and a sensation of true goodness, of *whiteness*."[247] When he picks it up, he realizes that the talisman is not just a doorway to other worlds, but also the worlds themselves and all the spaces between them. When he holds it, Jack becomes all of those things. King and Straub write: "Here was enough transcendentalism to drive even a cave-dwelling Tibetan holy man insane. Jack Sawyer was everywhere; Jack Sawyer was everything. [. . .] *He was God. God, or something so close as to make no difference.*"[248] The end of Jack's quest is a profound mystical experience; the boy sees clearly into the nature of all creation. In a brief coda, however, he begins to grow up and forget about the talisman, leaving the magic behind with his childhood. It's a telling commentary on the basic journey of everyman's life, and not a bad setup for a sequel.

King followed up with another coming-of-age fantasy, this one written for his daughter Naomi, who (according to the book's dust jacket) had "made it clear that she loves me, but has very little interest in my vampires, ghoulies, and slushy crawling things." In a 1986 interview, the author sarcastically labeled *The Eyes of the Dragon* the "kiss of death" for his writing career, noting embarrassedly, "It's not a fairy story exactly, but it's got dragons in it and things."[249] Around the same time, he defended the work by saying that "any children's story should be a story for grownups, like *Treasure Island* or *The Hobbit* or something, where you can read it to a child and child will love it, but you can see or hear reverberations in the story that maybe the

247 King: *Talisman* 698
248 King: *Talisman* 704
249 Schaefer 199

child doesn't hear because he doesn't have the same experience."[250] Certainly the tale had reverberations in King's later fiction.

The Eyes of the Dragon revolves around two brothers, heirs apparent to the throne of the kingdom of Delain—a place that seems to exist somewhere like The Territories or Mid-World (though King's official research assistant Robin Furth decisively asserts that *Eyes* "doesn't fit into the history of Roland's world"[251]). Peter, the older brother, seems destined to take the throne, and his prospective reign bodes well for the future. That future changes, however, when a wicked sorcerer named Flagg frames Peter for the murder of his father, which leads to the crowning of his weaker-willed brother Thomas.

The characterizations of Flagg and Thomas are the most mature aspects of the book. King plays off of his initial concept for the ageless villain of *The Stand*, depicting Flagg as a creature obsessed not merely with gaining power but rather with creating chaos. He writes:

> *Being a King did not interest [Flagg] because the heads of Kings all too often found their way to spikes on castle walls when things went wrong. But the advisors to Kings . . . the spinners in the shadows . . . such people usually melted away like evening shadows at dawning as soon as the headsman's axe started to fall. Flagg was a sickness, a fever looking for a cool brew to heat up. He hooded his actions just as he hooded his face.*[252]

Stephen King's brand of evil, "the conscious will to do harm," requires a vessel, and—as in *The Stand*—weak and lonely human beings serve the purpose quite naturally. In this case, Thomas becomes corrupted, taking the throne while his innocent brother wastes away in a tower dungeon. Despite Thomas's failures, the author urges us not to judge the younger brother too harshly: "Thomas was not exactly a good boy, but you must not think that made him a bad boy. He was sometimes a sad boy, often a confused boy [. . .] and often a jealous boy, but he wasn't a bad boy."[253] In the end, Peter outwits Flagg and Thomas comes around to his brother's side. Therein lies King's hidden "grownup" message: People *can* change. Such a possibility offers hope even for someone like Roland Deschain.

250 Blue 49
251 Furth 643
252 King: *Eyes* 41
253 King: *Eyes* 49

Cancer of the Pseudonym

For years, King's humanism was counterbalanced by his more cynical Richard Bachman persona, his "dark half." Accordingly, during the period when King was writing his most fantastic stories, Bachman remained mired in grim, naturalistic horror. The author explains in his second introduction to *The Bachman Books*:

> *Bachman had become a kind of Id for me; he said the things I couldn't, and the thought of him out there on his New Hampshire dairy farm—not a best-selling writer who gets his name in some stupid* Forbes *list of entertainers too rich for their own good, or his face on the* Today *show or doing cameos in movies—quietly writing his books, gave him leave to think in ways I could not think and speak in ways I could not speak."*[254]

Despite this claim, the fifth novel published under the Bachman moniker actually has more in common with *Pet Sematary*, published one year earlier, than it does with the earlier Bachman novels. *Thinner* is a straight-ahead horror story revolving around a gypsy curse—it's a werewolf story for weight watchers. It is also, like *Pet Sematary*, a complex morality tale. Rather than a story about simple good and evil, it is about global actions and consequences. "Everybody pays," the gypsy says, "even for things they dint do." This collusion of fate and chance clearly represents Stephen King's worldview, not Richard Bachman's. (One of the characters in the book even comments, accusingly, "You were starting to sound a little like a Stephen King novel for a while there...")

The similarities to King's earlier work were too glaring to go unnoticed, and an astute bookstore clerk named Steve Brown eventually blew the author's cover in an April 1985 exposé in *The Washington Post*. Six months later, all of Richard Bachman's early novels were back in print, collected in a single volume under the byline of Stephen King. At that point King pronounced his alter ego dead, citing "cancer of the pseudonym" as the cause of death. There was still, however, the matter of another novel that King's Id had been writing on that imaginary New Hampshire farm.

254 King: "Why"

King's childhood friend Chris Chesley has suggested that the specter of *Misery* had been with Stephen King since he was a kid. Chesley explained to Steven J. Spignesi, "He talks about a recurrent dream that he has. He says that when he's anxious, he has this dream where he's alone in an upstairs room in a house, and he's writing as fast as he can, and there's a woman with an axe trying to get in."[255] King places the origin of the story a bit later:

> *In the early 1980s, my wife and I went to London on a combined business/pleasure trip. I fell asleep on the plane and had a dream about a popular writer [. . .] who fell into the clutches of a psychotic fan living on a farm somewhere out in the back of the beyond. The fan was a woman isolated by her growing paranoia. She kept some livestock in the barn, including her pet pig, Misery. The pig was named after the continuing main character in the writer's best-selling bodice-rippers.*[256]

Around 1984, King began writing the story of author Paul Sheldon and his "number one fan" Annie Wilkes, with the plan of publishing it under his pseudonym.[257] At first, he thought it would be "about escape, pure and simple." Later, he realized that he was "actually talking about something as opposed to just telling a story."[258] He was, in fact, writing a book *about writing*. In a sense, King felt that Annie Wilkes represented the publishing world that was impatiently awaiting his next bestseller. She also represented the portion of his readership that wanted him to keep churning out *more of the same*.

In *Misery*, Paul Sheldon has earned fame and fortune by writing formulaic romance novels about a character named Misery Chastain. More recently, he has decided to kill off the character and discontinue the series in order to focus on more personal and prestigious writing projects. Enter Annie Wilkies, who literally burns Sheldon's literary passion project and forces him to write a new Misery novel for her. The parallels with King's career are obvious. The bestselling "horror writer" wanted to expand beyond the horror genre, but he was getting some resistance from his publisher

255 Spignesi: 'Talk" 51
256 King: *On Writing* 165
257 Edward Gross 32
258 Beahm: *Story* 138

and his constant readers. The publication of *Thinner* under the name Richard Bachman suggests that King knew he was not done with horror, but nevertheless wanted to separate himself from the easy (perhaps lazy) branding. One does not have to sympathize with a millionaire in order to understand the real anxiety that comes from high-pressure deadlines, high expectations and an inability to control one's future. These are the horrors that Paul Sheldon—and Stephen King—confront in *Misery*.

Echoing his sentiments about some of his earlier books, King says he initially envisioned a very bleak ending for *Misery*. He couldn't imagine how Paul Sheldon would escape from the trap he found himself in. As he wrote, however, King slowly worked out his fellow author's problems in his head and came to a surprising conclusion: "Paul Sheldon turned out to be a good deal more resourceful than I initially thought, and his efforts to play Scheherazade and save his life gave me a chance to say some things about the redemptive power of writing that I had long felt but never articulated."[259] Sheldon ultimately sacrifices his new Misery novel in order to escape from Annie. His freedom comes directly from the realization that it is the writing *process*, rather than the finished *product*, that defines him. The completed novel is for the fans, the act of writing is for the writer alone. Sheldon reflects:

> *It was good to be done—always good to be done. Good to have produced, to have caused a thing to be. In a numb sort of way he understood and appreciated the bravery of the act, of making little lives that weren't, creating the appearance of motion and the illusion of warmth. He understood—now, finally—that he was a bit of a dullard at doing this trick, but it was the only one he knew, and if he always ended up doing it ineptly, he at least never failed to do it with love.*[260]

In a 1986 interview with Charles Platt, King made a telling confession that he couldn't imagine himself as anything other than a writer. Ever since he was a kid, he said, writing had provided his only significant sense of self. He added, "And that's a danger, because you tie up your self-image, your masculinity, whatever, in being able

259 King: *On Writing* 168
260 King: *Misery* 288

to do this, which means that if you lose it, you have nothing left."[261] *Misery* reasserted his identity as a writer, but it also revealed another, more troubling truth to him.

Paul Sheldon's captivity represented another trap that Stephen King found himself in. The author explains his realization nakedly in his 2000 memoir *On Writing*: "Annie was coke, Annie was booze, and I decided I was tired of being Annie's pet writer." After completing *Misery*, King suddenly understood that ever since he had written *The Shining*, a story about an alcoholic writer, he had been an addict. This trap was more difficult to escape from, for one simple (but overwhelming) reason: "I was afraid that I wouldn't be able to work anymore if I quit drinking and drugging."[262] He couldn't quit because he feared he wouldn't be able to write; if he couldn't write, he feared he wouldn't exist. Stephen King simply couldn't imagine himself as anything other than a writer who was telling stories to stay alive. That's why, in spite of his overwhelming success, he was working harder than ever; he was simply afraid to stop. While making revisions on four novels slated for publication in 1986 and 1987 (*IT*, *Misery*, *The Dark Tower II: The Drawing of the Three* and *The Tommyknockers*), he frantically, perhaps desperately, pursued a second career as a filmmaker.

261 Platt 256
262 King: *On Writing* 98

The King of Hollywood (II)

In the early 1980s, Stephen King's brand had been overwhelmingly strong in Hollywood. In 1983 alone, three major film adaptations of his work were released into theaters: Lewis Teague's *Cujo*, David Cronenberg's *The Dead Zone*, and *John Carpenter's Christine*. They were quickly followed by *Children of the Corn* (1984) and *Firestarter* (1984). King was involved in the development of four out of five of the scripts, making it clear that he was very interested in a future in Hollywood. Eventually, producer Dino DeLaurentiis gave King free rein, allowing the author an unusual amount of authority over the productions of *Cat's Eye* (1985) and *Silver Bullet* (1985), and then granting the author a chance to make his directorial debut with *Maximum Overdrive* (1986). For King, all of these projects constituted a crash course in filmmaking.

Bolstered by his experience on *Creepshow*, King himself wrote the initial screenplay for *Cujo*, which was later revised by (and ultimately credited to) Don Carlos Dunaway and Lauren Currier. The biggest change between the book and screenplay was the ending of the story, as King explains:

> *The movie people came along and said, "What do you think about if the kid lived?" And I said fine, because movies are not books, and what they do doesn't bother me. I thought it would be fun to see what happened if he* did *live. Even though I knew that it wasn't real. That would be make-believe. The kid really died.*[263]

The new ending was a result of Lewis Teague's goal to convey "an entirely different theme" than the book, which he explained to Steven J. Spignesi:

> *I see them both as showing that most of our fears are imaginary, and that when we give credence to imaginary fears, they can then become self-fulfilling prophecies. Most of the fears that the family were suffering from in the story were imaginary. The husband was afraid of financial ruin because he'd lost one of his clients. The woman was afraid of growing old and wasting her*

263 Sherman 54

> *life away in this rural town after they moved out of there from New York. And all these fears were filtering down to the son, who began imagining that he could see monsters in the closet. I think the film shows what happens when people start believing in imaginary fears. And because all these fears had to do with the future—and no one can predict the future—none of those fears were real. But the family believed the fears and began to act on them as if they were real. And it's not until they face a real fear at the end—the fear of the rabid dog that's attacking the car—and face up to that, that they can put the rest of their fears in perspective.*[264]

Based on this perspective, Teague says, it would have been self-defeating to let the kid die, because then the theme about imaginary fears would have failed to resonate. King saw that the veteran director not only had a solid grasp on the story but also a remarkable knowledge of the techniques of terror, which he put to good use in the finished film. The author enthusiastically praised *Cujo* as a faithful adaptation of the book—"probably the first Stephen King novel *per se* that's been put on film"—and "one of the scariest things you'll ever see."[265]

The Dead Zone, produced by Dino DeLaurentiis and directed by David Cronenberg, is equally successful in its own right. The film is ultimately more of a character drama than a horror movie, but it didn't start out that way. According to Cronenberg, King delivered an initial screenplay that stripped away the heart of his own novel. The director explained to interviewer Chris Rodley, without mincing words:

> *Stephen King's own script was terrible. It was not only bad as a script, it was the kind of script that his own fans would have torn me apart for doing; they would have seen me as the one who destroyed his work. It was basically a really ugly, unpleasant slasher script. The Castle Rock killer in the middle of the movie becomes the lead, and it was "Let's show lots of his victims." It began with Greg Stillson torturing some kid in a back room, and it never went into Johnny's past.*[266]

264 Spignesi: "Dog" 572-573

265 Gagne 102, Grant: "Interview" 83

266 Rodley 113

Screenwriter Jeffrey Boam also wrote a competing draft in which Frank Dodd, the Castle Rock Killer, plays a much larger role.[267] Boam has said that he was trying to service a very different concept of the film, imparted by director Stanley Donen, who was attached to the project before Cronenberg came on board. Boam explains the eventual shift in focus from Dodd to Johnny Smith: "The basic difference between Stanley Donen's and David Cronenberg's approach to the material was that David ultimately wanted to see the story through Johnny's eyes. Stanley wanted it from an objective or outside point of view."[268]

Essentially, Cronenberg conceived *The Dead Zone* as a Frankenstein story, where "God is the scientist who experiments are not always working out [and] the Johnny Smith character is one of his failed experiments."[269] The quasi-religious elements of the novel, in which Johnny overtly questions his place in God's order, are mostly absent from the film. Perhaps that's why King has suggested that the adaptation, despite its technical accomplishments, is comparatively "thin" and "cold-blooded."[270] If Kubrick's *The Shining* is an atheist's take on an agnostic novel, then Cronenberg's *The Dead Zone* might be regarded as a vaguely deistic version of a vaguely Christian novel. Metaphysical philosophies aside, everyone seems to agree that the film is faithful to the *tone* of King's novel; it succeeds as both a character drama and an existential tragedy.

The third and most troubling Stephen King adaptation of 1983 was John Carpenter's *Christine*. Carpenter was originally supposed to helm a film adaptation of *Firestarter*, working from a screenplay by Bill Lancaster, but Universal scrapped that project (at least temporarily) after the commercial failure of Carpenter's 1982 film *The Thing*. Producer Richard Kobritz, who had worked with Carpenter previously on the TV movie *Someone's Watching Me!* (1979), turned Universal's loss into his gain, hiring the filmmaker to adapt *Christine* for Columbia Pictures.

Carpenter has since said that he was not very enthusiastic about the "haunted car stuff," believing that it would be difficult to make the picture genuinely scary.[271] In an attempt to take a subtler road

267 Conner 59
268 Rodley 114
269 Rodley 113
270 Wood: "Stephen" 44
271 Interview with the author 3/31/08

through the material, he and screenwriter Bill Phillips eliminated the specter of Roland LeBay from the story and began the film with a scene showing that Christine was "born" evil. Years later, Carpenter admitted that he regretted the decision, saying, "I made a big mistake by taking out Roland LeBay's rotting corpse in the back seat. I guess I was just tired of rotting corpses at the time, and I tried to do it all with the car. I failed."[272] To be fair, the finished film still boasts a captivating lead performance by Keith Gordon, as well as several impressive action sequences. Nevertheless, John Carpenter's *Christine* has its problems. Overall, King is fair in his final analysis:

> *The two main characters [John Stockwell as Dennis Guilder and Alexandra Paul as Leigh Cabot] were just sort of forgettable. They didn't generate any real magnetism among the three of them. [But] still there's a lot of Carpenter. There's some of the excitement that he can generate. When the car's going along the road, and it's in flames, and it's chasing these people, that's pretty good.*[273]

Unfortunately, *Christine* was not the box office bonanza that Columbia expected. Like *Cujo* and *The Dead Zone*, it earned roughly double its production cost in theatrical release—which is, in Hollywood terms, only a modest success. Most significantly, each of these three Stephen King adaptations earned slightly less than the previous one, a trend suggesting that the author's drawing power was already beginning to wane. That didn't stop other filmmakers from adapting his work, but it probably provided a greater sense of urgency.

In 1984, New World Pictures produced an ultra-low-budget adaptation of "Children of the Corn," based on a concept that had been floating around for years—ever since King sold the story rights to documentary filmmaker Harry Wiland in 1979. Wiland and King had collaborated on several early drafts of the script, including one with a "Vietnam subtext."[274] Later, screenwriter George Goldsmith (who received full credit for the finished film) took over, and tried to "make clearer, more linear, certain ideas [King] touched upon but did not develop."[275] Goldsmith felt so strongly about his contributions

272 Wood: "King's" 44
273 Wood: "King's" 44
274 Conner 82
275 Conner 83

that he petitioned the Writer's Guild for sole screenwriting credit on the film. King let him have it, thereby saving himself some embarrassment over the ham-handed results. Critics and viewers savaged the finished film, and in a 1985 issue of Castle Rock magazine, King himself called it one of the worst movies of all time, ranking it with Ed Wood's infamous *Plan 9 from Outer Space* (1959) and Herschell Gordon Lewis's *Blood Feast* (1963). (To be fair, he later softened his stance, telling Jesse Horsting that the film is "not as bad as it could be, but it's not very good."[276])

The filmmakers, however, weren't smarting for very long, since the profit margin for *Children of the Corn* turned out to be far greater than all of the previous year's Stephen King adaptations. As a result, the film has spawned a staggering seven direct-to-video sequels as well as a TV remake. In a 1985 interview, Stephen King described his feelings about this travesty by comparing movie adaptations of his work to sending a daughter off to college. He explained, "You hope she'll do well. You hope that she won't fall in with the wrong people. You hope she won't be raped at a fraternity party, which is really close to what happened to 'Children of the Corn,' in a metaphoric sense."[277]

A month after the *Children of the Corn* debacle, producer Dino DeLaurentiis released his second Stephen King adaptation. Unfortunately, *Firestarter* lacked the gravitas of *The Dead Zone*. In subsequent interviews King placed the blame on director Mark L. Lester, noting that the screenplay by Stanley Mann was "a masterpiece," but characterizing the finished film as "flavorless," "like cafeteria mashed potatoes."[278] At one point he even likened *Firestarter* to *Myra Breckinridge* (1970), a film that he had described elsewhere as "absolutely dreadful," like "watching slow-motion footage of a head-on collision."[279] His criticism sparked a heated exchange with Lester in the pages of *Cinefantastique* magazine. Lester asserted that King had been intimately involved with the production of the film and had praised the final cut, before going on to criticize it so ruthlessly.[280] King countered that his input during the production was minimal, and that "Mark's assertion that I saw the movie and

276 Horsting 122
277 Modderno 144
278 King: "King" 35, Ewing 109
279 Modderno 142, Cadigan 43, King: *Danse* 227
280 Wood: "Blasting" 34

loved it is erroneous."[281] The author did, however, change his stance a bit, attributing the film's failure to a combination of miscasting and bombastic producing—a series of small mistakes that added up to a perfect storm.[282] By the time he made these comments, in the wake of his own directorial debut, King presumably had a better understanding of how such things could happen.

King insists that he never intended to become so heavily involved in film adaptations of his own work. He initially refused to write the screenplay for *Cat's Eye* (1985), but was convinced by DeLaurentiis, who flew up to his home in Bangor for a private conversation. "I'm still not sure how he did it," the author quips. "I think it was a form of benign hypnotism. I started by shaking my head and saying it absolutely couldn't be done, my schedule was killing me already, and ended by nodding the fool thing and telling him I could have a first-draft screenplay for him in a month or so."[283] The finished film, directed by Lewis Teague, was a commercial dud, but DeLaurentiis was unbowed. He immediately started persuading King to write a screenplay adaptation of his mini-novel *Cycle of the Werewolf.* Once again, the author refused. Then he got an idea. "I happened to have the house to myself on an overcast Sunday afternoon," King remembers:

> *Lying on the sofa with the Sunday paper beside me, I was flicking through TV channels and happened on* To Kill a Mockingbird, *a movie I hadn't seen since I saw it in first run [. . .] When it ended I actually cried a little—it was the voice of the girl, mostly, recalling those events which were playing themselves out before my eyes. I turned off the TV and thought: What would happen if you tried to use that elegiac, retrospective, and rather gentle form of narration to tell the story of Marty Coslaw and his duel with the werewolf?*[284]

With that in mind, King agreed to write the screenplay for *Silver Bullet* (1985). The script, published as a supplement to a retitled edition of *Cycle of the Werewolf,* exhibits a surprising lack of visual detail. The resulting film, helmed by first-time director Daniel

281 King: "King" 35
282 Wood: "Blasting" 46
283 King: "Foreword," *Silver* 15
284 King: "Foreword," *Silver* 15

Attias, demonstrates the same lack of visual storytelling experience. Compounding the problem, the solemn and sentimental voiceover is at odds with the film's crude humor and cartoonish FX. When King saw the final cut, he opined that "it's either very good indeed or a complete bust."[285] *Silver Bullet* did so-so business in its theatrical release, but was mostly forgotten afterward.

After years of sitting on the sidelines while filmmakers directed his screenplays, King was understandably curious about whether or not he could successfully bring his own work to the screen. Dino DeLaurentiis was only too happy to grant him the opportunity to find out. When it came time for him to make his directing debut, King decided to adapt "Trucks," a short story about a group of truck-stop patrons that are stalked by driverless vehicles. "Trucks" is not one of King's best stories, but the theme of the story had become increasingly important to the author over the years. He explained in 1983, "Machines make me nervous. They just make me nervous. Because I live in a world that's surrounded by them. It's impossible to get away from them."[286] He figured that if he could translate this genuine fear to the screen, *Maximum Overdrive* might be the cinematic equivalent of Steven Spielberg's debut *Duel* (1971).

From day one, the experiment was an unwieldy one. In *Maximum Overdrive*, it's not just the vehicles that turn against humanity; every machine in the world begins to rebel. Electric knives, lawnmowers, toy cars, video games, even Coke machines turn into homicidal maniacs in the film. King sets up this idea—as well as the zany tone of the film—in the opening scene, which features the author himself as an obnoxious bumpkin (a role he had test-driven in George Romero's *Knightriders* and *Creepshow*) who gets into an altercation with a foul-mouthed ATM machine. That scene is followed by a cartoonish sequence in which a drawbridge opens while dozens of vehicles are crossing it. Instead of taking on a life of their own, the vehicles become props in a passive demolition derby. The filmmaker lovingly depicts the disastrous spectacle in slow motion, suggesting that what he really wanted to do was make a Hal Needham movie. That's not necessarily a worthless ambition, but it's not what audiences expected from Stephen King.

---

285 King: "Foreword," *Silver* 16
286 King: "Evening" 21

Instead of scaring viewers, King continued to pummel them with crude action, absurd humor, and generally vulgar characterizations—as if he was determined to preemptively spit in the eye of anyone who dared to take him seriously. In a 1986 interview, he described the resulting film as "a combination of Monty Python and Jack the Ripper."[287] That spirit of gleeful anarchy, however, was mostly overrun by lazy storytelling and campy filmmaking. After the film failed dismally at the box office, King blamed himself for over-preparing. He told Paul Gagne that by storyboarding every single shot in advance, "I went against every creative impulse that's ever moved me, which has always been intuitive."[288] His explanation to Tony Magistrale, many years later, seems more to the point. "The problem with that film," he said bluntly, "is that I was coked out of my mind all through its production, and I really didn't know what I was doing."[289]

Maximum Overdrive might have signaled the end of King's short reign in Hollywood, but director Rob Reiner's adaptation of "The Body" provided a new beginning. Given a very limited release only two weeks after King's high-profile fiasco, *Stand by Me* turned out to be the most successful screen adaptation of the author's work since *Carrie*—in both financial and artistic terms. King himself raved, "It's a wonderful picture. It's as simple as that."[290] Ironically, even though the film was based on one of the author's most personal stories, the distributors decided to downplay the connection to the bestselling author. Presumably they recognized that the Stephen King name brand might drive some audiences away from the film. The filmmakers—Reiner, along with screenwriters Bruce A. Evans and Andrew Scheinman—likewise downplayed the more horrific aspects of King's novella, eliminating hints of a ghost story in favor of defining the main character through his emotional isolation. *Stand by Me*, bolstered by remarkable performances from its cast of rising stars, became the surprise hit of the summer, and earned the author a new kind of credibility.

It was a few years before Hollywood was again ready to gamble on the Stephen King brand. The year 1987 saw the release of three

---

287 Strauss 209
288 Gagne 215
289 Magistrale 20
290 Edward Gross 36

theatrical King adaptations, but they were mostly reheated leftovers. Richard Rubinstein produced *Creepshow 2*, an anthology of King stories adapted by George Romero, while writer/director Larry Cohen concocted an unlikely *Return to 'Salem's Lot*. Even stranger was screenwriter Steven E. de Souza's transformation of Richard Bachman's *The Running Man* into a vehicle for Arnold Schwarzenegger. Few viewers or critics associated the sci-fi thriller with Stephen King, which was probably best for everyone concerned. The author's only contribution to the motion picture medium in the following year was an original teleplay for Rubinstein's TV series *Tales from the Darkside*. "Sorry, Right Number" was routine at best. For the time being, the Stephen King craze had abated in Hollywood.

The Mystery of Ka-Tet

In 1987, after the publication of his magnum opus *IT* and the failure of *Maximum Overdrive*, King was contemplating retirement. His most recent novels, *The Dark Tower II: The Drawing of the Three*, and *The Tommyknockers*, had prompted the writer to make a serious assessment of his creative life. In both the stories, the central characters are struggling to overcome substance abuse and addiction, and King realized that he was subconsciously writing about problems in his private life.

In *The Drawing of the Three*, the gunslinger named Roland Deschain literally gets inside the head of a New York drug addict named Eddie Dean. As the story unfolds, Roland suffers from a physical infection that requires treatment with prescription antibiotics; without drugs, he'll die. In contrast, Eddie is a heroin addict who senses that he is one hit away from a fatal overdose; if he keeps using, he'll die. Since both characters exist within the same body, the story reads like the symbolic confession of a reluctant drug addict. King understood the dual mindset only too well.

When his wife Tabitha staged an intervention to force him to get help or "get the hell out," the author remembers that he recognized the seriousness of the problem but nevertheless remained reluctant to change. In his mind, the effects of his addiction on his family and friends (not to mention his own body) weren't the only issue at play. Above all, he feared that if he stopped drinking and drugging, he would lose his mysterious access to the fictional worlds that defined him. In his mind, it was the illicit substances that allowed him to "flip" into his own Territories, and he wasn't prepared to give up that power.

King has always spoken of fiction writing as a mysterious process, likening it to telepathy and asserting that in some sense the stories control the writer more than the writer controls the stories. This vague idea suggests an essential faith in a power beyond the rational human mind—a faith that had become increasingly explicit in his work in the 1980s. If he gave up alcohol and drugs, King believed, he would need something that gave him the same access to those other worlds. He might have turned immediately to Alcoholics Anonymous, but he wasn't yet able to place his complete faith in a Higher Power.

During the seven-year period when he was writing *IT*, King granted a handful of interviews in which he ruminated on the topics of church and theology. Noting that he grew up in the Methodist church and was now "nonpracticing," he said in 1980, "I try to keep church in my heart. I don't want to say that I'm a pantheist or that I try to go out and look on Nature as the work of God—because it isn't like that. It's trying to feel what it is that the world has to tell us about something that is more than the world." In the same interview, he clarified his belief in a transcendent God: "I'm pretty convinced there is a God, an Oversoul, some kind of sentient being who's in charge of everything that goes on here." He also carefully added, "I haven't figured it out to my satisfaction."[291] In a 1982 interview, he told interviewer Bob Spitz that he felt "more religious now than ever in my life" but noted that "everything that I see about organized religion appalls me."[292]

Some of the details in *IT* suggest that King was striving for his own unique formulation of God, and in these sections he finally began to realize some of the key elements of the mythology of *The Dark Tower*. According to *The Dark Tower VI: Song of Susannah*, a 2004 novel that quotes King's personal journals from the 1980s, the formulation of a Higher Power came to the author the same way his stories always did—out of the depths of his subconscious—in November 1984. King writes in his journal:

> *I had a dream last night that I think breaks the creative logjam on* IT. *Suppose there's a kind of Beam holding the Earth (or even multiple Earths) in place. And that the Beam's generator rests on the shell of a turtle? I could make that part of the book's climax. I know it sounds crazy, but I'm sure I read somewhere that in Hindu mythology there's a great turtle that bears us all on his shell, and that he serves Gan, the creative overforce.*[293]

Within the context of *IT*, the frequent references to a cosmic Turtle do seem a bit odd, offering only oblique hints at a much larger

291 Freff 141
292 Spitz 187
293 King: *Song* 520

mythology that the author had not yet worked out. For the time being, King simply defines The Turtle as the creator of the known universe; according to Pennywise, The Turtle vomited it up and then withdrew into his shell. The Turtle, then, is a Deistic representation of a god that does not interfere with his creation. Bill Denbrough, however, senses a greater force—"the final Other," "perhaps the creator of the Turtle," "the author of all that is"—just beyond the reach of his imagination. After defeating the monster, Bill even hears the Voice of that "final Other." The voice says, "*Son, you did real good.*"[294]

King is careful not to get too specific about defining this paternal entity, but he carefully distinguishes it from the power of The White in *The Stand*. There is no *deus ex machina* in *IT*, no benevolent God intervening on behalf of the characters. The God-like force that arises at the end of *IT* is more abstract, and comes from the collective *belief* of the characters in some higher power that has brought them together. Because they *fight together*, the characters are able to overcome their fears and survive. Because they *believe together*, the characters actualize God as a real, active force in the world they live in.

King imports this collective-creative force into *The Dark Tower II: The Drawing of the Three* as the concept of "ka-tet," which serves as his solution to Roland's emotional isolation. "Ka-tet" designates a group of people brought together by "ka," a word that approximates duty + destiny. In the terms of King's story, "ka-tet" means that, unless Roland can learn to love and trust other people, his quest is doomed. The gunslinger's own thoughts echo this realization:

> *If you have given up your heart for the Tower, Roland, you have already lost. A heartless creature is a loveless creature, and a loveless creature is a beast. To be a beast is perhaps bearable, although the man who has become one will surely pay hell's own price in the end, but what if you should gain our object? What if you should, heartless, actually storm the Dark Tower and win it? If there is naught but darkness in your heart, what could you do except degenerate from beast to monster?*[295]

Or, to repeat the question in overtly Biblical terms:

---

294 King: *IT* 1048

295 King: *Dark Tower II* 265

> *For what will it profit a man if he gains the whole world and forfeits his soul?* (Matthew 16:26)

King might have been asking himself similar questions about his own fate. What if he sacrificed his wife and family for the sake of his writing? If he traveled the rest of his road alone, would he ever attain peace or satisfaction in his life? In a sense, the author answered himself in his next book, *The Tommyknockers*.

The Tommyknockers starts out as the story of two writers, Jim Gardner and Bobbi Anderson. Gard is a self-loathing booze hound who has all but given up on life until his only friend Bobbi suddenly develops a similar problem. After discovering a buried spaceship in her backyard, Bobbi falls under the spell of an alien force that instantly lights up her mind and gradually destroys her body. King explains: "What you got was energy and a kind of superficial intelligence (the writer, Bobbi Anderson, creates a telepathic typewriter and an atomic hot-water heater, among other things). What you gave up in exchange was your soul. It was the best metaphor for drugs and alcohol my tired, overstressed mind could come up with."[296] In the novel, King describes Bobbi's addiction as follows:

> *The urge, simple and elemental, had nothing to do with her forebrain. It came baking up from someplace deeper inside. It had all the earmarks of some physical craving—for salt, for some coke or heroin or cigarettes or coffee. Her forebrain supplied logic; this other part supplied an almost incoherent imperative:* Dig on it, Bobbi, it's okay, dig on it, dig on it, shit, why not dig on it awhile more, you know you want to know what it is, so dig on it till you see what it is, dig dig dig.[297]

The author remembers routinely digging on the novel "with my heart running at a hundred and thirty beats a minute and cotton swabs stuck up my nose to stem the coke-induced bleeding."[298]

In the novel, Bobbi is only the first member of her town to develop mild psychic abilities. After a few weeks, all of her friends and neighbors have a sense of common purpose—everyone except Gard. Bobbi tries to explain to him what he's missing: "Telepaths

296 King: *On Writing* 97
297 King: *Tommyknockers* 65
298 King: *On Writing* 96

are at least to some degree precognitives, Gard, and precognitives are more apt to let themselves be guided by the currents, both large and small, that run through the universe. 'God' is the name some people give to those currents, but God's only a word."[299] For most of the novel, Gardner denies this "God" and chooses to ignore the terrible things that are happening all around him. He prefers to drown his sorrows in booze rather than face his fears. It is only in the final pages of the novel that he finally seeks out God on his own terms. Realizing that the alien groupthink is destroying the souls (as well as the bodies) of the people he cares about, he asks for God's help to destroy the source of the malign influence. God answers, granting Gard the strength to save his soul, and the soul of his community, at the cost of his life.

Despite the initial strength of the characterizations, *The Tommyknockers* remains a chaotic novel—not simply a story about the damaging effects of addiction, but also a damaged product of addiction. King himself has called the novel "self-indulgent," acknowledging that he lost his focus as a storyteller.[300] Indeed, the story and its eventual hero meander aimlessly for several hundred pages before achieving any real sense of purpose. If *Misery* was a warning from the author's subconscious mind that his addictive behavior was holding him hostage, *The Tommyknockers* was a self-portrait of a man in denial and full of secret self-loathing. Confronted with this reality, the author finally acknowledged the need for a change. In the end, he chose to save his soul and his family, even though he feared it might mean his death as a writer.[301]

When *The Tommyknockers* was published in the fall of 1987, King told Waldenbooks that his latest novel "was the clearance sale," adding that he was taking a hiatus from writing and publishing.[302] Around the same time, he told journalist Tyson Blue that his priorities in life had changed: "I've got a family to take care of, to be with, and I gotta be alone with myself sometimes and stuff like that. You know, just sort of let the well fill back up."[303] Like Roland, he realized that he couldn't get where he wanted to go by traveling alone. He also couldn't continue to write if writing came at the expense of

299 King: *Tommyknockers* 649
300 Flewelling
301 King: *On Writing* 97
302 Beahm: *Companion* 295
303 Blue 49

real life. "Life isn't a support system for art," King says, reflecting on the turning point of his life. "It's the other way around." [304]

304 King: *On Writing* 94

The Last Castle Rock Stories

In a 1990 interview to promote his new novel *The Dark Half*, Stephen King said that the process of creative writing had always fascinated him because it revealed "the mechanics of belief." Many of the characters in his early novels, he noted, undergo experiences that prompt them to question their most deeply held beliefs about the nature of reality. On one level, those novels are about the dance that a rational mind must go through in order to accept the unacceptable. When writing, King says, he goes through that same dance himself: "Basically what a writer does is sit down and say, I'm going to do something that ordinary day-to-day life forbids under most circumstances. I'm going to entertain my fantasies and make them as believable as I can."[305] He compares his writing experiences to meditation, self-hypnosis, even telepathy; the essential idea being that, when the rational self surrenders, an *other* self takes over. The challenge for the author, as for the characters, is to integrate irrational beliefs into reality without becoming helplessly delusional. It's a delicate dance along the very thin line between faith and madness.

The Dark Half is about a novelist who tries to escape the threat of madness by discarding an old pseudonym. For Thad Beaumont, writing under the influence of "George Stark" means surrendering control to a mysterious *other*—something that has become much more *real* than simply a troubled subconscious—and he no longer feels safe doing that. The novel reveals, however, that the influence of George Stark is not so easy for him to shake off. King writes:

> *Hadn't there always been a part of him in love with George Stark's simple violent nature? Hadn't part of him always admired George, a man who didn't stumble over things or bump into things, a man who never looked weak or silly, a man who would never have to fear the demons locked away in the liquor cabinet? A man with no wife or children to consider, with no loves to bind him or slow him down? A man who had never waded through a shitty student essay or agonized over a Budget*

305 Langston 10

> *Committee meeting? A man who had a sharp, straight answer to all of life's more difficult questions?*[306]

Thad is essentially addicted to George Stark, because George Stark helps him to escape his real world problems and insecurities.

King had been writing under a comparable influence for many years; alcohol and drugs helped him to surrender his rationality to the mysterious creative process, but they also gradually took away his self-control in real life. In *The Dark Half*, King and Beaumont are both struggling to beat old habits. Beaumont ultimately fails, and George Stark takes over. "The dream of being a writer overwhelms the reality of being a man," the author explains, and "delusive thinking overtakes rationality completely, with horrible consequences."[307] The same thing happens again in King's 1990 novella "Secret Window, Secret Garden," which revolves around a writer suffering from a split personality disorder. Both stories read like bleak predictions of King's own potential future. On at least a subconscious level, the author recognized that he was very close to surrendering everything to his own Mr. Hyde. In the end he decided to "trade writing for staying married and watching the kids grow up."[308] As it turned out, he didn't have to give up writing; his belief that the writing and the substance abuse problem were inseparable turned out to be untrue.

It would be difficult and perhaps unfair to divide King's work from the late 1980s and early 1990s in terms of his struggle with substance abuse, but it is worthwhile to note some marked changes in the content and themes of the work he produced between 1987 (when he started writing *The Dark Half*) and the fall of 1994 (when he completed the novel *Rose Madder)*. During that interval, King finished five additional novels (*Needful Things*, *The Dark Tower III: The Waste Lands*, *Gerald's Game*, *Dolores Claiborne* and *Insomnia*), four novellas (collected as *Four Past Midnight*), and more than a dozen short stories. The earliest short stories came about during a period when he was newly sober and suffering from writer's block. "Rainy Season," a story about a ritualistic sacrifice to a seemingly sadistic God, opened the floodgates for traditional sci-fi/horror fantasies like "The Night Flier" and "The Langoliers," as well as unconventional

306 King: *Dark Half* 328
307 King: "Importance"
308 King: *On Writing* 98

stories like "Dedication" (about a mother who is willing to do *anything* for her son). The latter suggested a new direction for the author, merging fantasy with the harsh, sobering realities of physical and psychological abuse.

In his introduction to *Four Past Midnight*, King writes that the stories written during this time period stand apart from his fantasy fare because of their unremittingly horrific *realism*:

> *[They] are different because they came from a mind which found itself turning, at least temporarily, to darker subjects. Time, for instance, and the corrosive effects it can have on the human heart. The past, and the shadows it throws upon the present—shadows where unpleasant things sometimes grow and even more unpleasant things hide . . . and grow fat.*[309]

King may have been thinking in particular of the novella "The Library Policeman," which began as a *Twilight Zone*-style yarn about an undead librarian, and evolved into something much more serious and challenging. The story revolves around a businessman named Sam Peebles who gets caught up in the supernatural mystery of "the library policeman" only to uncover repressed memories that he was sexually molested as a boy. A helpful friend tells Sam that his real battle is not with the supernatural threat but with his own haunted mind. She suggests that he can only overcome the monster by overcoming his own repression and denial of the molestation, explaining, "I think the real opposite of fear might be honesty. Honesty and belief."[310] Indeed, for the hero of this particular story, the key to defeating the supernatural monster is admitting that real monsters actually exist, and must be confronted. It is not difficult to draw a parallel between the self-consciously metaphorical tale and King's own battle with addiction; the first step in the famous twelve-step program of Alcoholics Anonymous is admitting that you have a problem.

"The Library Policeman" set the stage for two subsequent novels that would explore the long-term psychological effects of child abuse. Building on the themes of the short story "Dedication," *Dolores Claiborne* contrasts a mother's unflagging devotion to her child with

309 King: "Straight" xiv
310 King: "Library" 558

a father's ultimate betrayal. The question at the heart of the tale is not whether Dolores is a murderer (she is), but whether she can be a murderer *and still be a good mother. Gerald's Game*, a novel that is connected to *Dolores Claiborne* through its use of a common setting and theme, tells a similar story from the perspective of the abused child. The novel is mostly set in the mildly schizophrenic mind of Jessie Burlingame, a middle-aged woman whose unwillingness to confront a childhood violation has caused her to become both psychologically and physically trapped in her adult life. King summed up the theme of the book in a 2007 *London Times* podcast: "It's an ordinary, grim story about a little girl who is abused by her father and grows up to be a certain kind of woman. She is chained to the bed because she has been chained in a certain kind of life."[311]

With these two novels, King refutes the cliché that "time heals all wounds" in favor of the traditional Gothic formulation about "the sins of the father" and real-life cycles of violence. There is nothing supernatural about his latest expression of the timeworn theme; in his new storytelling mode, King refused to fall back on the scapegoat of supernatural metaphors, choosing instead to examine these horrors in the cold and rational light of day. It was not an easy transition, as the author conceded in a 1995 interview: "For me at this point, to write on a non-supernatural level is like learning to talk after you've had a stroke."[312] Nevertheless he refuses to allow himself, or his characters, any easy outs. When Jessie wishes for madness as a means of escape, King writes, "Madness would be a relief, but madness would not come."[313] For Dolores and Jessie, as for Sam Peebles, the only true escape lies in acknowledging and confronting the past. Only once that is done can there be hope for the future.

King seems to have had an equally strong desire to achieve some kind of closure on his own past. He conceived the novella "The Sun Dog" (the fourth story in *Four Past Midnight*) as a prologue to *Needful Things*, which he intended to be his last supernatural horror novel. In 1991, the author explained why he needed to leave that type of writing behind him: "I'm sure that I could make a very nice living just being Stephen King, the master of the modern horror story, unquote, for the rest of my life. But if it came down to just

311 Rogak 168
312 Marotta 110
313 King: *Gerald's* 295

doing that, I would rather not write at all."[314] To force himself to change, he conceived the symbolic destruction Castle Rock, the fictional town that had served as the setting for "The Body," *The Dead Zone*, *Cujo*, and *The Dark Half*.

In *Needful Things*, an antiques dealer named Leland Gaunt creates an atmosphere of chaos in Castle Rock by offering residents their most coveted material possessions. In exchange, he asks for payment in the form of a mean-spirited "trick" played on their friends and neighbors. One person at a time, Gaunt "cross-wires" the entire town, turning locals against each other until violence spills out into the street. The plot is reminiscent of the *Twilight Zone* episode "What You Need," about a street peddler who always magically produces the right product at the right time, as well as Richard Matheson's short story "The Distributor," in which a cold-hearted man drives his neighbors to violence through a series of increasingly cruel tricks. King, however, puts his own spin on the basic concept. The author says he intended *Needful Things* as a satire on consumerism, and tried to illustrate his belief that ordinary, everyday Americans will practically sell their souls in exchange for material possessions: "I thought I'd written a satire of Reaganomics in America in the eighties. [...] I always saw Leland Gaunt, the shop owner who buys souls, as the archetypal Ronald Reagan: charismatic, a little bit elderly, selling nothing but junk but it looks bright and shiny."[315] Read in this light, *Needful Things* becomes a satirical Faustian parable—although King's Devil insists that he is *not* particularly interested in souls. Gaunt collects souls as keepsakes, like a serial killer collecting "trophies," but he claims it is the sheer "amusement" of generating chaos that feeds him.[316] Like Randall Flagg in *The Stand*, Gaunt is an instigator who literally feeds on mischief. (And, in that respect, both are perhaps more like the Greek god Loki than the Christian Devil.)

Luckily, Castle Rock sheriff Alan Pangborn sees Gaunt for what he is. Pangborn has a kind of sixth sense for irrational threats, born from his encounter with George Stark in *The Dark Half* and with Pop Merrill's supernatural camera in "The Sun Dog." In the end, Pangborn recognizes the real force behind Gaunt's "needful things":

---

314 Stroby
315 Lehmann-Haupt
316 King: *Needful* 319

> *Magic—wasn't that what this was all about? It was mean-spirited magic, granted; magic calculated not to make people gasp and laugh but to turn them into angry charging bulls, but it was magic, just the same. And what was the basis of all magic? Misdirection. It was a five-foot-long snake hidden inside a can of nuts.*[317]

The sheriff literally uses that can of nuts to expose Gaunt's illusory nature and run him out of town. On behalf of the hero, King invokes the magical power of the White to dispel the demon. It's a surprisingly heavy-handed ending, invoking an old remnant of King's evolving worldview. Perhaps for that reason, as the author himself observed, many of his constant readers dismissed the novel as an "unsuccessful horror novel" rather than embracing it as a satire.[318] This only increased the author's conviction that it was time to move away from horror.

317 King: *Needful* 562
318 Lehmann-Haupt

Excavating The Dark Tower

According to King's meta-fictional journals in *Song of Susannah* (2004), the author found himself on more comfortable ground with *The Dark Tower III: The Waste Lands*, a book that he claims practically wrote itself between October 1989 and January 1990. This third entry in the *Dark Tower* is a pivotal work for the author, creating a broad canvas for his future novels by solidifying the elaborate cosmology of the author's fictional universe, while putting Roland and his motley *ka-tet* on a discernible path. Much of the volume focuses on the psychic connection between Roland and his stepson Jake, both of whom are haunted by conflicting memories of alternate pasts—two in which Jake dies, and one in which Roland saves him. In the third variation, Roland rescues Jake from a haunted house much like the one in *'Salem's Lot*, a scenario suggesting that King now regarded his famous horror novels as a jumping-off point for more ambitious tales. The novel also makes oblique references to people, places and things in *The Stand* and *IT*, and hints that Roland's adventure extends into "other worlds," well beyond King's fiction. In the later part of the novel, for example, Roland and his ka-tet wander into the waste land of twentieth-century poet T.S. Eliot—a literary warehouse of ancient myths and religious ideas.

Eliot seems to have been an influence on King's work since the very beginning. In *Carrie*, the author alluded to Eliot's modernist poem *The Waste Land* in the following passage:

> *She closed her eyes, slept, and dreamed of huge, living stones crashing through the night, seeking out Momma, seeking out Them. They were trying to run, trying to hide. But the rock would not hide them; the dead tree gave no shelter.*[319]

In Eliot's poem, the phrase "the dead tree gives no shelter" is part of a heap of Biblical allusions, signifying desolation and despair. King adapts the line for his own purposes, to signify Carrie White's emotional despair within an overtly religious context. He is using Eliot's phrase the same way that Eliot himself used phrases from hundreds of literary predecessors, to contextualize and deepen his

319 King: *Carrie* 58

meaning. The comparison is fair: In *Carrie*, as in *The Waste Land*, the modern world is finally ravaged by purgatorial fire.

In *Pet Sematary,* Louis Creed remembers Eliot's poems "The Love Song of J. Alfred Prufrock" and "The Hollow Men" (in conjunction with George Romero's *Night of the Living Dead*) while digging up his dead son. King writes:

> *In this dull, exhausted aftermath, nothing seemed to matter. He felt like something less than human now, one of George Romero's stupid, lurching movie-zombies, or maybe someone who had escaped from T.S. Eliot's poem about the hollow men.* I should have been a pair of ragged claws, scuttling through Little God Swamp and up to the Micmac burying ground, *he thought and uttered a dry chuckle. "Headpiece full of straw, Church," he said in his croaking voice.*[320]

Although King conflates the two poems, the quote reveals something about the author's mindset. "Prufrock" is a poem about a man who feels undeserving of his humanity, and haunted by the seeming inevitability of genuine madness. In the midst of his self-analysis, Prufrock muses, "I should have been a pair of ragged claws / Scuttling across the floors of silent seas."[321] King's novel is about a man who surrenders his humanity and succumbs to madness. For the sake of everyone around him, Louis suggests, he should have been a pair of ragged claws, instead of a blasphemous Dr. Frankenstein. "The Hollow Men" is essentially a poem about the moral emptiness that follows such a surrender—the absolute darkness that has consumed everything by the end of *Pet Sematary.*

In *The Talisman*, King hints at Eliot's eventual answer to the spiritual despair of "The Hollow Men." Along his journey, Jack Sawyer adopts a phrase that becomes his mantra of hope: "All will be well and all manner of things will be well." The phrase originated in the journals of a fourteenth-century Christian mystic named Julian of Norwich. Eliot repeated it at the end of his overtly Christian masterpiece *Little Gidding*, to suggest a profound mystery beyond human understanding. Whether consciously or unconsciously, King seems to have done the same thing in *The Talisman*, using the phrase to

320 King: *Pet* 372
321 Eliot 5

invoke the ineffable God of the great mystics—"*God, or something so close as to make no difference.*"

As in Eliot's work, there is a progressive spiritual journey apparent in King's work in the early 1980s, moving from darkness to light as the author moves from horror to fantasy. The latter never replaces the former because—as the great mystics point out—light and dark, like good and evil, must exist in a kind of equilibrium. That equilibrium is precisely what's at stake in *The Dark Tower* series. In *The Waste Lands*, King reveals that the purpose of Roland's quest is to restore a cosmic balance that has shifted too far in one direction, threatening to destroy not just one world, but all worlds. Accordingly, King's characters adopt Eliot's apocalyptic visions as their own. When Jake looks into his future, he remembers a line from Eliot: "I will show you fear in a handful of dust."[322] When Susannah sees the abandoned city of Lud on the edge of King's waste lands, she remembers "a heap of broken images, where the sun beats and the dead tree gives no shelter."[323] Even Blaine the Mono (a sadistic variation on another literary relic, Charlie the Choo-Choo) seems obsessed with Eliot. As Blaine murders the last survivors in Lud using chemical and biological weapons, he glibly paraphrases Prufrock: "IN THE ROOMS THE PEOPLE COME AND GO, BUT I DON'T THINK ANY OF THEM ARE TALKING OF MICHAELANGELO."[324] Then he hijacks Roland's *ka-tet*, intent on carrying them to their doom.

The author took a lot of flak from his readers for leaving the characters stranded in Blaine's care at the end of *The Waste Lands*. In self-defense, King could only say that he didn't know yet what happened to them. He explained in his 1991 afterword to the novel:

> *Books which write themselves (as this one did, for the most part) must be allowed to end themselves, and I can only assure you, Reader, that Roland and his band have come to one of the crucial border-crossings in their story, and we must leave them here for a while at the customs station, answering questions and filling out forms. All of which is simply a metaphorical way of*

322 King: *Waste* 277
323 King: *Waste* 483
324 King: *Waste* 535

> *saying that it was over again for a while and my heart was wise enough to stop me from trying to push ahead anyway.*[325]

Some writers, King would have us believe, don't control their journeys any more than spiritual seekers do. When they start down a true path, they do not travel alone. They require help, and they can't control when or where that help arrives. King puts it another way, echoing Thomas Wolfe:

> *Actually, when I feel that I'm creating, I feel that I'm doing bad work. The best work that I've ever done always has a feeling of having been excavated, of already being there. I don't feel like a novelist or a creative writer as much as I feel like an archaeologist who is digging things up and being very careful and brushing them off and looking at the carvings on them [. . .] In the case of* The Dark Tower, *it's like excavating this huge fucking buried city that's down there.*[326]

Over the following years, the voice of the Dark Tower continued to haunt the author, finding its way into seemingly unrelated stories. In a 1991 interview, King revealed that he had recently completed a manuscript entitled *Insomnia*. On the surface, he said, it was a horror novel about a seventy-year-old man named Ralph Roberts, who begins seeing strange and frightening things in the not-so-sleepy town of Derry, Maine. His assessment of the manuscript was damning: "It's no good. It's not publishable . . . Things just don't connect, it doesn't have that novelistic roundness that it should have."[327] Based on observations about the published version of *Insomnia*, one may speculate that the author was initially dismayed by the intrusion of the *Dark Tower* mythology into a novel set in Derry. King had already established a connection between the *Dark Tower* mythology and Derry in the final pages of *IT*, but suddenly *everything* happening in Derry seemed to be related to Roland's quest.

Like *Needful Things*, *Insomnia* had much simpler origins—in this case, a criticism of abortion rights. Ralph Roberts's troubles begin when he witnesses an altercation involving his neighbor Ed Deepneau, a vehement pro-lifer who warns him about a mysterious

325 King: "Afterword," *Waste* 590
326 Stroby
327 Stroby

menace called The Crimson King. According to Deepneau, the Crimson King is a supernatural entity that "jumps from body to body and generation to generation like a kid using stepping-stones to cross a brook . . . always looking for the Messiah."[328] Ralph initially assumes that his neighbor is simply delusional . . . but then he begins suffering from insomnia, and having vaguely mystical experiences that seem to be related to Deepneau's warnings. He gradually comes to understand his experiences as *hyper-reality*, fleeting moments of "heightened sensory awareness . . . like taking an LSD trip without having to ingest any chemicals."[329] King offers the following description of Ralph's experience:

> *Things and people, particularly the people, had auras, yes, but that was only where this amazing phenomenon began. Things had never been so brilliant, so utterly and completely there. The cars, the telephone poles, the shopping carts in the Kart Korral in front of the supermarket, the frame apartment buildings across the street—all these things seemed to pop out at him like 3-D images in an old film. All at once this dingy little strip-mall of Witcham Street had become wonderland, and although Ralph was looking right at it, he was not sure what he was looking at, only that it was rich and gorgeous and fabulously strange.*[330]

Ten years earlier, Stephen King said in an interview that he did not believe that mind-altering substances like LSD could expand human consciousness. "I've never bought the argument of Aldous Huxley that hallucinogens open the doors to perception," he asserted, adding, "That's mystical self-indulgence, the kind of bullshit Timothy Leary used to preach."[331] In *Insomnia*, Ralph Roberts initially shares the same rational reservations about the "doors of perception," but he also expresses a yearning to believe that such transcendence is possible. Although an inner-voice cautions Ralph that the visions aren't real, still he can't help wondering if maybe, *just maybe*, chronic insomnia has "afforded him a glimpse of a fabulous dimension just

328 King: *Insomnia* 82
329 King: *Insomnia* 127
330 King: *Insomnia* 133
331 Norden 44

beyond the reach of ordinary perception."[332] Once again King seems to be treading the thin line between faith and madness.

As the novel progresses, the author tries to resolve Ralph's intellectual crisis by crafting an explanatory mythology—one that turns out to be vitally connected to the *Dark Tower* universe. King introduces three "little bald doctors" who serve as agents of death. Two of those doctors are "*physicians of last resort*," whose actions help to endow life and death with Purpose. The third doctor is "*an agent of the Random*," whose actions on behalf of the mysterious Crimson King have begun to threaten the natural balance of all worlds. In the final pages of the novel, Ralph makes a leap of faith in order to prevent an act of terrorism. King insists that his actions have (somehow) saved The Dark Tower, but Ralph never has any intellectual understanding of the greater significance of his heroics; he merely acts on blind faith. In a sense, it seems, the author was doing the same thing. At that point, he didn't know how Ralph's actions might relate to the Dark Tower narrative, but he believed that he would see the big picture in due time.

Within the context of King's subsequently published *Dark Tower* novels, *Insomnia* makes sense. When it was first published, however, readers were understandably frustrated. Until he was able to provide a proper context for Ralph's sacrifice, even King himself dismissed *Insomnia* as a "stiff, trying-too-hard" novel.[333] He knew that he had botched this particular excavation . . . perhaps by excavating it too fast or too soon.

King followed up *Insomnia* with *Rose Madder*, a schizophrenic novel about a woman who runs away from her abusive husband, then lures him to his death in the surreal world of a mythic painting. The author has called it simply a "bad book," and "the one book that I really sort of regret."[334] To be fair, it's not a bad book—it's just unbalanced, failing to effectively fuse the realism of novels like *Dolores Claiborne* and *Gerald's Game* with the fantasy of books like *The Waste Land* and *Insomnia*. Its biggest problem may be that it relies too heavily on classical Greek mythology instead of developing King's own personal mythology. There is a passing reference to the *ka* of the *Dark Tower* universe, but most of the story seems like

332 King: *Insomnia* 135
333 King: *On Writing* 169
334 Lehmann-Haupt, Mason

a magical realist's misguided version of the Julia Roberts vehicle *Sleeping with the Enemy* (1991).

In the introduction to his 1993 short story collection *Nightmares & Dreamscapes*, King confided, "I have days when I think this old Wang word-processor stopped running on electricity about five years ago; that from *The Dark Half* on, it's been running completely on faith."[335] With *Insomnia* and *Rose Madder*, the author had reason to worry about where that faith was taking him. Stories kept coming, but they were more and more often a heap of broken images. King was unwilling to repeat the past, but so far he had not been able to see the future clearly. As it turned out, he was waiting for a character he'd created almost twenty years earlier to show him the way forward.

335 King: "Myth" 2

King of Hollywood (III)

It's easy to understand how King might have felt suffocated by his own legacy, particularly since more and more audiences knew him better for film adaptations of his work than for his novels. After a brief lull in the late 1980s, Stephen King adaptations made a strong comeback in the early 1990s. The commercial success of *Pet Sematary* (1989), a down-and-dirty horror film adapted by the author himself and shot in his home state of Maine, gave rise to the equally gruesome monster movies *Graveyard Shift* (1990) and *Sleepwalkers* (1992). Rob Reiner's comparatively restrained adaptation of *Misery* (1990), which earned star Kathy Bates an Academy Award, inspired more sophisticated works like *The Dark Half* (1993), *Needful Things* (1993), and *The Shawshank Redemption* (1994). The ABC miniseries *Stephen King's It* (1990) cast an even longer shadow, paving the way for a long line of TV adaptations, including *Sometimes They Come Back* (1991), the *Golden Years* series (1991), *The Tommyknockers* miniseries (1993) and *The Stand* miniseries (1994). On top of this, a handful of ripoffs—including two direct-to-video sequels to *Children of the Corn* and an in-name-only adaptation of *The Lawnmower Man* (1992)—guaranteed that no one was safe from King's legacy.

The omnipresent author has never hesitated to share bold critical assessments of the film and television work that carries his name. In a 1991 assessment of *Pet Sematary*, he told journalist Gary Wood that, although he felt that the performances of Dale Midkiff and Denise Crosby lacked the necessary "warmth" to make the film as emotionally effective as the novel had been, the film still did "what horror movies are supposed to do." Calling *Pet Sematary* "an outlaw picture," he noted that the taboo subject matter and the explicit gore had upset and offended many viewers, and insisted, "That's exactly the effect that the horror movie seeks."[336] To be fair, the film still had enough warmth (thanks in large part to Fred Gwynne's performance as the grandfatherly Jud Crandall) to illustrate the comparative coldness of a film like *Graveyard Shift*. King himself later opined that his original short story was "gruesome, fast, and fun," while the film

336 Wood: "King's" 39

adaptation was "gruesome and fast, but unfortunately not much fun."[337] The author was equally disappointed with *Sleepwalkers*, which was based on his first original screenplay since *Creepshow*. He placed the blame on the producers, saying: "[Director] Mick [Garris] didn't have enough power, and I didn't have enough time, to stop Columbia from whittling it down to something about two critical cuts above *Dr. Giggles*."[338] Summing up his observations about the latest round of King pics, the author's formula for a successful adaptation of his work was simple:

> *Human beings are not secondary to the theme of horror. That's an important thing to remember: You cannot scare anyone unless you first get the audience to care about these make-believe characters. They have to become people with whom you identify. After all, they are only as thick as the screen, which means about as thick as your thumbnail. We go to the movies with the understanding that we are watching people who are not real. But if we come to like them, and we recognize the things they are doing are also part of our own lives, if they are reacting the way in which we would react under similar circumstances, then we become emotionally invested. Once this happens, it is possible to frighten the audience by putting the character in frightening situations.*[339]

In contrast to the excesses of the less successful adaptations, Rob Reiner's *Misery* was a subtle character study—a horror film relying on genuine mystery and suspense rather than simply shock and gore. Just as Reiner had eliminated any hint of the supernatural from King's novella "The Body" in order to produce *Stand by Me*, so he and screenwriter William Goldman eliminated the more explicit horrors of *Misery* (including a show-stopping scene involving an ax and a blowtorch) to produce a nuanced psychological thriller. The film appealed to non-horror audiences as well as die-hard Stephen King fans, and its critical and commercial success bolstered the name brand.

A few years later, when Reiner's production company Castle Rock brought *Needful Things* to the screen, the filmmakers were not as successful in downplaying the overtly supernatural elements or crafting character drama. Screenwriter W.D. Richter (building on an

337 King: "Introduction," *Carrie* ix
338 Bill Warren: "Long" 86
339 Magistrale 14-15

early draft by *Carrie* screenwriter Lawrence D. Cohen) humanized the heroic Alan Pangborn by giving him a temper, thereby making him more vulnerable to Leland Gaunt's machinations. At the same time, however, he eliminated the backstories of both Pangborn and his leading lady Polly Chalmers, and reduced many of the other supporting characters to walk-on roles. When it came time for the townfolk to fight for their souls, the thinness of the characters became painfully apparent. An extended cut of the film, which aired on the TNT television network, acknowledged the problem but didn't entirely fix it.

Director George A. Romero and screenwriter Lawrence D. Cohen faced a similar challenge in adapting *IT* to the screen. In the novel, King spent more than 1,000 pages fleshing out his seven main characters as well as the town they grew up in. Cohen aimed to do the same thing in his screenplay for a six-hour miniseries, and the director was pleased with the results. Later, the network trimmed the miniseries to four hours, prompting Romero to abandon the project. At this point, Cohen methodically restructured King's story, dividing it neatly into a two-part shooting script.[340] The first half, revolving around the characters' childhoods, works well as a series of vignettes, bolstered by Tim Curry's deliciously mad performance as Pennywise. The second half struggles with the increasingly abstract nature of King's ultimate boogeyman and fails to replicate the emotional crescendo of the novel. The author was generally pleased with the miniseries, but like most viewers he was disappointed by the climactic battle with "this sort of Tonka toy spider."[341] Regardless, the miniseries earned high ratings for ABC, and insured Stephen King's future on network television.

A year later, producer Dino DeLaurentiis made one last foray into the Stephen King universe, hiring director Tom McLoughlin to helm an adaptation of the short story "Sometimes They Come Back" for CBS. McLoughlin's challenge wasn't condensing the story but expanding it, and the filmmaker forthrightly admits that the initial script (by Lawrence Konner and Mark Rosenthal) "wasn't fleshed out properly," relying too heavily on borrowed moments from better-known Stephen King stories.[342] Thankfully, heartfelt performances

340 Jones 64
341 Ashton-Haiste 71
342 Maddrey

from Tim Matheson and Brooke Adams held the story together, and McLoughlin managed to amplify the emotional resonance of the piece. The movie was "about love," the director explains, "[about] losing somebody you love."[343] The end result was successful enough to inspire two direct-to-video sequels.

That same year, King conceptualized his first completely original TV series. The author appreciated the advantages of the longer storytelling format, recognizing that it provided more opportunities than a feature film to "control the viewer the way that it's possible sometimes to control readers, to bring them into the story, to make them care." Accordingly, his goal was to produce "a novel for television."[344] In that respect, *Golden Years* was a success. With memorable performances by a superb cast including Keith Szarabajka, Frances Sternhagen, and Felicity Huffman, the character development in the series is on par with the best of King's novels. Unfortunately, the novelistic pace of the series put off many viewers. Ratings fell as the series progressed, and CBS opted not to continue the story after the seventh episode. A truncated version of the series was eventually released on VHS, featuring an abrupt and confusing finale. King told interviewer Wallace Stroby that the ending was "basically a condensed version of my concept of how the thing should have ended with a lot of the intervening stuff taken out."[345] The "intervening stuff," apparently, was the logic.

In 1993, ABC returned to the miniseries format, relying on Lawrence D. Cohen to adapt *The Tommyknockers*. Once again Cohen substantially altered the structure of the novel—this time creating a more sensible balance between the story of the two main characters and the stories of the supporting characters. In King's novel, Bobbi and Gard exist almost entirely independent of the town of Haven. In the miniseries, Bobbi becomes the de facto leader of Haven, enlisting the help of her fellow abductees to unearth the spaceship buried in her backyard. Critics justifiably compared the results to Jack Finney's "The Body Snatchers," Nigel Kneale's *Quatermass and the Pit*, and *Twilight Zone* scribe Jerry Sohl's TV movie *Night Slaves* (1970). Derivative or not, *The Tommyknockers* earned solid ratings

343 Maddrey
344 Applebome
345 Jones 72

and set the stage for the most successful Stephen King miniseries of the decade.

The Stand has long been regarded as the fan favorite among all of King's novels, and the author had been struggling for more than a decade to bring it to the screen under the stewardship of director George A. Romero and producer Richard Rubinstein. After writing three prospective screenplays for the film in the mid-1980s, the author gave up on adapting his own novel and Romero redirected his attention to *The Dark Half*. Undaunted, Rubinstein commissioned several more screenplays in a desperate attempt to translate the mammoth novel into a viable feature film project. In 1991, he told journalist Gary Wood that he had acquired a producible feature film script from screenwriter Rospo Pallenberg, who explained that, rather than condensing King's story, he had "collapsed and reinvented" it into a two-hour structure.[346] Two years later, however, it was King's latest draft that finally got the green light—as the basis for a six-hour miniseries on ABC.

King nominated Mick Garris, the director of *Sleepwalkers*, to take on the intimidating job of shooting a 460-page script on a 100-day production schedule. He explained his choice to journalist Bill Warren:

> *Mick has an understanding of Americana, and I like that. He has as good a visual sense as Steven Spielberg, and I like that too. And he was willing to basically serve as a conduit for the script. He is not the kind of director who would come to me and say, "Well, look, this one sequence here, I have a little idea. . . ." Mick understood that this was going to say "Stephen King's* The Stand*" and not "Mick Garris's* The Stand.*"* [347]

King believed that *The Stand* would be the most time-consuming and "important" film project of his career. For that reason, he said, he wanted it to live or die on his terms: "If *The Stand* fails, it's going to be my failure, no matter who is involved in the various elements."[348] According to Garris, the author was on the set for "at least half" of the production.[349] He even played a supporting character in the

346 Wood: "Adapting" 28
347 Bill Warren: "Long" 86
348 Bill Warren: "Stephen" 97
349 Galluzzo

latter part of the film. The end result was a monumental ratings success for ABC. Garris remembers: "It had 50 million people a night watching, and more every night of the four nights. They just added on. It became the water-cooler show. It was the *Jurassic Park* of television."[350] King was mostly pleased with the results, summing up, "There are some things I wish we could change; I look at the climax, and I wish that it were a little bit hotter, that the emotional temperature was a little higher, but I don't know exactly how [we could have done that]. The big five-alarm climax has never been my forte; I've always felt I fell about one alarm short. But I think it's good."[351] Amazingly, the miniseries was followed by an even bigger cinematic success.

The Shawshank Redemption didn't arrive with the kind of promotion and fanfare that surrounded *The Stand*. Instead, Frank Darabont's film made its debut in a limited theatrical release and struggled to make back its budget. Marketing was a problem; the film's distributor simply didn't know how to get audiences excited about a prison melodrama. The story seemed so grim that even Stephen King practically dismissed the venture, noting that his source novel was "a moody tale with more thinking than action in it . . . not the sort of thing that usually makes a good movie."[352] Nevertheless Darabont turned "Shawshank" into one of the most profoundly moving films in modern cinema. The author credits the filmmaker with creating, first and foremost, "a film about human beings."[353] Darabont clearly recognized the beating heart of the original story, and structured his adaptation to highlight the spiritual content of key passages like the following:

> *Andy was the part of me they could never lock up, the part of me that will rejoice when the gates finally open for me and I walk out in my cheap suit with my twenty dollars of mad-money in my pocket. That part of me will rejoice no matter how old and broken and scared the rest of me is.*[354]

350 Galluzzo
351 Bill Warren: "Stephen" 94
352 King: "Rita" xi
353 Magistrale 14
354 King: "Shawshank" 99

In the film, Morgan Freeman's dignified voiceover drives home this message, which is at the heart of many of King's best tales: "Get busy living or get busy dying."

What *The Shawshank Redemption* and *The Stand* illustrate clearly is the author's essential faith in humanity to rise above bad circumstances and base instincts. In *Shawshank*, it's Andy Dufrense who demonstrates that indomitable spirit. In *The Stand*, Glen Bateman does the same thing by proposing a vision quest to help him and his friends recharge and recover a clear, spiritual view of life. In the fall of 1994, King took Bateman's advice. His publisher arranged a ten-city book tour, in part so that the author to take a cross-country trip on his motorcycle. Along the way, the troubled novelist unearthed his next story.

Miracle Mile

In his 1992 book *The Stephen King Story*, George Beahm quotes a then-recent interview in which King talks about five prospective novels he would like to write, including "a novel about an evangelist [or] about religion," and a novel "about Christ."[355] The author's interest in religion, and Christianity in particular, eventually provided the backdrop for three transitional works in the mid-'90s: *Desperation*, *The Regulators* and *The Green Mile*. *Desperation* is more overtly religious than any of King's novels since (and including) *The Stand*. *The Regulators* is a companion piece and, in some ways, a rebuttal of *Desperation*. *The Green Mile* rounds out this strange trilogy of faith by revisiting the themes of *The Shawshank Redemption*, and expanding on them. Although the author had a sense of the themes before he started writing, each of these stories surprised him.

According to a 1994 news article, King spent "a couple of days" in northern Nevada at the tail end of his *Insomnia* book tour, traveling from Sun Valley, Idaho, to Santa Cruz, California, along a desolate stretch of highway known as the "loneliest road in America."[356] The author remembers the trip vividly:

> *It was this real overcast day, and I go through this little town. And there was nobody on Main Street. Main Street was totally deserted. There are a couple of cars in the slant parking spaces, but otherwise nobody on the sidewalk, and I'm thinking, where are they all? And right away, the voice in the back of my mind, that's been waiting, says, "All dead." And I go, "Oh, are they? Why are they all dead?" And the voice says, "Sheriff killed them. Sheriff went crazy and killed everybody in town." I'm going, "He couldn't kill everybody," and the voice says, "He did." So I go, "How did he do it?"*[357]

To answer the question, King began writing *Desperation* in November 1994. At that point, he not only had an unlikely villain in mind but also an unlikely hero.

355 Beahm: *Story* 252
356 Kramer
357 Ulin

The main villain of *Desperation* is Collie Entragian, a cop with a habit of stopping travelers on the highway, then executing them or taking them hostage in a nearby mining town. Eventually we learn that Entragian's body is merely a physical vessel for a malevolent entity that escaped from one of the old mines. King dubs this entity "Tak," and suggests that it is a spiritual Dracula for the Wild West. (At one point, Tak/Entragian even communicates with a pack of wild coyotes, saying, "My children of the desert! The *can-toi*! What music they make!") Like Dracula, Tak is essentially immortal, but unlike Dracula, his body is weak. Most of the human bodies he inhabits tend to break down after only a few days of possession, which is why Tak always keeps a fresh supply of hostages on hand.

One of his latest hostages is Johnny Marinville, a Harley-riding novelist whose literary reputation has "gone slipping through his fingers in the last five years," following a well-publicized substance abuse scandal.[358] Although he's now stone cold sober, Johnny is a mess. His ex-wife is bored with him, his three kids want nothing to do with him, and his work has "degenerated into self-parody or outright drivel."[359] Out of sheer desperation, Johnny has taken to the open highway to seek some kind of redemption. When he encounters Entragian, the cop mocks his self-important suffering. "You've never written a truly spiritual novel," the cop/killer barks, adding, "It is your great unrecognized failing, and it is the center of your petulant, self-indulgent behavior. You have no interest in your spiritual nature. You mock the God who created you, and by doing so you mortify your own *pneuma* and glorify the mud which is your *sarx*."[360] Johnny takes the criticism to heart, because he knows what this archaic language means: He has suffocated his own soul.

The similarities between John Edward Marinville and Stephen Edwin King are unavoidable (though King told one interviewer, "I'd like to think that if you went out to dinner with me, you'd like me better than you'd like this guy"[361]), and it is for that reason that King can't cast Marinville as the hero of the tale. In both cases, the writer himself needs rescuing, and an eleven-year-old boy named David Carver comes to his aid. David's advice is simple: *Pray*.

---

358 King: *Desperation* 56
359 King: *Desperation* 58
360 King: *Desperation* 87
361 Marotta 110

None of the other hostages is particularly religious. In fact, several of them are determinedly anti-religious; the cruelty of Tak seems to some of them like hard evidence *against* the existence of a benevolent God. David, however, maintains his faith, insisting that "God's cruelty is refining" and that "life is more than just steering a course around pain."[362] David prays not for rescue or relief or even understanding, but for the strength to fulfill God's purpose, whatever it might be: "*See in me, God. Be in me. And speak in me, if you mean to, if it's your will.*"[363] Eventually, he realizes what that purpose is: God has brought them all to Desperation to stop Tak, and Johnny has a crucial role to play.

At that point in the story, Johnny's lack of faith becomes an obstacle to God's Higher Purpose. Hardened and embittered by a lifetime of experiences, he decides to flee instead of fighting, saying, "I trust God about as far as I can sling a piano."[364] This conflict of belief, King says, was the main reason for writing the novel:

> *The idea of using God as a character in* Desperation *was sort of what made the book go. I was thinking to myself that I had read so many books that are about EVIL! For example, one of the characters will say, "There is something 'EVIL' in this town!" They root out the vampires and they use the garlic and the crosses, which I've done myself. I'm not trying to set myself up as someone who's better. I think it's all like kryptonite, all the trappings of religion are like kryptonite. I thought to myself, "What if you treat God and the accoutrements of God with as much belief, awe and detail as novelists do the 'EVIL' part of it?"*[365]

King was trying to sort out his own ideas and beliefs about God in the most natural way he knew how—by telling a story about it. This self-conscious agenda becomes a bit overbearing at times, but the author's conclusions are nevertheless thought-provoking. Here's how King sums up the meaning of his novel:

> *God doesn't always let the good guys win. I always wanted to say that you can still reconcile the idea that things are not*

362 King: *Desperation* 424
363 King: *Desperation* 365
364 King: *Desperation* 447
365 Mauceri

> *necessarily going to go well without falling back on platitudes like "God has a plan" and "This is for the greater good." It's possible to be in pain and still believe that there is some force for good in the universe.*[366]

Neither Stephen King nor Johnny Marinville explicitly embrace the tenets of organized religion, but they both express faith in the existence of a "force for good" that is beyond human understanding and traditional dualistic theology. Johnny Marinville rediscovers his sense of purpose, and David Carver gives voice to King's concept of God, saying, "I guess he's sort of… Everything."[367] It is essentially the same conclusion that Jack Sawyer came to at the end of *The Talisman*. By echoing that note of childlike faith in *Desperation*, King redeems his fictional counterpart, allowing Johnny to finally escape from his dark half.

Although *Desperation* suggests a quasi-religious awakening (or at least a desire for one), King's next novel reads like a rally crying from his dark half—the writer known as Richard Bachman. The author says he conceived his pseudonym's latest novel while still working on *Desperation*:

> *The idea was to take characters from* Desperation *and put them into* The Regulators. *In some cases, I thought, they would play the same people; in others, they would change; in neither would they do the same things or react in the same ways, because the different stories would dictate different courses of action. It would be, I thought, like the members of a repertory company acting in two different plays. Then an even more exciting idea struck me. If I could use the rep company concept with the characters, I could use it with the plot itself—I could stack a good many of the* Desperation *elements in a brand-new configuration, and create a kind of mirror world.*[368]

The "mirror world" of *The Regulators* is a quiet suburban street where Johnny Marinville, David Carver, and Collie Entragian are neighbors. Johnny remains a has-been novelist suffering a mid-life crisis, but this time David can't help him redeem himself. By the end

366 Cruz
367 King: *Desperation* 547
368 King: "Importance"

of the first chapter, David is dead—the victim of a mysterious drive-by shooting. Collie Entragian, an ex-cop with a history of anger management problems, rallies the neighbors to figure out what's going on. Eventually we learn that Tak has returned as well—this time taking up residence inside the head of an autistic eight-year-old boy named Seth, and giving him the power to turn his favorite TV shows into a menacing reality. (Imagine the *Twilight Zone* episode "It's a Good Life" as a Sam Peckinpah movie.) And God? Well, as King sarcastically says, the only God in *The Regulators* is television.[369]

There's something both fascinating and frustrating about the way the author overlaps these two stories. The fact that the same characters end up in approximately the same circumstances suggests that the author believes in fate; the fact that the characters are comparatively passive and ineffectual in the second story suggests an equally strong cynicism about the idea that *anything* happens for a reason. Because of its relationship with *Desperation*, *The Regulators* comes across as the work of a storyteller in his own state of desperation, quickly backsliding from a hard-won intellectual (if not genuinely spiritual) battle for personal faith. In the latter novel, a disembodied voice advises King's surrogate, "You need to double back in your head... To the time when you felt good. *Were* good." One gets a sense that the author may be trying to achieve the same sort of "double back" in his writing career.

On one level, *The Regulators* is quite literally a return to an earlier time, when King conceived an idea for a feature film called *The Shotgunners*. The setup, he says, was straight out of *The Twilight Zone* episode "The Monsters Are Due on Maple Street." It's summertime in suburbia, and the living is easy, right up until the idyllic setting is shattered by a drive-by shooting. What happens next is pure Stephen King: "The people are pinned down in their houses. Night starts to fall and some of the people go down to the bottom of the street, but the rest of the world is *gone*! It just ends at the end of the block, both ways."[370] King explains that his original idea was that "the shotgunners" are enacting kind of supernatural revenge for a hanging that occurred in the town a century earlier—an idea similar to Clint Eastwood's horror-western *High Plains Drifter* (1973). It's no wonder, then, that western filmmaker Sam Peckinpah was

369 Mauceri
370 Wood: "Shotgunners"

once attached to the script. According to King, the legendary director gave him notes on how to restructure the story. Unfortunately, Peckinpah died soon after, and King didn't revise his story until a decade later—by which time he had developed completely new ideas about what the story should be. Unlike King's unproduced script, *The Regulators* is not a story about supernatural revenge; it's just a convoluted, needlessly gimmicky *Twilight Zone* episode. After this, King apparently realized that he needed to try a new method of doubling back.

The author says that he has always written his best stories like a reckless driver, sans outline and "with the pedal all the way to the metal."[371] That's exactly how he wrote *The Green Mile*, publishing individual chapters as he wrote them instead of allowing himself time to rewrite and revise. The result is an exploratory story, completely reliant on instinct and intuition rather than intellect. When the first installment was published, the author says, he didn't even know how the tale ended. He knew that he doing a high-wire act without a safety net . . . and he loved it. In a 1996 AOL chat, he explained:

> *I wrote like a madman, trying to keep up with the crazy publishing schedule and at the same time trying to craft the book so that each part would have its own anti-climax, hoping that everything would fit, and knowing I would be hung if it didn't. There was less margin for screwing up, it had to be right the first time.* [372]

Although it is clear that many of King's novels have benefitted from multiple draft revisions, which is when the author usually develops his theme, *The Green Mile* works amazingly well as a stream of consciousness narrative, revealing the author's core beliefs with straightforward honesty.

The story began simply enough, with King's longtime fascination with death row stories, and gradually evolved into a novel about Jesus Christ. The storyteller is Paul Edgecomb, a 105-year-old man who once worked as a prison guard on death row during the Great Depression. At the outset, Edgecomb explains that he has never

371 King: "Foreword," *Two* xiii
372 Rogak 187

believed in the effectiveness of the death penalty, because he doesn't believe that people are inherently evil: "Old Sparky never burned what was inside them, and the drugs they inject them with today don't put it to sleep. It vacates, jumps to someone else, and leaves us to kill husks that aren't really alive anyway."[373] Perhaps for that reason, Edgecomb performs the duties of his job with a kind of emotional resignation—until the arrival of a prisoner named John Coffey.

Coffey is what the old-timers call a faith healer, a man who can cure people of physical ailments simply by touching them. When he cures Edgecomb's bladder infection, Edgecomb says: "I remember thinking the name of the Savior—Christ, Christ, Christ, over and over, like that."[374] Later, he watches Coffey physically absorb the sickness from other people, and then expel it from his own body as a cloud of black insects. In such moments, Edgecomb realizes that he's in the presence of God, and reflects:

> *For one to rejoice at the sick made well is normal, quite the expected thing, but the person healed has an obligation to then ask why—to meditate on God's will, and the extraordinary lengths to which God has gone to realize His will. What did God want of me, in this case? What did He want badly enough to put healing power in the hands of a child-murderer?*[375]

From this point forward, Edgecomb feels a need for atonement, or "balancing." He has suddenly become aware of his place in a cosmic tug-of-war, and understands that he has greater responsibilities than the fulfillment of his job requirements. King obviously shares this sense of duty, noting in the introduction to his serial novel that Edgecomb is "a Stephen King narrator if ever there was one."[376] If Johnny Marinville is an intellectual self-portrait of King, Paul Edgecomb is an emotional self-portrait. Edgecomb expresses the author's worldview as follows:

> *I believe there is good in the world, all of it flowing in one way or another from a loving God. But I believe there's another*

373 King: *Green* 16
374 King: *Green* 184
375 King: *Green* 192
376 King: "Foreword," *Two* xii

> *force as well, one every bit as real as the God I have prayed to my whole life, and that it works consciously to bring all our decent impulses to ruin. Not Satan, I don't mean Satan (although I believe he is real, too), but a kind of demon of discord, a prankish and stupid thing that laughs with glee when an old man sets himself on fire trying to light his pipe or when a much-loved baby puts its first Christmas toy in its mouth and chokes to death on it.*[377]

King has, of course, made his career telling stories about this "demon of discord," otherwise known as Randall Flagg, Leland Gaunt, Atropos, etc. In each case, he has counterbalanced that chaos through the actions of ordinary, good-hearted people who—if only for a moment—channel the power of the White, the ultimate force for good that emanates from a loving God. While most of King's novels take place in the midst of the ongoing struggle between good and "discord," *The Green Mile* contextualizes and reflects on the human condition with even greater profundity. The beating heart of the story is Edgecomb's acute awareness of John Coffey's Christ-like nature, and of his suffering.

When it comes time for Coffey's execution, the prisoner says that death will be a blessing:

> *I'm rightly tired of the pain I hear and feel, boss. I'm tired of bein' on the road, lonely as a robin in the rain. Not ever havin' no boddy to go on with or tell me where we's coming from or goin' to or why. I'm tired of bein' ugly to each other. It feels like pieces of glass in my head. I'm tired of all the times I wanted to help and couldn't. I'm tired of bein' in the dark.*[378]

Repeating this monologue many years later, Edgecomb understands exactly what Coffey meant—because Coffey died so that Edgecomb and his fellow guards could see the world the same way he saw it: with boundless empathy for every other living thing. By writing *The Green Mile*, King attempts to do the same things for his readers. In his proudest moments, the horror author embraces the mystic's realization that "all will be well and all manner of things will be well." In his own way, he shares the same irrational philosophy of

377 King: *Green* 399
378 King: *Green* 491

non-dualism: "Sometimes there is absolutely no difference at all between salvation and damnation."[379]

Having made his peace with traditional Christianity, King confidently returned to his own mythology in *Wizard and Glass*, an extended prologue to the first three *Dark Tower* novels. With this installment, the author says he realized that he was working on his ultimate statement about the nature of the universe. In the afterword, he explained himself:

> *I have written enough novels and short stories to fill a solar system of the imagination, but Roland's story is my Jupiter—a planet that dwarfs all the others (at least from my own perspective), a place of strange atmosphere, crazy landscape, and savage gravitational pull. Dwarfs the others, did I say? I think there's more to it than that, actually. I am coming to understand that Roland's world (or worlds) actually contains all the others of my making; there is a place in Mid-World for Randall Flagg, Ralph Roberts, the wandering boys from* The Eyes of the Dragon, *even Father Callahan, the damned priest from* 'Salem's Lot, *who rode out of New England on a Greyhound Bus and wound up dwelling on the border of a terrible Mid-World called Thunderclap.*[380]

In essence, King was suggesting that *all* of his work so far was an extended prologue to the remaining chapters of *The Dark Tower*. Recent short stories like "Everything's Eventual," about a writer whose tales always come true, and "Little Sisters of Eluria," in which the gunslinger is nursed by vampires, merely hinted at things to come.

379 King: *Green* 593
380 King: "Afterword," *Wizard* 695

The King of Hollywood (IV)

Even as King was building what he perceived as the pinnacle of his literary career, filmmakers continued to mine his older material, with dubious results. In May 1995, ABC aired an adaptation of "The Langoliers," written and directed by Tom Holland. The two-part miniseries suffered from bland performances, stilted dialogue and unconvincing visual effects. King opined, "The best thing about it was that it gave Tom Holland and [producer] Richard Rubinstein the *bona fides* they needed to get Spelling Productions to go ahead with [a feature film adaptation of] *Thinner*."[381] No doubt King was enthusiastic about the fact that *Thinner* (1996) would be shot entirely in his home state of Maine, but unfortunately that film also turned out to be a dud. Holland shot a black comedy, but the final edit made most of the humor seem unintentional; the result was a film with a frustratingly uncertain tone. King placed the blame on "the suits at Spelling," telling journalist Bill Warren, "I don't know who finally made the creative editing decisions, except they *weren't* creative decisions—they were made by people who have no sense of humor."[382]

Castle Rock's *Dolores Claiborne* (1995) was a respectable, if equally humorless, affair. It boasted striking cinematography and excellent performances by Kathy Bates and Jennifer Jason Leigh, but King compared it to Kubrick's *The Shining*, saying that although it was "a remarkably beautiful film," it was a "flawed" adaptation that softened the rough-hewn edges of his story. The biggest mistake, he argued, "was the decision on the part of the filmmakers to try to tack on this artificial reconciliation between Dolores and her daughter."[383] In the author's opinion, the screenplay by Tony Gilroy transformed a genuinely gritty horror story into a predictable melodrama.

Tobe Hooper's *The Mangler* (1995) was comparatively bold, but its mean-spirited horror drove audiences away. The movie earned less than two million dollars in theatrical release, despite the marketing power of three modern-day masters of horror (King, Hooper

381 Marotta 103

382 Jones 108

383 Magistrale 18-19

and actor Robert Englund, of *A Nightmare on Elm Street* fame). As for the sequels . . . King once joked about a possible sequel to *Christine* that would star a homicidal Cuisinart made from the remains of the original monster.[384] The filmmakers of *The Mangler 2* (2002) and *The Mangler Reborn* (2005) apparently took this joke seriously. Or tried to.

Even more confounding was an attempt to remake Stephen King's most embarrassing filmmaking debacle. Writer/director Chris Thomson presumably meant for *Trucks* (1997) to show the author where he had failed in adapting his own short story as *Maximum Overdrive*. King was not humbled.

Despite so many lackluster or downright embarrassing adaptations of his work, King's name still carried enough weight with viewers to justify yet another miniseries. This time, the author convinced ABC to wrangle the rights to *The Shining* so that he could fulfill his longtime dream of creating a more faithful screen adaptation than Stanley Kubrick's film. Once again he hired Mick Garris to be the medium for his message, and the duo set out to create a more conflicted Jack Torrance, as well as a smarter and stronger Wendy Torrance. Bringing the story back to its roots, they shot the miniseries at the Stanley Hotel in Estes Park, Colorado, where the author had conceived *The Shining* twenty years earlier. The new adaptation earned solid television ratings, but did little to erase the collective memory of Kubrick's adaptation.

Garris went on to adapt King's short story "Chattery Teeth," using the same crew from *The Shining*. His goal, according to King, was to create "a kind of pilot for a series [. . .] where there would be two episodes every week with the same cast of actors, but they'd be different stories."[385] Instead, "Chattery Teeth" ended up on a double bill with a Clive Barker adaptation, in the video release *Quicksilver Highway* (1997). King, meanwhile, contributed an episode to the paranormal TV series *The X-Files*, a show that may have drawn some initial inspiration from the author's own series *Golden Years*. In the end, the author was dismayed by his lack of control over that particular project. "I did two or three drafts of a script," he later explained, "and [showrunner Chris Carter] rewrote me entirely."[386] Although

384 Lofficier 62
385 Marotta 106
386 Jones 180

King was complimentary of Carter, it was a discouraging experience for a storyteller who had become accustomed to dictating his terms and controlling his own material. The finished episode, about a killer doll, failed to please either King fans or *X-Files* viewers.

King was more enthusiastic about *The Night Flier* (1997), a stylish adaptation by writer/director Mark Pavia that aired on HBO. According to Stephen Jones, the author handpicked the director and served as "story editor" on the project.[387] The resulting film boasts compelling performances by Miguel Ferrer (as reporter Richard Dees, a character who first appeared in *The Dead Zone*) and newcomer Julie Entwistle, and the expanded story is a significant improvement on King's perfunctory short story—elaborating brilliantly on his recurring theme of faith vs. madness.

Whereas *The Night Flier* benefited from the expansion of its source story, director Bryan Singer's 1998 film adaptation of "Apt Pupil" suffered from unnecessary truncation. The original novella charts a teenage boy's descent into madness, culminating with a desperate leap from serial murder to spree killing. Following a recent spate of comparable shootings in American high schools, the author felt that the ending would hit too close to home for contemporary moviegoers, and encouraged the filmmakers to adapt only the first act of his story.[388] The result was a rather lightweight film that carefully placated conservative critics who are always eager to blame media violence for real-world violence.

King expressed his feelings on this subject in May 1999, when he spoke about his decision to discontinue the publication of his early novel *Rage* based on concerns that the book may have been a blueprint for a high school shooting in West Paducah, Kentucky:

> *Do I think that* Rage *may have provoked [shooter Michael] Carneal, or any other badly adjusted young person, to resort to the gun? It's an important question, because it goes to the very heart of the wrangle over who's to blame. You might as well ask if I believe that the mere presence of a gun makes some people want to use that gun. The answer is troubling, but it needs to be faced: in some cases, yes.*[389]

387 Jones 111

388 Jones 118

389 King: "Stephen King's Keynote"

King later clarified his response in his 2013 essay *Guns*:

> *According to* The Copycat Effect, *written by Loren Coleman (Simon and Schuster, 2004), I also apologized for writing* Rage. *No, ma'am, I never did and never would. It took more than one novel to cause [Jeff] Cox, [Dustin] Pierce, [Barry] Loukaitis, and Carneal to do what they did. These were unhappy boys with deep psychological problems, boys who were bullied at school and bruised at home by parental neglect or outright abuse [. . .] My book did not break Cox, Pierce, Carneal, or Loukaitis, or turn them into killers; they found something in my book that spoke to them because they were already broken. Yet I did see* Rage *as an accelerant, which is why I pulled it from sale.*[390]

King's makes his own sense of moral responsibility clear, and in both of these instances he goes on to raise questions about the moral responsibility of a *community*. The same questions are at the heart of his next miniseries *Storm of the Century* (1999), about a small town held hostage by its own demon of discord. The visitor, who calls himself Andre Linoge, is a hybrid of erudite serial killer Hannibal Lector (*Silence of the Lambs*) and Leland Gaunt (*Needful Things*). After committing a series of murders to demonstrate his supernatural power, Linoge offers a deal to the citizens of Little Tall Island: "Give me what I want and I'll leave." What he wants is for them to *willingly* surrender one of their children to him as a ritualistic sacrifice. If they don't, he promises to kill everyone. The scenario is reminiscent of King's short story "Rainy Season," about a small Maine town where people condone the periodic sacrifice of tourists in order to protect themselves from a perceived greater threat. In both stories, most characters view the welfare of the town as their greatest responsibility. Only one character dares to question the nature of their sacrifice, and ask the necessary question: *Are the townfolk making a utilitarian judgment or are they merely acting out of fear?* More importantly: What is the *psychological* cost of giving in to this kind of spiritual terrorism? King's suggests that living with guilt and regret over immoral decisions is worse than dying afraid.

390 King: *Guns*

Fin de siècle

In May 1997, while he was between drafts of *Storm of the Century*, King began work on another dark tale about moral responsibilities. *Bag of Bones* was his first grand-scale ghost story since *The Shining*, and like the earlier tale, *Bag of Bones* revolves around a struggling writer who is tested by supernatural forces. It also shows King doubling back to his early gothic horror work, with a more mature outlook on life.

The setup of the novel is relatively straightforward. After the tragic death of his pregnant wife, bestselling author Mike Noonan (jokingly referred to as "V.C. Andrews with a prick") is overcome by a kind of existential panic. He retreats to his summer home in the rural community of TR-90, where he suffers a debilitating case of writer's block. For him, as for King in the late 1980s, writer's block is the equivalent of death-in-life—because, he says, "without my wife *and* my work, I was a superfluous man living alone in a big house that was all paid for, doing nothing but the newspaper crossword over lunch."[391] Noonan soon realizes, however, that he's *not* alone in the house, as he begins uncovering clues that his wife's death is related to a century-old murder mystery.

King took his main inspiration from traditional gothic literature—most notably Daphne du Maurier's 1938 novel *Rebecca*—and so *Bag of Bones* revisits the most indelible of Gothic themes. The author says:

> *It's an Old Testament idea and not very palatable to us in Western culture, but generally speaking, evil does not die, and evil acts are visited on generation after generation, so that a child who's beaten grows up to be a beater, and a child who's abused grows up to be an abuser. Then, there's the whole idea of sacrifice in* Bag of Bones, *the sacrifice of the innocents in order to expiate guilt. That goes back to the Old Testament as well.*[392]

This gothic plot (echoed by the philosophy of Alcoholics Anonymous) is compelling enough, but what really brings the

391 King: *Bag* 43
392 Ulin

book to life is the first-person narrative of Mike Noonan. As his experiences in TR-90 become increasingly inexplicable, the writer undergoes an intense reevaluation of personal beliefs. At first, he refuses to accept the reality of ghosts. Later, when the evidence of a supernatural haunting becomes impossible to deny, he has to change his belief system in order to maintain his sanity.

The author had already explored the idea that a *building* can be haunted (in *The Shining*) and he reiterates his working theory here: "I think houses live their own lives along a time-stream that's different from the ones upon which their owners float, one that's slower. In a house, especially an old one, the past is closer."[393] In *'Salem's Lot* and *Storm of the Century*, King had also proposed that the collective subconscious of a community can be haunted, and Mike Noonan comes to the same conclusion about TR-90: "There is such a thing as town consciousness—anyone who doubts it has never been to a New England town meeting. Where there's a consciousness, is there not likely to be a subconscious?"[394] As in those earlier works, the town in *Bag of Bones* has a very *guilty* subconscious.

What seems to interest King the most, however, is the haunting of an individual psyche. *Bag of Bones* builds on the ponderings of King's novels about the link between creativity and madness, faith and desperation—and with an intimacy and immediacy that is reminiscent of his earliest work. Noonan muses, "When an imaginative person gets into mental trouble, the line between seeming and being has a way of disappearing."[395] That's exactly what happens to him as the story unfolds. Dreams conflate with reality, to the point that Noonan no longer thinks of supernatural experiences as waking dreams (or, more to the point, products of the imagination) but as "*spiritual time-travel*."[396] To him, ghosts have become as much a part of the fabric of reality as anything he can experience with his natural senses. King insists this is a perfectly *natural* leap for the creative mind to make:

> *That's what writers do. They create ghosts and watch them walk around the room. [. . .] You have to remember that what we do, people who don't get paid for, or published, end up in lunatic*

393 King: *Bag* 124
394 King: *Bag* 530
395 King: *Bag* 87
396 King: *Bag* 494

asylums for. We see things that aren't there, which of course is the definition of seeing ghosts.[397]

The real challenge for a creative mind, of course, is keeping the ghosts from taking over. In *Bag of Bones*, ghosts threaten every aspect of Mike Noonan's life, until he finally figures out what they want from him. Once he has done that, he is able to exorcise the spirits and reassert control of his life.

For King, the arc of Mike Noonan's growth toward a new kind of belief—the belief that the living are more powerful than the dead, and that the present is more powerful than the past—reveals the theme of the novel and represents the author's own personal convictions:

I was trying to say that writing is not life. There is a certain unstated scripture that I think most liberal arts majors take with them from school. A lot of liberal arts students take the idea with them that art is life, that writing is life, that painting is life, that sculpture is life, that architecture is life. Creativity is not life. Love is life. Carpentry is life. Regular bowels are life! Most of all, love is life.[398]

At the end of the story, Noonan overcomes his dependence on writing for a sense of self. Even though his wife is gone, he remains a loving husband. Even though he is not a biological father, he becomes a loving caregiver to a child who needs him. His roles as a husband and father, he concludes, are more important than any fiction he could ever create.

By the late 1990s, Stephen King had reached the same conclusion, as he explained in the BBC documentary *Stephen King: Shining in the Dark*:

The first thing I am is a husband. The second thing I am is a father. And there's a time when I probably would have put fatherhood ahead of husbandhood, when the kids were small. The third thing that I am is, I'm a man of my place and my time and my community. And I have to be all those things first because, if I want to be a writer, everything trickles down.

397 King: "Night" 396
398 King: "Evening" 398

At the end of the novel *The Shining*, Jack Torrance sacrifices himself to save his son from the ghosts of the Overlook Hotel. At the end of *Bag of Bones*, Mike Noonan fights off the ghosts of TR-90 to save his adopted daughter. The major difference between the two endings is that Noonan survives and remains a good parent, breaking the gothic cycle of violence. King has effectively "doubled back," and rewritten the future.

Considering this revisionist quality of the novel, which shows how King had matured since the time when he thought of himself as a writer above all else, *Bag of Bones* might have provided a natural stopping point for the author. Unlike Mike Noonan, however, King was not ready to retire. In fact, at the end of *Bag of Bones*, immediately after Noonan's declaration that he is putting down his pen forever, King teased his next book—a story that had been germinating in his subconscious since the late 1960s, when he was a student at the University of Maine. It was a story about being a man of a particular place, time and community.

For years, the author had thought of writing a book about his generation, but he was overwhelmed by the prospect of trying to capture the essence of 1960s America. In *Danse Macabre* (1981), he wrote:

> *I've purposely avoided writing a novel with a 1960s time setting because all of that seems, like the pulling of [a] surgical dressing, very distant to me now—almost as if it happened to another person. But those things did happen; the hate, paranoia and fear on both sides were all too real.*[399]

What he didn't want to do, as he explained in the afterword to *Bag of Bones*, was write a book full of clichés: "I wasn't able to imagine, for instance, writing a story in which a character flashed a peace sign or said, 'Hey . . . groovy!'"[400]

Hearts of Atlantis, a collection of short stories about a generation's coming of age, emerged gradually. The writing process began with a 1993 short story called "Blind Willie," about a Vietnam vet who lives a secret life as a blind beggar—doing penance for the horrible things he did at home and abroad when he was a young man. The

399 King: *Danse* 168
400 King: "Afterword," *Bag*

subsequent "Hearts in Atlantis," a short story written between drafts of *Bag of Bones*, is a more autobiographical tale, based on an incident King observed during his freshman year in college. It follows a group of college boys in 1966 that manages to avoid the fact that the world is changing around them, until one of their peers makes an anti-war statement that rattles the entire community and demands a serious reaction. King says that this particular story became his "way in" to the book about his generation: "I began to see a way I might be able to write about what we almost had, what we lost, and what we finally ended up with."[401]

Next, the author went back even further in time, to tell the story of a kid named Bobby Garfield. Bobby came of age in 1960 when a kind stranger named Ted Brautigan introduced him to literature (beginning with *Lord of the Flies* and culminating with *Of Mice and Men*), telepathy (the B-movie *Village of the Damned* makes a convenient tutorial) and the nature of evil. In "Low Men in Yellow Coats," Bobby learns that evil can come from outside sources as well as from inside the human heart. Brautigan knows all about outside evil, but Bobby recognizes that the old man's heart is pure. On the other hand, Bobby's mother has been corrupted by a lifetime of abuse and betrayal; through her, Bobby comes to understand that people—even the people we love the most—can be broken. It is unclear exactly how devastating this revelation is to Bobby, or what will become of him later in life. King offers only vague hints at an answer; subsequent stories illustrate how Bobby is vitally connected to the dreams and disappointments of an entire generation, so we can assume that he will have his fair share of hopes and failures.

The fourth story in *Hearts in Atlantis*, "Why We're in Vietnam," provides the author's most explicit commentary on hippie-cum-yuppie culture. A disillusioned war veteran, speaking in 1999, reflects:

> *I like lots of people our age when they're one by one, but I loathe and despise my generation, Sully. We had an opportunity to change everything. We actually did. Instead we settled for designer jeans, two tickets to Mariah Carey at Radio City Music Hall, frequent-flier miles, James Cameron's* Titanic, *and retirement portfolios. The only generation even close to us in pure, selfish self-indulgence is the so-called Lost Generation of*

401 King: "Afterword," *Bag*

the twenties, and at least most of them had the decency to stay drunk. We couldn't even do that.[402]

This character gives voice to the author's own disappointment, but the overall tone of *Hearts in Atlantis* shows that King is not predominantly bitter. Mostly he seems melancholy, and quietly amazed by the realization that life's joys are intermixed with so much pain and sadness. Like Paul Edgecomb at the end of *The Green Mile*, King conveys immense sorrow for the human condition—but, like the children in his stories, he remains awed by the very real possibilities for change. "Heavenly Shades of Night Are Falling" ends the *Hearts in Atlantis* collection on a hopeful note and a simpler message, repeating Bobby Garfield's most important lesson: "Hearts are tough. Most times they don't break. Most times they only bend."[403] In his most deeply personal work since "The Body," King's essential faith in humanity continues to shine through. Like *Bag of Bones*, *Hearts in Atlantis* suggests closure by bringing the author back to the themes of his early work, and examining them from a more mature perspective. Life is an endurance contest, King says, and *hearts endure.*

King confidently reiterates his belief in a Higher Power in his subsequent novel *The Girl Who Loved Tom Gordon*, a simple story about fear, faith and baseball. This is how one character sums up:

> *I believe in the Subaudible . . . I don't believe in any actual thinking God that marks the fall of every bird in Australia or every bug in India, a God that records all of our sins in a big golden book and judges us when we die—I don't want to believe in a God who would deliberately create bad people and then deliberately send them to roast in a hell He created—but I believe there has to be something [. . .] Some insensate force for the good."*[404]

These words resonate in the mind of nine-year-old Trisha McFarland when she gets lost in the dense woods of western Maine. In reality, King says, the odds of Trisha's survival are grim, but the story asserts that odds don't necessarily apply to the faithful. Trisha, like

402 King: *Bag* 639
403 King: *Hearts* 514
404 King: *Girl* 65

her father, like baseball enthusiast Stephen King, places her faith in Red Sox pitcher Tom Gordon. Gordon can't save her, of course, but her *faith* in him does. King's message (which would be reiterated a few years later in *Faithful*, his non-fiction chronicle of the 2004 Red Sox winning season) is simple: Miracles *do* happen.

After completing the final draft of *Tom Gordon* in the spring of 1999, Stephen King left his winter home in Florida and headed north to Maine. He had said all he wanted to say for the time being, and had no plans to start another novel anytime soon. His next story, however, was lying in wait for him. King explains that the opening scene of *From a Buick 8* came to him when he stopped at a quaint little gas station off the Pennsylvania Turnpike. He chewed the fat with the gas station attendant for a few minutes, then went around to the back of the building to use the restroom. Afterwards he wandered down to a nearby stream—and nearly disappeared, just like Trisha McFarland. King remembers:

> *There were still patches of snow on the ground. I slipped on one and started to slide down the embankment. I grabbed a piece of someone's old engine block and stopped myself before I got fairly started, but I realized as I got up that if I'd fallen just right, I could have slid all the way down into that stream and been swept away. I found myself wondering, had that happened, how long it would have taken the gas station attendant to call the State Police if my car, a brand-new Lincoln Navigator, just continued to stand there in front of the pumps. By the time I got back on the turnpike again, I had two things: a wet ass from my fall behind the Mobil station, and a great idea for a story.*[405]

As it turned out, it was the story that swept him away. King spent the next two months writing the first draft of a novel about a group of Pennsylvania State Troopers who are drawn together as caretakers of an abandoned car. As the story unfolds they learn that the car is utterly *foreign*, and extremely dangerous. The narrative itself hinges on unanswerable questions: *Where did the car come from? What is its purpose? What will happen if they try to destroy it?*

Years later, King explained that the story naturally evolved into a "meditation on the essentially indecipherable quality of

405 King: *On Writing* 228-229

life's events, and how impossible it is to find coherent meaning in them."[406] The story is about how one simple event—the discovery of a Buick on the side of the road—can profoundly and permanently change the lives of everyone involved. In this case, the event burdens each and every character with a terrible mystery that will haunt them for the rest of their lives. They can no more solve the mystery than they can explain the meaning of life or death. On the surface the mystery is simply an alien car (Christine by way of The Tommyknockers), but it is also the Thing that awaits all of us at the bottom of an icy slope: the great and inescapable Unknown.

The author once said that if he had to restrict everything he'd ever said or written about the horror genre to one statement, it would be this: "Death is when the monsters get you."407 In his last novel of the twentieth century, death appeared in the guise of a car. A few short months after completing his first draft of *From a Buick 8*, the author confronted the same monster in real life.

406 King: "Author's Note" 484
407 King: *Danse* 205

A Clarifying Effect

Late in the afternoon on June 19, 1999, Stephen King was walking along the edge of Route 5 near his summer home in Lovell, Maine, when he was hit from behind by a van. After he regained consciousness, the author remembers, "I'm lying in the ditch and there's blood all over my face and my right leg hurts. I look down and see something I don't like: my lap now appears to be on sideways, as if my whole lower body has been wrenched half a turn to the right."[408] The next thing he recalls is being loaded into an ambulance and rushed to a hospital in nearby Bridgton, where doctors determine that his injuries (a broken hip, a completely shattered right leg, a chipped spine, four broken ribs, and a severe scalp laceration) are too extreme for them to treat at that facility. King was then airlifted to the Central Maine Medical Center in Lewiston. On the way, his right lung collapsed.

Five weeks and five surgeries later, King was fearful that he would never have the strength and presence of mind to write again. His wife Tabitha urged him on, and King spent the rest of the summer working to complete his memoir *On Writing*, which explains how writing sustained him through the dark days of his recovery: "Writing did not save my life—Dr. David Brown's skill and my wife's loving care did that—but it has continued to do what it has always done: it makes my life a brighter and more pleasant place."[409] For that reason, above all others, he kept going.

In 2013, when *Fresh Air* host Terri Gross asked King if he felt that his work had changed since the accident, the author said he honestly didn't know. "I'm on the inside," he responded, "[so] I am not the best person to ask." He did suggest, however, that his near-death experience might have had a "clarifying effect."[410] Certainly it made him more acutely aware of his mortality, and prompted him to carefully consider what he wanted to accomplish with his remaining years. Although King insists that he writes at a much slower pace than he did before the accident, he spent the subsequent decade

408 King: *On Writing* 256
409 King: *On Writing* 269
410 Terri Gross

and a half producing a significant body of work that expanded the worlds he created in the 1970s, '80s and '90s—tying up loose ends, developing ideas that had previously overwhelmed him, and proving that his power as a storyteller has not diminished.

In the initial months after the accident, however, that future was uncertain. Amidst pervasive rumors about the extent of his injuries, the author promptly addressed his readers' concerns via his official website. On November 2, 2000, he wrote:

> *Since the accident I have finished my book on writing, I have written a novelette called "Riding the Bullet," and have begun work on an original miniseries for TV. This is called* Rose Red *and is an expansion of a screenplay I wrote some years ago. I have also begun talking with Peter Straub about finally writing a sequel to* The Talisman*—we jokingly called this project T2, although I doubt if there will be a part for Arnold Schwarzenegger.*[411]

Obviously, King had lost neither his writing ability nor his sense of humor. As if to further quell reader anxieties, he released three new short stories (presumably written before his accident) in an audio collection called *Blood and Smoke*. One of the stories, a ghost story called "1408" quickly became a fan favorite. A few months later, he released "Riding the Bullet" in an e-book format. A good old-fashioned Stephen King horror story, it charted a young man's unexpected night journey to the Central Maine Medical Center in Lewiston. A messenger of death follows him the whole way, forcing him to question his personal beliefs and assess the value of his own life.

Oddly, King's teleplay for the haunted house miniseries *Rose Red* paid very little attention to questions of belief. The characters in *Rose Red* express no initial disbelief about the existence of ghosts, so when ghosts appear in front of them (which happens very early in the story) their reactions are ludicrously casual. King has never shied away from showing the monsters onscreen, but he *has* generally been more mindful of characterization and suspension of disbelief. *Rose Red* focuses more on imaginative set pieces than on people, and

411 King: "Messages"

that's a disappointment from one of the world's most successful storytellers.

Thankfully, King quickly returned to his natural medium, and began writing a horror novel that would draw on his own close encounter with death. "When I sat down to work on *Dreamcatcher*," the author remembers,

> *I was in terrible pain, taking all these heavy drugs by the jarful, and I was on crutches, a brace on my leg, and all I knew was when I went to bed at night, I would lie there and I'd think of this guy on a hunter stand, in a tree, like a shooter's platform, where you go when you've been hurt sometimes. And I thought here's this guy, it's starting to snow, he wants to get his deer because it's hunting season, and here comes this thing he thinks is a deer, but it's a person . . . That's all I had.*[412]

When he started writing, King identified the man in the tree as Gary Jones, a college professor struggling to cope with chronic pain in the wake of a near-fatal accident. Like King, Jonesy was hit by a moving vehicle and his injuries were severe: a fractured skull, two broken ribs, and a shattered hip. Over time, the wounds have healed and his pain is subsiding, but Jonesy's recovery has taken a tremendous psychological toll on him. When he goes on an annual hunting trip into the wilds of northern Maine with three friends, he realizes that he no longer has any interest in hunting; he already feels too close to death.

Nearly suicidal, Jonesy views the trip as a desperate final attempt to reconnect with the only truly meaningful thing in his life: his friendship with childhood chums Pete, Henry, and The Beav. Although each one's hopes and dreams have withered over the years, the four friends are bolstered by something they did together when they were growing up in Derry. Like the quartet of friends in "The Body" or the seven "losers" in *IT*, they brought out the best in each other once upon a time. King insists that this is still the case: "Together they are still good."[413] As it turns out, however, that childhood magic also makes them especially vulnerable to a new threat.

412 Adams
413 King: *Dreamcatcher* 32

The first few hundred pages of *Dreamcatcher* succeed in creating an atmosphere of palpable dread. King writes about the invisible presence of an alien menace with the same intensity that author Whitley Strieber described his alien abduction in the memoir *Communion*. What's so terrifying about both accounts is the narrator's acute sensitivity to the Unknown, or perhaps the Unknowable. This is not the first time that King has written about the possibility of alien invasion (see *IT*, *The Tommyknockers*, and *From a Buick 8*), but it is the first time that he crafted such an intimate response to the idea. In *Dreamcatcher*, it is not just the Maine woods that are invaded; the bodies and minds of the main characters are invaded as well, making the horror inescapable.

At first, the alien invaders make their presence known in a manner worthy of an early David Cronenberg movie. King once wrote that "you can't write about a monster that has anything to do with the excretory functions or anything like that," but he breaks his own rule here.[414] His goal, he insists, was not to be crude or gross but to convey the nature of real-life body horror:

> *I thought to myself that no one in novels, let alone in movies, talks about one of the primal fears that we have: That one day we will stand up from taking a shit and discover that the toilet bowl is full of blood. This event could signal many things: It could just be a hemorrhoid, or it could be colon cancer.*[415]

In *Dreamcatcher*, it signals a type of alien invasion that would make Ridley Scott shudder. Suddenly, burping and farting is no longer a product of male bonding, but of an affliction much worse than cancer.

Once the alien threat has been identified, the story follows a more traditional route, updating and reflecting on scenarios from stories like *The War of the Worlds* and *The Body Snatchers*. A character aptly named Kurtz (an obvious allusion to Joseph Conrad's *Heart of Darkness*) leads Uncle Sam's war, targeting not only the invading alien "cancer" but also the Constitutional rights of rural Maine's citizens. The author's characterization of the American military leadership is none too subtle. Kurtz rants:

414 Schaefer 113
415 Magistrale 10

> *We are going to wipe these invading assholes out, my friend, and if they ever come back to Terra Firma, we are going to rip their collective gray head and shit down their collective gray neck; if they persist we will use their own technology, which we are already well on our way to grasping, against them, returning to their place of origin in their own ships or ships built like them by General Electric and DuPont and praise God Microsoft and once there we will burn their cities or hives or goddamn anthills, whatever they live in, we'll napalm their amber waves of grain and nuke their purple mountains' majesty, praise God,* Allah akhbar, *we will pour the fiery piss of America into their lakes and oceans...*[416]

Despite Kurtz's fiery rhetoric, the real battle is waged in Jonesy's mind, because King's aliens are not little green men but an advanced consciousness that exists independent of physical bodies.

In a 1999 appearance, the author confessed that he didn't much believe in little green (or gray) men: "UFOs, Hanger 51, all that *X-Files* stuff, I don't think so. I think the aliens among us are the Ted Bundys and the Jeffrey Dahmers and the John Wayne Gacys. I think they really are alien."[417] In a way, the author's disbelief in aliens as an outside threat becomes the hero's greatest weapon in *Dreamcatcher*. Jonesy is able to fight back once he realizes that human imagination is the vector for the alien cancer. As soon as he stops believing in *physical* alien creatures, those creatures cease to exist on a physical level; his mind overcomes the external threat the same way a person's mind can overcome pain, by refusing to give it power. It's an ambitious, if slightly confounding, ending that approximates Whitley Strieber's own tentative conclusions about the force(s) that invaded his own consciousness. Strieber writes, "Either what is happening is that visitors are actually here, or the human mind is creating something that, incredibly, is close to physical reality."[418] King writes, of Jonesy, "What you caught was an intention . . . a kind of blind imperative. Fuck, there's no word for it, because there's no word for *them*. But I think it got in because you *believe* it was there."[419] Through sheer force of will, Jonesy survives. Likewise, once King

416 King: *Dreamcatcher* 431
417 King: "Evening" 395
418 Strieber 4
419 King: *Dreamcatcher* 874

realized that he could imagine his way *through* his pain, he realized that he could still be an effective writer. That gave him the clarity and strength to tackle an unfinished project that had been hanging over his head for more than two decades.

Saving The Dark Tower

In 1995, following the release of the fourth *Dark Tower* book *Wizard and Glass*, the author expressed his concerns that he might not be able to complete his epic saga, posting the following comment on his publisher's website:

> *I want to finish it. But there are no guarantees in this business. I can walk out of here today and get hit by a bus and that would be the end of that. Unless it came into somebody by Ouija board, which is always a possibility. But the other thing is, I can try and find out that the words aren't there anymore. I don't think that will happen, but you never know 'til you open the cupboard.*[420]

Clearly nervous about the prospect of reopening the cupboard, the author chose to focus on other, smaller projects during the following years, only to find elements of his epic saga creeping into seemingly unrelated stories.

In the 1997 short story "Everything's Eventual," King introduced a character named Dinky Earnshaw, an antisocial high school dropout with a wild talent for killing people by writing about them. (Dinky writes in symbols—something like Runic script—and those symbols cast a deadly spell on their intended recipient.) Like Charlie McGee in *Firestarter*, Dinky is pursued by a shadowy organization that wants to use his supernatural power for their own ends. For a while, Dinky is content to work as a high-paid assassin, grateful that his supernatural gifts can be put to some practical use. "This is what I was put on Planet Earth for," he rationalizes. "Can I be blamed for doing the thing that finishes me off, that completes me?" King answers, "Absolutely."[421] In the end, Dinky doesn't stop writing, but he does start taking responsibility for his actions. That resolution draws him into *The Dark Tower*, where the Crimson King is amassing an army of "wild" children called Breakers to help destroy the nexus of all worlds.

---

420 Beahm: *America's* 208
421 King: "Everything's" 260

In the 1998 story "Low Men in Yellow Coats" (the longest segment of *Hearts in Atlantis*), King had introduced a character with similar supernatural powers. Ted Brautigan, the paternal stranger who teaches Bobby Garfield some hard truths about life, is a telepath—one of the strongest in the world. Because of this talent, Ted is pursued by a group of inhuman strangers that he refers to as "low men." When they catch up with him, the low men put him to work for the Crimson King, as a Breaker. The author explains, "There is a Tower [that] holds everything together. There are Beams that protect it somehow. There is a Crimson King, and Breakers working to destroy the Beams . . . not because the Breakers want to but because it wants them to."[422] When Brautigan gets pulled into Mid-World at the end of the story, his plight beckoned the author to return to the *Dark Tower* series, to find out what happens when Roland's *ka-tet* meets the Breakers.

King did not follow immediately, but he was not deaf to the call. In a February 1999 interview for the *San Francisco Chronicle*, he articulated his sense of responsibility to the fans, saying, "I can't retire until I finish the *Dark Tower* books, because there are people out there who would slaughter me if I didn't finish."[423] Later he developed an even stronger sense of responsibility to the characters and to the tale itself. In the final *Dark Tower* book, the author describes *Hearts in Atlantis* as a symbol of his own lazy reluctance to complete the *Dark Tower* series, noting that by the summer of 1997 he already knew the story of the fifth book but chose to write *Hearts in Atlantis* instead because returning to the path to the Dark Tower "seemed like too much work."[424]

A few months later, the author's brush with death almost prematurely sealed the fate of Roland and his *ka-tet*. When King recovered, he began thinking that perhaps he had survived the accident *in order to* complete *The Dark Tower* series; that perhaps the Tower had, in some profound sense, kept him alive. The notion would eventually find its way into the final books of the series, which fuse King's real-world autobiography with Roland's quest. For the time being, however, the author remained reluctant to write the fifth book. In the fall of 2000, after a second e-book experiment ("The Plant"), he

422 King: *Hearts* 292
423 Rogak 200
424 King: *Dark Tower VII* 212

chose to focus his attention on a sequel to *The Talisman*, cowritten with Peter Straub . . . only to find that The Dark Tower would not leave him alone.

Unlike *The Talisman*, *Black House* reads like a book written by two different writers. The first part of the novel is a gritty and gruesome murder mystery set in the fictional town of Tamarack, Wisconsin. The setting (near Straub's childhood home) and the narrative voice (a reflective "we" that distances the reader from the action) suggest that this early section is drawn largely from Straub's imagination. Stephen King appears to confirm the theory in a September 2000 interview. When asked whose voice was dominating the book-in-progress, he answered, "At the moment to me the voice that this book has seems more Peter Straub, so I'm trying to wrestle it back a bit."[425] His way of "wrestling it back" was to introduce elements of *The Dark Tower* mythology. According to one interview, it was Straub who actually suggested the overlap. King responded, "I'm glad you said that, because I don't know if I can keep it out."[426] Just as *The Talisman* reads like a dry run for King's epic fantasy, *Black House* often seems like an excuse for the author to delve back into the Dark Tower mythology without the psychological pressure of starting a new *Dark Tower* novel. Like "Everything's Eventual" and "Low Men in Yellow Coats," *Black House* is a story not about Roland and his ka-tet but about the forces lying in wait for them.

In *Black House*, Jake Chambers is an ex-homicide detective who gets drawn into the search for a kidnapped child. Gradually he comes to realize that the missing boy, Tyler Marshall, is telekinetic. Because of his history with "other worlds," Jake also realizes that Tyler has been abducted by servants of the Crimson King, and later has a vision of what will happen if the Crimson King is allowed to use the boy's power to destroy the Beams and collapse the Dark Tower: All worlds, including Mid-World and the Territories (described in this book as a "borderland" near Mid-World), will be cast into an apocalyptic furnace. With that in mind, Jake and his friends set out to rescue Tyler and preserve the Tower—at least until Roland and his ka-tet can get there to finish the job. Here again, the author's subconscious mind seemed to be telling him he had a job to finish . . . and that he was running out of time.

425 Adams

426 Zaleski

Black House was published just prior to September 11, 2001, and the events of that day may have enhanced King's feelings about his fictional Tower. Soon after, the author resolved to complete the *Dark Tower* series. In hindsight, he said, "I knew it was going to be like crossing the Atlantic in a bathtub [but] I thought I'm just going to keep on working, because if I stop I'll never start again."[427] For roughly three years, he devoted himself entirely to Roland's journey. The culmination of the epic quest finally appeared in three volumes: *Wolves of the Calla* (published in 2003), *Song of Susannah*, and *The Dark Tower* (both published in 2004). Almost immediately, King began characterizing the finished series as his masterwork, and the text itself offered a unique interior perspective on his career as a writer.

Wolves of the Calla brings King full circle to one his earliest novels. At the outset of the book, Roland and his fellow travelers encounter Father Donald Callahan, the priest who was cursed by the vampire Barlow at the end of *'Salem's Lot*. It's no accident that the old vampire hunter is in Mid-World, because many of the soldiers in the Crimson King's army are vampires. For the time being, however, vampires are not Callahan's main concern; the priest is trying to protect a village called Calla Bryn Sturgis from an army of werewolves. In much the way that King modeled *The Gunslinger* on Sergio Leone's Man-with-No-Name westerns, he takes some inspiration for *Wolves of the Calla* from the John Sturges western *The Magnificent Seven*, about a group of mercenary gunslingers who pledge to protect a town of poor farmers. Father Callahan joins Roland's ka-tet as they go into battle.

As the story draws to a close, *Wolves of the Calla* becomes saturated with references to other works of popular fiction, including J.K. Rowling's *Harry Potter* series, the *Star Wars* movies, and Marvel's *Spider-Man* comics. This was King's way of illustrating that Roland's quest is bigger than any one imagination. In a sense, the narrator suggests, "Stephen King" is no longer the creator, but now only a character in *The Dark Tower* mythos. This strange fusion of fiction and biography (academics would call it meta-fiction, but King detests that term) is a kind of humbling prayer to whatever mysterious life

427 Jeffries

force allows great writers to write great stories—an invocation of the Muses. King's typewriter was once again running on faith.

In *Song of Susannah*, Roland and Eddie travel through time and space to visit the bestselling author at his home in Bridgton, Maine, in 1977, and convince him of his duty to complete *The Dark Tower*. At that point in the story, the character "Stephen King" admits that he once had a full outline for the entire saga, but lost it. He also confesses that he is afraid of the power of this particular saga, and proposes that *something* might be trying to stop him from telling it. The narrator suggests the existence of a force that works *against* artistic inspiration, stifling confidence and imagination and thereby diminishing the magic of life. The writer (and the character) Stephen King knows this from personal experience, remembering how he suffered writer's block when he gave up drinking and drugs, and again after his near-fatal accident. The moral of *Song of Susannah* is that the artist has a responsibility to rise above such "counter-forces," to "go on" and do the work they are supposed to do.

From this point forward, details of Stephen King's life become inextricably intertwined with the Dark Tower myth. The line between fact and fiction breaks down completely because the story is no longer a simply a story, but a real-life quest. For a writer like King, who believes that his vocation is to *excavate* stories rather than simply create them, the writer must believe in the world of imagination just as surely as he believes in the world he experiences with his five senses. When a writer surrenders the distinction between fact and fiction, reality and fantasy (along with fragments of personal biography) get mysteriously shuffled with ideas and impressions to produce a *hyper-reality* that is more vital than memory or imagination alone.

In the final book of *The Dark Tower*, King invokes a lifetime's worth of fictional creations, including Patrick Danville and Ed Deepneau's daughter (*Insomnia*), Dinky Earnshaw ("Everything's Eventual") and Ted Brautigan ("Low Men in Yellow Coats"), Randall Flagg (*The Stand*) and Pennywise the Clown (*IT*). The reason is simple: It is not just what Roland and his ka-tet have done, but *everything that Stephen King has done over the course of his writing career*, that has led to this point. In the words of one character, "From the spring of 1970, when he typed the line The man in black fled across the desert and the gunslinger followed [...] very few of the things Stephen King wrote were 'just stories.'" The narrator says they were "messages in a bottle," always meant to reach Roland and help him along way. In King's words: It is the Tale that matters, not He Who Tells It. Story is sacred.

King's perspective is similar to the spiritual beliefs of the Navajo Indians, who regard stories not as entertainment, but as powerful rites to stave off illness and death, and give meaning to everyday life. *The Dark Tower* might be viewed as the author's variation on the Holy Grail legend, or the ancient fertility myths that preceded it. For storytellers, these are not simply diversionary tales, but religious narratives with practical meaning. They reveal that the too-rapid course of human progress can dry up the creative wellsprings of life; and that, when the well runs dry, water must be rediscovered through a sacred quest, so that it can be preserved for future generations. King's grasp of this universal myth has been apparent since at least 1989, when he summed up the meaning of the first *Dark Tower* book for interviewer Janet Beaulieu:

> *Everybody in* The Gunslinger *kind of shrugs and says, "Well, the world's moved on." But the point is that if nobody tries to stop the world from moving on, inertia will take care of all our problems. The whales will be gone, the ozone layer will be depleted. There'll be a degeneration where technology continues to progress and there's no morality to keep it in check, as though machines would somehow solve all of our problems.*[428]

The same idea is articulated in *Song of Susannah*:

> *Great men of thought, anyway, that's what I mean, great men of* deduction—*these came together and created the machines which ran the Beams. They were great machines but they were* mortal *machines. They replaced the* magic *with* machines, *do ya kennit, and now the machines are failing. In some worlds, great plagues have decimated whole populations... The Crimson King's Breakers are only hurrying along a process that's already in train. The machines are going mad. You've seen this for yourself. The men believed there would always be more men like them to*

428 Beaulieu

> *make more machines. None of them foresaw what's happened. This . . . this universal exhaustion.*[429]

The purpose of the hero's journey—in King's myth as in other timeless myths—is to restore the magic. In the author's view, we are all here to serve a purpose higher than our own. We are connected to each other by what the author calls *ka*—a timeless mystery that is more complicated than the popular concepts of fate, destiny, or God. We are also connected to worlds that interpenetrate and transcend ours. It is the writer's (or, more broadly, the artist's) responsibility to remind us of this hidden truth, the twilight zone of our everyday reality.

One could scarcely imagine a more all-encompassing quest. No doubt that's why King stated in his afterword to *The Dark Tower* that he finally felt like he could retire in peace. "In a sense," he wrote, "there's nothing left to say now that Roland has reached his goal."[430] Of course it was not the first time he had made this bold statement and, as it turned out, it was not the last time he had to swallow his words. Like Roland, King had only reached the conclusion of a particular cycle—the end of the second phase in his career, which began with the completion of *IT*. Having relieved himself of the psychological burden of finishing Roland's quest, the author once again faced a blank slate. Instead of leaving him dry, *The Dark Tower* renewed his creativity and set him at a new beginning.

429 King: *Song* 147
430 King: "Afterword," *Dark Tower VII* 1048

The King of Hollywood (V)

While Stephen King was striving to complete his *Dark Tower* saga, his best-known work was being rebooted for a new generation of viewers, ensuring his continued popularity. In March 2002, Sci-Fi Channel produced the lukewarm sequel *Firestarter 2: Rekindled*, featuring Marguerite Moreau as an adult Charlie McGee. A few months later, the USA network unveiled *The Dead Zone* TV series, starring Anthony Michael Hall in the role of Johnny Smith. The first two episodes closely followed King's source novel, up to the point where Johnny identifies the Castle Rock Strangler. Beyond that, the series writers developed their own narrative threads, slowly unraveling Johnny's relationship with Greg Stillson over the course of six seasons and eighty total episodes.

No doubt NBC was hoping for an equally long run when the network produced a 2002 remake of *Carrie* as a backdoor series pilot. With the exception of the ending (which leaves the title character alive and repentant), screenwriter Bryan Fuller's adaptation is remarkably faithful to King's novel, restoring several scenes that were absent from DePalma's film, and adding depth to all of the female characters. Despite solid performances by Patricia Clarkson and Angela Bettis as Margaret and Carrie White, however, the movie lacks the panache of DePalma's vision. Perhaps for that reason, it failed to inspire an ongoing series.

In 2004, the TNT network followed suit with a remake of *'Salem's Lot*, starring Rob Lowe as Ben Mears, Donald Sutherland as Richard Straker, and Rutger Hauer as the vampire Barlow. Once again, the storytellers strived to remain faithful to King's story and themes, particularly his insights about the conspiratorial nature of small town life and the dangerous repercussions of harboring too many secrets. Screenwriter Peter Filardi doesn't shy away from the thematic darkness of King's material, but there is a hamminess in some of the performances that kept the miniseries from being as unsettling as Tobe Hooper's 1979 adaptation.

King's more recent stories have inspired equally mixed results on the big screen. Legendary screenwriter William Goldman, who adapted *Misery*, wrote scripts for two new Castle Rock productions: *Hearts in Atlantis* (2001) and *Dreamcatcher* (2003). Both were poorly received during their theatrical runs, but for very different reasons. *Hearts in Atlantis* is a sentimental coming-of-age movie, structured similarly to *Stand by Me*. In adapting King's book, Goldman opted to focus on the "Low Men in Yellow Coats" segment, and particularly on the relationship between Bobby Garfield and his childhood sweetheart Carol Gerber. While such streamlining was undoubtedly necessary, it reduces King's emotionally complex study of a generation into a comparatively lightweight nostalgia trip. And, as Goldman has pointed out, audiences were in no mood for nostalgia at the time the film was released—just two weeks after September 11, 2001.[431]

Dreamcatcher is a very different beast. In a 2002 introduction to Goldman's screenplay, Stephen King not only pronounces the finished film "one of the very, very good adaptations of my work," but also hails it as "a classic suspense film that will eventually go on the same shelf with movies like *Jaws* and *Alien*."[432] Rarely has the author's opinion been so wildly out of sync with the reaction of audiences. *Dreamcatcher* went on to become one of the most reviled Stephen King adaptations—and for many of the reasons that the author himself professes to love the film. It plays out like a big-budget version of a Bert I. Gordon B-movie.

Of course, the film's failure did not diminish the author's presence in Hollywood. Two years later, writer/director David Koepp adapted King's novella "Secret Window, Secret Garden" into *Secret Window*, a stylish and grisly thriller. Later the same year, Mick Garris personalized "Riding the Bullet," turning King's protagonist into a young artist who romanticizes death until he's confronted with it directly. King, meanwhile, decided to try adapting someone else's work for a change, tackling a remake of Lars von Trier's Danish television series *The Kingdom* for ABC.

The pilot episode of *Kingdom Hospital* was partly drawn from the author's own experiences, featuring a brutal opening sequence in which renowned painter Peter Rickman gets struck by a van while jogging. In his semi-conscious state, Rickman looks down

431 Goldman
432 King: "All" ix-x

and sees his lower torso in a terrifyingly unnatural position. Even more disturbing, he begins to suffer hallucinations of a telepathic ant-eater with razor sharp teeth! The creature (a harbinger of death later named Antubis) follows Peter to the hospital, where the painter also begins seeing visions of a young female ghost. And that's far from the strangest thing that happens inside Kingdom Hospital, a place that is literally built on historic tragedy.

The premiere of the quirky series drew a huge audience, but unfortunately, King wasn't able to enjoy the ratings victory. When the episode aired on March 3, 2004, he was once again fighting for his life. The author remembers, "I thought I was all better [from the 1999 accident], but it turned out that the bottom part of my lung was still all crumpled up. I got pneumonia, and they ended up taking my lung right out of my chest in order to repair it. I almost died. It was really close."[433] After he recovered, this second brush with death provided material for his first new novel since the completion of *The Dark Tower*.

433 Lehmann-Haupt

Return to the Myth Pool

If King's near-death experiences have had a "clarifying effect," it is not just because he recognized how close he came to dying, but also because began to imagine the world after his death. With *Lisey's Story*, the writer who built his career on "what if?" scenarios asked "*What if I already died?*" The question came to him when he returned home from the hospital in 2004 and found his home office completely empty. His wife Tabitha had decided to redecorate the room while he was away, and had removed everything, transforming the workspace into a ghostly version of what he remembered. King stared at the empty room and thought, "Maybe I died. This is what the study would look like after I died."[434]

From that simple and sobering thought emerged *Lisey's Story*, the fictional tale of Lisey Landon, widow of famous author Scott Landon. In King's mind, the story of the woman who had loved and supported Scott for so long emerged naturally as a tribute to the woman who had loved and supported *him* for so long. He summed up for *The New York Times*: "*Lisey's* supposed to be about finding somebody who understands what it's like to live that life of the imagination. Not everybody is comfortable with that, and when you find somebody who is—in that sense Tabby is like Lisey."[435] Like Stephen King, Scott Landon routinely jokes that he became rich and famous by documenting personal "delusions and visions" and selling them to an eager public. Lisey, however, understands that her husband's writings are not simply the products of wild imagination. She alone sees the dark side of his writing process, which is also a conscious rejection of conventional sanity in favor of creative madness.

All his life, Scott has been aware of "a world right next door to this one," a world of imagination that is both awesome and dangerous.[436] He calls it Boo'ya Moon, and that's where he goes to drink the sustaining waters of "the myth-pool." King first mentioned this evocative term in his non-fiction book *Danse Macabre*, crediting it to his mentor Burton Hatlen, who defined the myth-pool as "that

434 Lehmann-Haupt
435 Rich
436 King: *Lisey's* 346

body of fictive literature in which all of us, even the nonreaders and those who do not go to the films, have communally bathed."[437] In *Lisey's Story*, King elaborates:

> *It's the pool where we all go down to drink, to swim, to catch a little fish from the edge of the shore; it's also the pool where some shady souls go out in their flimsy wooden boats after the big ones. It is the pool of life, the cup of imagination, and [Lisey] has an idea that different people see different versions of it, but with two things ever in common: it's always about a mile deep in the Fairy Forest, and it's always sad. Because imagination isn't the only thing this place is about. It's also about* (giving in) *waiting. Just sitting . . . and looking out over those dreamy waters . . . and waiting.* It's coming, *you think.* It's coming soon, I know it is. *But you don't know exactly what and so the years pass.*[438]

To extend the metaphor: King's myth-pool is the place where big dreamers search for the immortal, and where all dreamers eventually drown. Scott goes there not simply because he can, but because he must. His "delusions and visions" are both a gift and a curse; they sustain him but they will also inevitably destroy him.

Both Scott Landon and Stephen King imagine their most important story as a posthumous narrative, written to one specific reader: their wives. Landon's final manuscript, like the novel *Lisey's Story* itself, is an intimate confession about the life-consuming compulsion to write, as well as an expression of overwhelming gratitude for the women whose love and understanding makes it possible to fulfill that need without getting hopelessly lost in fictional worlds. Considering the intimacy of such a confession, it's no surprise that King was initially reluctant to publish *Lisey's Story*. In 2006, he told an interviewer:

> *I'm inside it, and to me it feels like a very special book. To the point where I don't want to let it out into the world. This is the only book I've ever written where I don't want to read the reviews, because there will be some people who are going to be*

437 King: *Danse* 51

438 King: *Lisey's* 437

> *ugly to this book. I couldn't stand that, the way you would hate people to be ugly to someone you love. And I love this book.*[439]

When he finally published the novel that fall, most of the negative reader responses were related to the way that Scott and Lisey communicate, using code words that hold special meaning only for them. King had used the technique to illustrate the intimacy of the central couple's relationship—when one of the two is gone, the other cannot be fully understood—but it inevitably alienated some readers. Still, others recognized that the story was not about casual comprehension but about the universal human need to *connect* on the deepest level, the difficulty of making such a genuine connection, and the amazing bond that is formed when two people really manage to do so. As King says, "To some degree this is a book about myth, depression, and story-making, but it's also a story about marriage and faithfulness."[440]

At the same time he was writing this intimate tribute to his wife, the renewed mythmaker also began working on a more accessible novel that would speak to the legion of fans that will always regard him as America's master of horror. On its simplest level, *Cell* is a zombie story, a natural project for an author who claims Richard Matheson as his biggest writing influence and George Romero as a close friend. According to King, however, *Cell* did not originate with a conscious desire to return to horror or to exploit a trend; it began with one of those all-important "what if?" ideas:

> *I came out of a hotel in New York and I saw this woman talking on her cell phone. And I thought to myself, What if she got a message over the cell phone that she couldn't resist, and she had to kill people until somebody killed her? All the possible ramifications started bouncing around in my head like pinballs. If everybody got the same message, then everybody who had a cell phone would go crazy. Normal people would see this, and the first thing they would do would be to call their friends and families on their cell phones. So the epidemic would spread like poison ivy.*[441]

439 Lehmann-Haupt
440 Lehmann-Haupt
441 Lehmann-Haupt

The famously technophobic author imagined the scenario unfolding like events in *Night of the Living Dead*, which follows a group of strangers who band together against an army of sub-human creatures. The biggest difference between King's story and Romero's story is that King's characters respond to the crisis by seeking an explanation, whereas Romero's are focused mainly on survival. King proposes that his pseudo-zombies are the results of an electro-magnetic pulse that has erased the "software" inside human brains, leaving only the basic operating system—survival instincts and little else. One of the characters in *Cell* embraces this cursory explanation and expands it into a cynical philosophy about human nature:

> *At bottom, you see, we are not Homo sapiens at all. Our core is madness. The prime directive is murder. What Darwin was too polite to say, my friends, is that we came to rule the earth not because we were the smartest, or even the meanest, but because we have always been the craziest, most murderous motherfuckers in the jungle. And that is what the Pulse exposed five days ago.*[442]

Of course not all of King's characters subscribe to this theory—because King, at his core, is a humanist.

The author suggests that his "phone crazies," like Romero's zombies, may actually represent a better way of life. In *Cell*, the crazies demonstrate not only *sub-human* instincts, but also *super-human* telepathic abilities that allow them to co-exist as a species without fighting amongst themselves. In essence, they represent an evolutionary leap forward as well as a regression to primitive instincts. This revelation does not transform the monsters into noble creatures, but it does allow some characters (and readers) to contemplate the possibility that such a crisis could contribute to a kind of enlightenment, by forcing us to define "civilization" in a new context. From that perspective, King's story captures one of the dominant themes of Romero's zombie films: The phoenix can't rise, except from ashes.

For many readers, the publication of *Cell* in January 2006 signaled King's long-awaited return to the horror genre. That may not have been the author's intention, but he has in subsequent years continued to produce the kind of genre storytelling that he is best

442 King: *Cell* 206

known for. He has also returned to short story writing, a talent that he claimed to have "forgotten" until he was tapped to edit the 2007 edition of the annual anthology book *The Best American Short Stories*. Between December 2005 and January 2007, the author says, he read hundreds of new short stories that stimulated his imagination. The assignment was, he claimed, a necessary reminder about what makes stories work:

> *Talent can't help itself; it roars along in fair weather or foul, not sparing the fireworks. It gets emotional. It struts its stuff. In fact, that's its job. And if these stories have anything in common—anything that made them uniquely* my *Best American stories—it's that sense of emotional involvement, of flipped-out amazement. I look for stories that care about my feelings as well as my intellect, and when I find one that is all-out emotionally assaultive [. . .] I grab that baby and hold tight.*[443]

The discovery of so many "emotionally assaultive" tales inspired King to write some of his most vivid and energetic short stories in years. Stories like "Willa" and "*The New York Times* at Special Bargain Rates" revel in the same kind of flipped-out amazement that define the work of Jack Finney, Ray Bradbury, Rod Serling, and the young Stephen King. These stories (collected in the 2008 publication *Just After Sunset*) also stand as reminders that the most convincing writers are those who dream as they write, letting their subconscious minds do most of the work.

The same philosophy informs *Duma Key*, King's 2008 novel about a maimed painter whose latest work of art haunts him like a phantom limb. *Duma Key* is essentially a ghost story, like *The Shining* and *Bag of Bones*, but even more than that it is a story about recovery and rediscovery. King contextualizes the novel as a counterpart to *Dreamcatcher*, explaining, "The two books are really the polarities of my recovery from my accident. I was feeling a lot better by the time that I wrote *Duma Key*, and I think it shows."[444] Just as *Key* protagonist Edgar Freemantle escapes from pain and depression through art, so the author apparently rediscovered his own ability

443 King and Pitlor
444 Cruz

to create subconsciously. King explains this revelatory experience through the voice of his protagonist:

> *I saw no one and spoke to no one but myself. The extraneous dropped away almost entirely, and when that happens, you begin to hear yourself clearly. And clear communication between selves—the surface self and the deep self is what I mean—is the enemy of self-doubt. It slays confusion.*[445]

Under the best circumstances, the real world and the world of the artist's imagination fall into perfect alignment through a mysterious process that is—as Freemantle notes—"at least partially supernatural."[446] Focus and confidence renewed, King found it perfectly natural to return to the subject matter for which he is best known. *Duma Key* represented the first stage in the creative renaissance of America's literary boogeyman.

445 King: *Duma* 132
446 King: *Duma* 382

The Wheel

Onscreen, the "classic King" revival got underway with the release of two new movie adaptations. In June 2007, Dimension Films released a gonzo adaptation of the author's short story "1408," starring John Cusack as a skeptical journalist who experiences a violent supernatural assault. In November, the same studio released director Frank Darabont's fourth Stephen King adaptation, *The Mist*. Both films pleased the author, who confidently cited them in his updated version of *Danse Macabre* as laudable examples of twenty-first century horror cinema.

The Mist is particularly harrowing because Darabont treats the subject matter with deadly seriousness—right up to an ending that, King promises, "will tear your heart out."[447] Reportedly, Darabont sought permission from the author to change the ending of the novella, and King responded enthusiastically:

> *I thought it was terrific but it jarred me. I knew what was coming the first time that I looked at the movie in rough cut, and it still jarred me. I took a second viewing to get used to the idea that it was probably the only ending in terms of the world that had been created in that story.*[448]

King's original ending suggests a glimmer of hope for the future: Darabont's dashes that hope entirely. The director later confessed that he was venting personal frustrations about the state of American life and politics in the early 2000s: "This is an angry cry from the heart of a humanist who is really pretty pissed off about the fact that all the reasonable people seem to be marginalized, ground under the heel of the extremists."[449]

King vented similar frustrations with his next novel, *Under the Dome*. The story, about a small Maine town that inexplicably becomes trapped inside a giant snow globe, had been lurking in the back of the author's imagination since 1976. At that time, the author remembers, he wrote seventy-five pages before becoming

447 King: *Danse* xxx
448 Rogak 239
449 Hennon

overwhelmed by the scope of the tale. When he returned to the story in the early 1980s, after completing *IT*, he wrote a 450-page (dome-less) variation called "The Cannibals."[450] Several chapters of this version were later published on the author's official website, but King never completed the manuscript. Finally, in November 2007, he started again from scratch and updated the story as a reflection on contemporary America. The new version, he says, was a product of the times:

> *I didn't believe there was justification for going into the war in Iraq. And it just seemed at the time, that in the wake of 9/11, the Bush Administration was like this angry kid walking down the street who couldn't find whoever sucker punched him, and so turned around and punched the first likely suspect. Sometimes the sublimely wrong people can be in power at a time when you really need the right people. I put a lot of that into the book.*[451]

Specifically, King embodied the Dick Cheney philosophy of leadership in the character of Jim Rennie, a manipulative town selectman who uses religion and intimidation to create a culture of fear. Only a handful of people under the dome dare to oppose Rennie, and their opposition stimulates a full-scale war, with the innocent and the ignorant caught in the crossfire. King voices his usual concerns about big government and organized religion, and also makes a case for gun control and climate change. In the end, *Under the Dome* is not about the cause of the crisis but about the effects of such a crisis on everyday people and everyday life in twenty-first century America. Just as George Romero has said over the years that the zombies in his Dead films could be "any natural disaster," one can easily read *Under the Dome* as a microcosm of life in twenty-first century America. King's prognosis is bleak: "Here are these people, they're in this situation, they can't get out, and if you think that we're all in that situation, then you're right."[452]

King followed up with a collection of equally bleak novellas called *Full Dark, No Stars*—proof that he could still deliver intense, naturalistic horror—before turning his attention to another long-germinating project. The origins of *11/22/63* extend even further

450 Winter: *Stephen* 192
451 Cruz
452 Mulkerrins

back than *Under the Dome*, to 1971. That was when King first asked himself the following question: "What if a person could go back in time and prevent the assassination of President John F. Kennedy?" This particular "what if?" was more than a casual *Twilight Zone* scenario for the young writer, because much of his adult worldview, and the worldview of his generation, began to coalesce around the events of November 22, 1963. Reflecting on the significance of that day in a 1984 interview, King said:

> *All the macabre things that I can remember, and that come out of reality rather than from something I made up, started with the Kennedy assassination in 1963. I don't have any bad memories from the Fifties. Everything was asleep. There was stuff going on, there was uneasiness about the bomb, but on the whole, I'd have to say that people in the Fifties were pretty loose.*[453]

In his book *Danse Macabre*, King added that the Kennedy assassination and the following three-day mourning period seemed to him to be "the closest any people in history has ever come to a total period of mass consciousness and mass empathy and—in retrospect—mass memory: two hundred million people in a living frieze."[454] With such a broad scope in mind, it's no wonder that the young writer was intimidated by the prospect of building a work of fiction around the event.

For years, King continued to mull over the question. No doubt it echoed in his mind when one of his characters posed a similar question *("If you could jump into a time machine and go back to 1932, would you kill Hitler?")* to Johnny Smith in *The Dead Zone*. The original question, however, continued to echo after King's accident in 1999. In *Dreamcatcher*, one of his characters muses:

> *You can't go back, can't kill your own grandfather, can't shoot Lee Harvey Oswald as he kneels at a sixth-floor window of the Texas School Book Depository, congealing fried chicken on a paper plate beside him and his mail-order rifle aimed. . . .*[455]

---

453 Lofficier 61

454 King: *Danse* 8

455 King: *Dreamcatcher* 380

In the later books of *The Dark Tower* series, Father Callahan invokes the name of the murdered president, claiming that he has considered using the magic of Mid-World to travel back in time and stop Oswald. "If there was ever a watershed moment in American life," Callahan opines, "that was it. Change that, change everything that came after. Vietnam . . . the race riots . . . everything." Eddie responds to him by asking "what if you did it and changed things for the *worse*?"[456] King apparently couldn't bear to leave the question unanswered any longer.

In *11/22/63*, schoolteacher Jake Epping travels back in time from modern-day Lisbon Falls, Maine, (by way of the fictional town of Derry) to 1960 Dallas, Texas. He stays at the Adolphus Hotel, visits the Book Depository in Dealey Plaza, and becomes overwhelmed by the uncanny feeling that these places harbor a timeless curse. In effect, he is experiencing a haunting in reverse. For the rest of the novel, Jake is tormented not only by his knowledge of things that haven't happened yet but by a looming question about the nature of the universe: *Do bad things happen for a good reason?* King has built a career on this basic question, and has answered it in many different ways. *11/22/63* reaffirms his belief that there is no definitive answer for all people in all times. If science or philosophy could provide a final answer, there might be no need for faith. If religion could provide a final answer, King might be a preacher instead of a storyteller. The writer's answer is that there will always be a basic human need for speculation. There will always be a need for stories that prompt us to ask important questions and to answer them for ourselves, even if our answers are never "final."

Over four and a half decades after his earliest publications, Stephen King continues to write—and he remains prolific, versatile and extremely popular in multiple mediums. Between 2009 and 2013, he published several new e-books and comic books as well as multiple short stories and novels, including an unexpected eighth *Dark Tower* book. Meanwhile, his older works continue to provide inspiration for new films and television series, including a remake of *Carrie* (2013) and the CBS series *Under the Dome*. The latter has proven to be King's most successful foray in television, earning consistently high ratings as it took on a narrative life completely

456 King: *Wolves* 607

independent of the source novel. In a June 27, 2013, letter on his official website, King wrote enthusiastically about the opportunity to help reshape his own story:

> *It's best to think of that novel and what you're seeing week-to-week on CBS as a case of fraternal twins. Both started in the same creative womb, but you will be able to tell them apart. Or, if you're of a sci-fi bent, think of them as alternate versions of the same reality.*[457]

Riding this new wave of success, King also released two novels in 2013, the murder mystery *Joyland* and a long-awaited sequel to *The Shining* called *Doctor Sleep*. Like *Under the Dome* and *11/22/63*, the novels brought the author full circle to the early days of his writing career. *Joyland* revisits King's original idea to set *The Shining* in an amusement park. In a May 2013 interview with NPR's Terri Gross, the author said he rediscovered the idea on a trip to Canobie Lake Park in New Hampshire, which became his model for Joyland, a "nice and clean and sunlit" amusement park that "wasn't too big."[458] The novel follows a twenty-one-year-old college student named Devin Jones, who takes a summer job at Joyland and encounters several people there who change his life. One of those people is a disabled boy named Mike, who has the gift of precognition and a supernatural ability to communicate with ghosts. Another one is a murderer, whose latest victim haunts the amusement park's House of Horrors.

The story is, on its most superficial level, a ghost story. More than that, however, it is a story about growing up and facing the world as a responsible adult. King waxes nostalgic about being twenty-one, when life was spread out in front of him like a roadmap, and mourns the inevitable realization that "no summer is endless."[459] *Joyland* emerges as a bittersweet celebration of life at its best and worst. Unlike the author's early work, it anticipates death with more wonder than fear—a reflection of the writer's own changing perspective, which he explained to Gross:

---

457 King: "A Letter"

458 Terri Gross

459 King: *Joyland* 184

> *I think we'd all like to believe that after we shuffle off this mortal coil, that there's going to be something on the other side because for most of us, I know for me, life is so rich, so colorful and sensual and full of good things, things to read, things to eat, things to watch, places to go, new experiences, that I don't want to think that you just go to darkness.*[460]

King concludes that belief in the afterlife is a choice, and he suggests that the choice itself makes all the difference in what lies beyond.

For the protagonist of *Joyland*, death is not the end; Devin Jones has seen proof to the contrary. The same is true for Danny Torrence in *Doctor Sleep*. As a hospice caregiver with the power to look beyond the everyday physical world, Danny helps people let go of the fear at the moment of their death. What he offers them is reassurance that "there are other worlds than these," a conviction born of his personal experiences with the dying. King writes: "In those gateway moments, Dan had always felt in the presence of some not-quite-seen enormity. They slept, they woke, they went somewhere. They went on. He'd had reason to believe that, even as a child."[461]

Danny, of course, has plenty of reasons to be afraid of death and the afterlife. As a child, he barely survived the events of *The Shining*, a book that expressed King's own deepest, darkest fears as a young adult—fear of his failure as a man, a husband and a father; fear that the only thing awaiting him beyond those failures was a horrible death where "the monsters get you." Dan initially suffers the same debilitating doubts that ultimately destroyed his father, but because Stephen King's worldview has changed profoundly since *The Shining*, *Doctor Sleep* does not automatically repeat the gut-wrenching horrors of that earlier novel. In fact, the new novel has more in common with *Bag of Bones*. Both are stories about a man's ability to escape from the negative influences of the past by taking full responsibility for the future. Dan is at first grateful that he has no family of his own (no "hostages of fortune," like his father had at the Overlook Hotel), but later he willingly becomes a father-figure to a young girl named Abra, whose wild talents are exponentially greater than his ever were. Dan is no longer the "wild child." He has become the teacher, the protector.

460 Terri Gross
461 King: *Doctor* 300

Doctor Sleep completes an arc that many of King's most notable characters have followed, from innocence and vulnerability to fear and self-doubt, finally arriving at a place of duty and acceptance. By compiling some of King's most familiar story tropes and tendencies, the novel gives voice to his most enduring personal beliefs. The author believes in the innocence of children, and in the raw power of their imaginations. He believes in family, and in the responsibility of parents and teachers to protect and nurture their children, so that those children can in turn do the same for *their* children one day. He believes that there is real evil in the world—often hidden in cults and bureaucracies; always taking, never giving—but he also believes that evil can be overcome by those who are essentially honest, those who believe in themselves, those who summon the strength to stand up for what is right, regardless of the risk to themselves. He believes that the past can exert a very real and damaging influence, but only if we allow it to. He believes in regret and in confession, but only as ways to learn from the past so that we can live in the present and face the future without fear. Reading *Doctor Sleep*, one gets the sense that King no longer fears for his characters (or himself) as much as he once did. People face dangers that are real, and may even prove fatal, but that does not necessarily keep them from living a rewarding life and standing tall when it matters most.

Like Dan Torrence, King himself has become a teacher. His work and his worldview have influenced countless readers and writers, not least of whom are his own children. Although his son Owen has so far avoided writing genre fiction, insisting that his worldview wouldn't "support" that type of storytelling, son Joe Hill has eagerly embraced the horror genre.[462] In 2013, Hill published his third novel *N0S4A2*, a tale with strong links to his father's fictional universe. The tale of a supernaturally-gifted child-turned-novelist who does battle with an ageless psychic vampire in an alien car, *N0S4A2* bears obvious similarities to *Firestarter*, *The Talisman*, *Christine*, and *From a Buick 8*, as well as allusions to *Doctor Sleep*, *The Stand*, and especially *IT*. Like *IT*, Hill's novel is primarily about the world of imagination that children and novelists inhabit, and about the wonders and dangers they find there. One character sums up:

462 Ghomeshi

*Everyone lives in two worlds [. . .] There's the real world, with all its annoying facts and rules. In the real world, there are things that are true and things that aren't. Mostly the real world s-s-s-suh-*sucks. *But everyone also lives in the world inside their own head. An* inscape, *a world of thought. In a world made of thought—in an inscape—*every *idea is a fact. Emotions are as real as gravity. Dreams are as powerful as history. Creative people, like writers, and Henry Rollins, spend a lot of their time hanging out in their thoughtworld.* S-s-strong *creatives, though, can use a knife to cut the stitches between the two worlds, can bring them together."*[463]

Stephen King is unquestionably one of the strongest creatives in our world today, and his legacy is even bigger than his brand name. Many of his fictional creations, like Carrie and Cujo, have become shorthand in everyday reality, even for those who have never read the books or seen the movies. More significantly, his essential belief in the ability of ordinary, good-hearted people to overcome extraordinary, potentially soul-crushing experiences has given hope to those who travel the darkest roads, in fiction and fact. In his afterword to *N0S4A2*, Joe Hill writes of his father, "I guess I have been cruising his back roads my whole life. I don't regret it."[464] Those same roads have been—and continue to be—traveled by millions of dreamers. After all these years, they are as real to us as anything that matters in life.

463 Hill 100
464 Hill 688

Bibliography

Adams, Tim. "Stephen King interview, uncut and unpublished." *The Guardian* (London). September 14, 2000. Online.

Allen, Mel. "The Man Who Writes Nightmares" (1979). *Bare Bones: Conversations on Terror with Stephen King*. Ed. Tim Underwood and Chuck Miller. New York: Warner, 1988.

Applebome, Peter. "TV Gets a New Poltergeist: Stephen King." *The New York Times*. July 14, 1991.

Ashton-Haiste, Brad. "Bleedful Kings." *Fangoria: Masters of the Dark*. Ed. Anthony Timpone. New York: Starlog, 1997.

Bandler, Michael J. "The King of the Macabre at Home" (1982). *Feast of Fear: Conversations with Stephen King*. Ed. Tim Underwood and Chuck Miller. New York: Warner, 1989.

Beahm, George W. *Stephen King: America's Best-Loved Boogeyman*. Kansas City: Andrews, 1998.

---. *The Stephen King Companion*. Kansas City: Andrews, 1989.

---. *The Stephen King Story*. Kansas City: Andrews, 1991.

Beaulieu, Janet. "Castle Rock News Interview (March 1989)." *Stephenking.com: The Official Website.*

Blue, Tyson. "The Truth about 'IT'." *Rod Serling's The Twilight Zone Magazine*. Volume 6, Number 5. December 1986.

Bradbury, Ray. *Something Wicked This Way Comes*. New York: Avon, 2006.

Bright, David. "Hampden Teacher Hits Jackpot with New Book" (1973). *Feast of Fear: Conversations with Stephen King*. Ed. Tim Underwood and Chuck Miller. New York: Warner, 1989.

Cadigan, Pat & Marthy Ketchum & Arnie Fenner. "Has Success Spoiled Stephen King? Naaah!" *Feast of Fear: Conversations with Stephen King*. Ed. Tim Underwood and Chuck Miller. New York: Warner, 1989.

Chesley, Chris. "Death Scenes: Going to the Movies with Stephen King." *The Complete Stephen King Encyclopedia: The Definitive Guide to the Works of America's Master of Horror*. Ed. Stephen J. Spignesi. Chicago: Contemporary, 1991.

Childs, Mike and Alan Jones. "DePalma Has the Power!" (1977). *Brian DePalma: Interviews*. Ed. Laurence F. Knapp. Jackson: UP of Mississippi, 2003.

Christian, George. "Eyeglasses for the Mind" (1979). *Feast of Fear: Conversations with Stephen King*. Ed. Tim Underwood and Chuck Miller. New York: Warner, 1989.

Chute, David. "King of the Night" (1979). *Feast of Fear: Conversations with Stephen King*. Ed. Tim Underwood and Chuck Miller. New York: Warner, 1989.

Conner, Jeff. *Stephen King Goes to Hollywood*. New York: New American Library, 1987.

Cruz, Gilbert. "Stephen King on His 10 Longest Novels." *Time.com*. November 6, 2009.

Eliot, T.S. "The Love Song of J. Alfred Prufrock." *The Complete Poems and Plays, 1909-1950.* New York: Harcourt, 1971.

Ewing, Darrell and Dennis Myers. "King of the Road" (1986). *Feast of Fear: Conversations with Stephen King*. Ed. Tim Underwood and Chuck Miller. New York: Warner, 1989.

Finney, Jack. *Invasion of the Body Snatchers*. New York: Simon & Schuster, 1998.

Flewelling, Lynn. "King working on book he believes could be his best." *Bangor Daily News*. September 11, 1990.

Freff. "The Dark Beyond the Door: Walking (Nervously) into Stephen King's World" (1980). *Bares Bones: Conversations on Terror with Stephen King*. Ed. Tim Underwood and Chuck Miller. New York: Warner, 1988.

Furth, Robin. *Stephen King's The Dark Tower: The Complete Concordance (Revised and Updated)*. New York: Scribner, 2012.

Gagne, Paul R. "Interview with Stephen King" (1989). *Feast of Fear: Conversations with Stephen King*. Ed. Tim Underwood and Chuck Miller. New York: Warner, 1989.

Galluzzo, Rob. "ICONS Interview with writer/director Mick Garris—*The Stand, Psycho IV, Sleepwalkers, The Shining*." *IconsofFright.com*. September 2008.

Ghomeshi, Jian. "Stephen King and son Owen King on fiction and family." *Q with Jian Ghomeshi*. October 24, 2013. Online.

Goldman, William. "Adapting King." *Dreamcatcher: The Shooting Script*. New York: Newmarket, 2003.

Grant, Charles L. "I Like to Go for the Jugular" (1981). *Feast of Fear: Conversations with Stephen King*. Ed. Tim Underwood and Chuck Miller. New York: Warner, 1989.

---. "Interview with Stephen King" (1985). *Bares Bones: Conversations on Terror with Stephen King*. Ed. Tim Underwood and Chuck Miller. New York: Warner, 1988.

Gross, Edward. "Stephen King Takes a Vacation." *Fangoria: Masters of the Dark*. Ed. Anthony Timpone. New York: Starlog, 1997.

Gross, Terri. "Stephen King, Author of 'Joyland': On Growing Up, Believing in God and Getting Scared." *Fresh Air*. National Public Radio. May 28, 2013.

Hatlen, Burton. "Stephen King and the American Dream: Alienation, Competition, and Community in Rage and The Long Walk." *Reign of Fear: The Fiction and the Films of Stephen King*. Ed. Don Herron. Novato: Underwood, 1988.

Hennon, Blake. "*The Mist*: Frank Darabont, Thomas Jane on 'angry, bleak' ending." *Hero Complex. The Los Angeles Times*. May 12, 2013.

Hill, Joe. *NOS4A2*. New York: William Morrow, 2013.

Horsting, Jesse and Mike Stein. "Interview with Stephen King and George Romero" (1989). *Feast of Fear: Conversations with Stephen King*. Ed. Tim Underwood and Chuck Miller. New York: Warner, 1989.

Jackson, Shirley. *The Haunting of Hill House*. New York: Penguin, 1959.

James, Henry. *The Turn of the Screw*. New York: Modern Library 1991.

Jeffries, Stuart. "Dark Rider." *The Guardian*. September 17, 2004. Online.

Jones, Stephen. *Creepshows: The Illustrated Stephen King Movie Guide*. New York: Billboard, 2001.

Ketchum, Marty, Pat Cadigan and Lewis Shiner. "Shine of the Times" (1979). *Bares Bones: Conversations on Terror with Stephen King*. Ed. Tim Underwood and Chuck Miller. New York: Warner, 1988.

Kilgore, Michael. "Interview with Stephen King" (1986). *Bares Bones: Conversations on Terror with Stephen King*. Ed. Tim Underwood and Chuck Miller. New York: Warner, 1988.

King, Stephen. "Afterword." *Bag of Bones*. New York: Pocket, 1999.

---. "Afterword." *The Dark Tower: The Dark Tower VII*. New York: Pocket, 2006.

---. "Afterword." *The Waste Lands: The Dark Tower III*. New York: Signet, 2003.

---. "Afterword." *Wizard and Glass: The Dark Tower IV*. New York: Signet, 2003.

---. "All Story, No Bacon" (2002). *Dreamcatcher: The Shooting Script*. New York: Newmarket, 2003.

---. "Author's Note." *From a Buick 8*. New York: Pocket, 2003.

---. *Bag of Bones*. New York: Pocket, 1999.

---. *Blaze*. New York: Pocket, 2008.

---. "The Body." *Different Seasons*. New York: Signet, 1983.

---. *Carrie*. New York: Anchor, 2013.

---. *Cell*. New York: Pocket, 2006.

---. *Cujo*. New York: Signet, 1982.

---. *Danse Macabre*. New York: Gallery, 2010.

---. *The Dark Half*. New York: Signet, 1990.

---. *The Dark Tower: The Dark Tower VII*. New York: Pocket, 2006.

---. *The Dark Tower II: The Drawing of the Three*. New York: Signet, 2003.

---. *The Dead Zone*. New York: Signet, 1980.

---. *Desperation*. New York: Signet, 1997.

---. *Doctor Sleep*. New York: Scribner, 2013.

---. *Dreamcatcher*. New York: Pocket, 2001.

---. *Duma Key*. New York: Pocket, 2008.

---. "An Evening at the Billerica Library." *Bare Bones: Conversations on Terror with Stephen King*. Ed. Tim Underwood and Chuck Miller. New York: Warner, 1988.

---. "Everything's Eventual." *Everything's Eventual: 14 Dark Tales*. New York: Scribner, 2002.

---. *The Eyes of the Dragon*. New York: Viking, 1987.

---. "Foreword." *Night Shift*. New York: Anchor, 2011.

---. "Foreword." *Silver Bullet*. New York: Signet, 1985.

---. "Foreword." *The Two Dead Girls*. New York: Signet, 1996.

---. *Gerald's Game*. New York: Signet, 1993.

---. *The Girl Who Loved Tom Gordon*. New York: Pocket, 2000.

---. *The Green Mile*. New York: Pocket, 1996.

---. *Guns*. Brilliance Audio, 2013.

---. *Hearts in Atlantis*. New York: Pocket, 2000.

---. "The Horror Market Writer and the Ten Bears: A True Story" (1973). *Secret Windows: Essays and Fiction on the Craft of Writing*. New York: Book-of-the-Month Club, 2000.

---. "How *IT* Happened" (1986). *Secret Windows: Essays and Fiction on the Craft of Writing*. New York: Book-of-the-Month Club, 2000.

---. "The Importance of Being Bachman." *Liljas-library.com.*

---. *Insomnia*. New York: Signet, 1995.

---. Interview. "Bad House: The Making of Rose Red." Lions Gate.

---. Interview. *Stephen King: Shining in the Dark*. BBC.

---. "Introduction" (1981). *The Arbor House Treasury of Horror and the Supernatural.* Ed. Bill Pronzini, Barry N. Malzberg, Martin H. Greenberg. New York: Arbor, 1981.

---. "Introduction" (1999). *Carrie*. New York: Pocket, 1999.

---. "Introduction" (1999). *The Green Mile: The Screenplay*. New York: Scribner, 1999.

---. "Introduction" (1978). *Signet Classics: Frankenstein; Dracula; Dr. Jekyll and Mr. Hyde*. New York: Signet, 1978.

---. *Joyland*. London: Hard Case, 2013.

---. "King on Firestarter: Who's to Blame?" *Cinefantastique*. February 1991.

---. "A Letter from Stephen." (July 27, 2013) *Stephenking.com: The Official Website.*

---. "The Library Policeman." *Four Past Midnight*. New York: Signet, 1991.

---. *Lisey's Story*. New York: Pocket, 2007.

---. "Messages from Stephen—12:47pm, November 2, 1999." *StephenKing.com: The Official Website.*

---. *Misery*. New York: Viking, 1987.

---. "Myth, Belief, Faith, and Ripley's Believe It or Not!" *Nightmares & Dreamscapes*. New York: Signet. 1994.

---. *Needful Things*. New York: Signet, 1992.

---. "A Night at the Royal Festival Hall." *Secret Windows: Essays and Fiction on the Craft of Writing*. New York: Book-of-the-Month Club, 2000.

---. "On Becoming a Brand Name" (1980). *Secret Windows: Essays and Fiction on the Craft of Writing.* New York: Book-of-the-Month Club, 2000.

---. *On Writing: A Memoir of the Craft.* New York: Scribner, 2000.

---. *Pet Sematary.* New York: Signet, 1984.

---. *Rage. The Bachman Books: Four Early Novels by Stephen King.* New York: Signet, 1986.

---. "Rita Hayworth and the Darabont Redemption" (1995). *The Shawshank Redemption: The Shooting Script.* New York: Newmarket, 1996.

---. "Rita Hayworth and the Shawshank Redemption." *Different Seasons.* New York: Signet, 1983.

---. *Roadwork. The Bachman Books: Four Early Novels by Stephen King.* New York: Signet, 1986.

---. *'Salem's Lot.* New York: Anchor, 2011.

---. *The Shining.* New York: Anchor, 2012.

---. *Song of Susannah: The Dark Tower VI.* New York: Pocket, 2006.

---. *The Stand.* New York: Anchor, 2012.

---. "Stephen King's Keynote Address, Vermont Library Conference, VEMA Annual Meeting—May 26, 1999." *Horrorking.com.*

---. "Straight Up Midnight: An Introductory Note." *Four Past Midnight.* New York: Signet, 1991.

---. *The Tommyknockers.* New York: Signet. 1988.

---. *The Waste Lands: The Dark Tower III.* New York: Signet, 2003.

---. "What Stephen King Does for Love" (1990). *Secret Windows: Essays and Fiction on the Craft of Writing.* New York: Book-of-the-Month Club, 2000.

King, Stephen. "Why I Was Bachman." *Liljas-Library.com.*

---. *Wolves of the Calla: The Dark Tower V.* New York: Pocket, 2006.

King, Stephen and Heidi Pitlor, ed. *The Best American Short Stories 2007.* Boston: Houghton, 2007.

King, Stephen and Peter Straub. *The Talisman.* New York: Berkley, 1985.

Konstantin, Phil. "An Interview with Stephen King." *The Highway Patrolman.* July 1987. *Americanindian.net.*

Kramer, Staci D. "The Stand: Stephen King Gives Independent Bookstores a Boost." *Chicago Tribune.* October 26, 1994.

Langton, Mark. "Stephen King Scares Himself." *Image.* September 9, 1990.

Lehmann-Haupt, Christopher and Nathaniel Rich. "Stephen King, The Art of Fiction No. 189." *The Paris Review,* No. 178 (Fall 2006).

Lofficier, Randy. "Stephen King Talks about Christine" (1984). *Feast of Fear: Conversations with Stephen King.* Ed. Tim Underwood and Chuck Miller. New York: Warner, 1989.

Lovecraft, H.P. "The Rats in the Walls." *The H.P. Lovecraft Archive*. Online.

---. *Supernatural Horror in Literature* (1927). *The H.P. Lovecraft Archive*. Online.

Maddrey, Joseph. "Art Imitates Life… and Death: A Conversation with Filmmaker Tom McLoughlin." *The Modest Proposal*. Spring 2011. Online.

Magistrale, Tony. *Hollywood's Stephen King*. New York: Palgrave, 2003.

Marotta, Linda. "Stephen King Shines On." *Fangoria: Masters of the Dark*. Ed. Anthony Timpone. New York: Starlog, 1997.

Mason, Anthony. "Stephen King and his compulsion to write." *CBS News*. June 30, 2013.

Mauceri, Joseph B. "Joseph B. Mauceri Interviews King." *The World of Fandom. Horrorking.com.*

Modderno, Craig. "Topic: Horrors!" (1985). *Bare Bones: Conversations on Terror with Stephen King*. Ed. Tim Underwood and Chuck Miller. New York: Warner, 1988.

Mulkerrins, Jane. "Stephen King: 'We all live under the dome.'" *The Telegraph* (London). August 19, 2013.

Munster, Bill. "Stephen King: A 1981 Interview." *Feast of Fear: Conversations with Stephen King*. Ed. Tim Underwood and Chuck Miller. New York: Warner, 1989.

Murari, T.N. "Cosmo Talks to: Stephen King" (1985). *Feast of Fear: Conversations with Stephen King*. Ed. Tim Underwood and Chuck Miller. New York: Warner, 1989.

Norden, Eric. "Playboy Interview: Stephen King" (1983). *Bare Bones: Conversations on Terror with Stephen King*. Ed. Tim Underwood and Chuck Miller. New York: Warner, 1988.

Peck, Abe. "Stephen King's Court of Horror" (1980). *Bare Bones: Conversations on Terror with Stephen King*. Ed. Tim Underwood and Chuck Miller. New York: Warner, 1988.

Perakos, Peter S. "Stephen King on *Carrie, The Shining*, etc." (1978). *Feast of Fear: Conversations with Stephen King*. Ed. Tim Underwood and Chuck Miller. New York: Warner, 1989.

Phelan, Charlotte. "Scaring People All the Way to the Bank" (1979). *Feast of Fear: Conversations with Stephen King*. Ed. Tim Underwood and Chuck Miller. New York: Warner, 1989.

Platt, Charles. *Dream Makers: Science Fiction and Fantasy Writers at Work*. New York: Ungar, 1987.

Pouncey, Edwin. "Would You Buy a Haunted Car from This Man?" (1983). *Bare Bones: Conversations on Terror with Stephen King*. Ed. Tim Underwood and Chuck Miller. New York: Warner, 1988.

Rich, Motoko. "Stephen King Explores Joy in Marriage, Grief in Loss." *The New York Times*. October 4, 2006.

Robertson, William. "Reality Too Frightening, Horror King Says" (1984). *Feast of Fear: Conversations with Stephen King*. Ed. Tim Underwood and Chuck Miller. New York: Warner, 1989.

Rodley, Chris, ed. *Cronenberg on Cronenberg*. New York: Faber, 1992.

Rogak, Lisa. *Haunted Heart: The Life and Times of Stephen King*. New York: St. Martins, 2008.

Schaefer, Stephen. "The Director is King" (1986). *Feast of Fear: Conversations with Stephen King*. Ed. Tim Underwood and Chuck Miller. New York: Warner, 1989.

Shelley, Mary Wollstonecraft. *Frankenstein, or The Modern Prometheus. The Library of Classic Horror Stories.* Philadelphia: Running Press, 2001.

Sherman, David. "The Stephen King Interview" (1984). *Feast of Fear: Conversations with Stephen King.* Ed. Tim Underwood and Chuck Miller. New York: Warner, 1989.

Spignesi, Stephen J. "Dog (and Cat) Days: An Interview with Lewis Teague." *The Complete Stephen King Encyclopedia: The Definitive Guide to the Works of America's Master of Horror.* Chicago: Contemporary, 1991.

---. *The Lost Work of Stephen King: A Guide to Unpublished Manuscripts, Story Fragments, Alternative Versions, and Oddities.* Secaucus: Birch Lane, 1998.

---. "A Talk with Stephen King's *True* First Collaborator: An Interview with Chris Chesley." *The Complete Stephen King Encyclopedia: The Definitive Guide to the Works of America's Master of Horror.* Chicago: Contemporary, 1991.

Spitz, Bob. "Penthouse Interview: Stephen King" (1982). *Bare Bones: Conversations on Terror with Stephen King.* Ed. Tim Underwood and Chuck Miller. New York: Warner, 1988.

Stewart, George R. *Earth Abides.* New York: Ballantine, 2006.

Stoker, Bram. *Dracula. The Library of Classic Horror Stories.* Philadelphia: Running Press, 2001.

Strauss, Robert. "Interview with Stephen King" (1986). *Feast of Fear: Conversations with Stephen King.* Ed. Tim Underwood and Chuck Miller. New York: Warner, 1989.

Strieber, Whitley. *Communion.* New York: Avon, 1987.

Stroby, Wallace. "Digging Up Stories with Stephen King. *Writer's Digest.* 1991.

Terrell, Carroll F. *Stephen King: Man and Artist.* Orono: Northern Lights, 1991.

Tolkien, J.R.R. *The Fellowship of the Ring: Being the First Part of The Lord of the Rings.* New York: Mariner, 2012.

---. *The Return of the King: Being the Third Part of The Lord of the Rings.* New York: Mariner, 2012.

---. *Tree and Leaf.* Boston: Houghton, 1965.

Ulin, David L. "King of the Thrill: Stephen King Reflects on His Literary Aspirations, the Nature of Evil and the Relentless Voices Inside His Head." *Los Angeles Times.* October 9, 1998.

Vincent, Bev. *The Dark Tower Companion: A Guide to Stephen King's Epic Fantasy.* New York: NAL, 2013.

Warren, Alan. *This is a Thriller: An Episode Guide, History and Analysis of the Classic 1960s Television Series.* Jefferson: McFarland, 1996.

Warren, Bill. "The Long Road to *The Stand.*" *Fangoria: Masters of the Dark.* Ed. Anthony Timpone. New York: Starlog, 1997.

---. "Stephen King Takes *The Stand.*" *Fangoria: Masters of the Dark.* Ed. Anthony Timpone. New York: Starlog, 1997.

Wiater, Stanley. "Three Interviews with Stephen King and Peter Straub (1979—1984). *Bare Bones: Conversations on Terror with Stephen King*. Ed. Tim Underwood and Chuck Miller. New York: Warner, 1988.

Winter, Douglas E. *Faces of Fear: Encounters with the Creators of Modern Horror*. New York: Berkley, 1985.

---. *Stephen King: The Art of Darkness*. New York: Signet, 1986.

Wolfe, Thomas. "The Story of a Novel." *Short Stories*. New York: Penguin, 1947.

Wood, Gary. "Adapting Stephen King's *The Stand*." *Cinefantastique*. February 1991.

---. "Blasting Stephen King." *Cinefantastique*. February 1991.

---. "King's Vision on the Screen." *Cinefantastique*. February 1991.

---. "Shotgunners: King & Peckinpah." *Cinefantastique*. February 1991.

---. "Stephen King & Hollywood." *Cinefantastique*. February 1991.

Zaleski, Jeff. "Going Solo: PW Talks with Peter Straub." *Publisher's Weekly*. August 20, 2001.

Zicree, Marc Scott. *The Twilight Zone Companion*. Beverly Hills: Silman-James, 1989.

Index

Lightning Source UK Ltd.
Milton Keynes UK
UKHW02f2047301117
313661UK00017B/990/P

9 781593 93591